WITHDRAWN

Spinoza

SPINOZA

Alan Donagan

THE UNIVERSITY OF CHICAGO PRESS

The University of Chicago Press, Chicago 60637
Harvester Wheatsheaf, Hemel Hempstead

© 1988 by Alan Donagan
All rights reserved. Published 1988
University of Chicago Press edition 1989
Printed in Great Britain
98 97 96 95 94 93 92 91 90 89   5 4 3 2 1

Library of Congress Cataloging-in-Publication Data

Donagan, Alan,
   Spinoza.

   Bibliography: p.
   Includes index.
   1. Spinoza, Benedictus de, 1632–1677.   I. Title.
B3998.D66 1989   199′.492   88-27896
ISBN 0-226-15569-2

FOR
WILLIAM AND MARTHA KNEALE

Table of Contents

Preface xi
Acknowledgements xv
Abbreviations xvii

1. Spinoza in Context

    1.1. Spinoza's Writings 1
    1.2. Reconstructing Spinoza's Thought from his Writings 5
    1.3. What Students of Spinoza's Thought Need to Know about his Life, and What They Need Not 8

2. Judaism Naturalized

    2.1. Searching the Scriptures: Interpretation and Criticism 13
    2.2. Revelation as Practical, not Philosophical 21
    2.3. Judaism and Christianity 26
    2.4. The New Science as Key to True Religion 32

3. *Cogitatio*

    3.1. The New Way of Ideas 36
    3.2. The Structure of Representative Ideas: Descartes's Examples 41
    3.3. Ideas as Affirmations: Spinoza Emends Descartes 46
    3.4. Ideas and Words 49
    3.5. The Linkage of Ideas: Behind the Geometrical Method 53

4. The Elements of the Idea of Nature as God

    4.1. Reinterpreting Necessary Existence 57

4.2. Causation: Immanent and Transient	60
4.3. Cognition, Conception and Causation	64
4.4. The Fundamental Disjunctions	65
4.5. Substances in General	69
4.6. Necessity: a note on Spinoza's Rationalism	73

5. God as Absolutely Infinite Substance

5.1. Spinoza's Principle of Plenitude	77
5.2. What the Proofs of *Ethics*, I, 11 Prove	80
5.3. The Rejection of Monadism	84
5.4. The Constitution of God's Essence	86
5.5. Panentheism	89

6. God as Cause and as Effect

6.1. Perfection Naturalized	96
6.2. The Modal System and its Causation	102
6.3. Motion, Eternity and Time	107
6.4. The Non-Contingency of Finite Modes	113
6.5. Spinoza's Dualism: Pairing Within the Divine Attributes	116

7. Human Beings (I): Cognition

7.1. Human Individuals: Body and Mind	122
7.2. Representation Without Adequate Cognition	125
7.3. Extra-Cogitative Parallelism (I): Imagination	130
7.4. Extra-Cogitative Parallelism (II): Reason	135
7.5. Intra-Cogitative Parallelism: Ideas of Ideas	140
7.6. Human Error	142

8. Human Beings (II): Action and Passion

8.1. Human Individuals as Functional Entities	146
8.2. Persevering in One's Own Being	152
8.3. The Derivation of Affects that are Passions	155
8.4. *Servitus Humana*	161
8.5. *Ductus Rationis*	163

9. Human Freedom

9.1. Living by the Dictates of Reason	169
9.2. Why Free Human Beings Need to Live *in Statu Civili*	173

9.3. Liberty and Political Stability — 180
9.4. The Mind's Power Over the Affects — 183

10. Last Things

   10.1. Problems in Interpreting *Ethics* V, 21–42 — 190
   10.2. The Identity of Individual Human Minds — 191
   10.3. God's Cognition of Non-Existent Individuals — 194
   10.4. The Human Mind Without Relation to the Human Body — 197
   10.5. *Mentis Humanae Summa Beatitudo* — 200

Bibliography of Works Cited by Short Titles — 208
Index — 215

Preface

Spinoza is unique among seventeenth-century philosophers. Even today, it is possible seriously to wonder whether his philosophy, restated in terms of twentieth-century science, is substantially true, although it is quite impossible to entertain such a thought about even the greatest of his near-contemporaries, Descartes and Leibniz. Yet modern philosophical technique owes much to them, and virtually nothing to him.

The reason for this is complex. Spinoza was the first major modern philosopher to believe that nature exists in its own right, and needs no supernatural being to create or to sustain it. In his own day, to the applause of natural scientists, his fellow philosophers competed in supplying new versions of the scholastic proofs that nature depends on supernature. In our day, those who believe that nature depends on supernature do not believe it to be philosophically demonstrable that it does. What was last has become first. However, Spinoza's seventeenth-century form of naturalism does not fall short philosophically as today's varieties of it do. Today's naturalism is materialist; his is not. Yet the research programme of materialism—either to analyse thinking, the distinctive human activity, in terms of the concepts of the physical sciences, or to replace the concept of thinking with those of activities that can be so analysed—has led nowhere. More importantly, except in treating the discoveries of modern natural science, perhaps the greatest of the achievements of the human mind, today's naturalism is culturally barren. To questions about why human life matters and how it should be lived its answers are either evasive or contemptible. Spinoza's non-materialist naturalism not only provides answers to those questions that extort respect if not assent, but it incidentally lays the foundation of an historical explanation of the pre-naturalist answers to them that were accepted in the Judaeo-Christian religious traditions of his own European culture.

Although Spinoza is admired in the analytic tradition which I consider central to western philosophy, most analytic philosophers who study him regretfully conclude that his seventeenth-century tools were inadequate to what is now seen as his twentieth-century project. That is Jonathan Bennett's conclusion in his *Study of Spinoza's* Ethics, to which I owe much. It is inevitable if, like Bennett, you insist on wrestling with Spinoza's texts directly, inquiring neither into the writings by his predecessors on which he drew or which he opposed, nor into the nature of the contemporary audience he was addressing. Here his masterpiece, the *Ethics*, because of the *mos geometricus* he followed in writing it, turns out to be a trap. Most of its propositions, apart from their proofs, have senses that seem natural to twentieth-century readers; and that encourages them to interpret those that do not by the light of nature. While many of its propositions, thus interpreted, seem true or possibly true, others seem probably false, and yet others not only certainly false, but contrary to Spinoza's own naturalism. Worse, even granting his axioms and other principles, his proofs often appear fallacious, and sometimes grossly so (that of *Ethics* II, 49, for example). Nor do his answers to correspondents who confront him with difficulties inspire confidence: he usually fails to meet the point, even when he does not miss it.

Even within the analytic tradition, however, this approach is sometimes rejected as anachronistic. Frederick Pollock, the nineteenth-century jurist and philosopher who pioneered the study of Spinoza in the English speaking world, honoured Spinoza as a thinker who, at the beginning of the modern scientific movement, divined what its direction would be, and so produced a philosophy for the succeeding centuries. In doing so, Pollock pointed out, Spinoza employed the philosophical and theological language of his time giving it such new meanings as his naturalist purposes demanded; and he cannot be understood without ascertaining what those meanings were. Thus, while analytic philosophers today tend to approach the axiomatic system of Spinoza's *Ethics* with logicist preconceptions ultimately derived from Leibniz, Pollock did not. He presented Spinoza's metaphysics as continuous with his physics, and recognized that its necessary principles are not offered as reducible to truths of logic, even by infinite analyses.

Although Pollock's common-sense was for a time disregarded, in 1969 Edwin Curley returned to it in his *Spinoza's Metaphysics*; and was ultimately followed by most students of Spinoza in the analytic tradition. Curley himself brought out the affinities of Spinoza's naturalism with the atomism of the early Wittgenstein. In his recent *Beyond the Geometrical Method: A reading of Spinoza's* Ethics, Curley deepens his earlier work, while reaffirming the ideas that inspired it. Paradoxically, Pollock and Curley rescue Spinoza for the the twentieth century by restoring him to the seventeenth. Read in his own seventeenth-century terms, many of Spinoza's propositions are not what historically uninformed twentieth century readers imagine they are, and neither are their proofs. Useful inquiry cannot begin into whether Spinoza's philosophy can be adapted to the thought of our day until it has been reconstructed in its relation to the thought of his.

In the last thirty years, much more work on Spinoza has been done in continental Europe and in Israel than in the English-speaking world, and it teaches the same lesson. Incidentally, it also teaches that whatever divisions there may be between the analytical and the non-analytical philosophical traditions, they do not separate students of Spinoza. Pollock would certainly have rejoiced to read Martial Gueroult's *Spinoza*, left unfinished at his death, and Alexandre Matheron's *Individu et Communauté chez Spinoza*. Nothing in English on Spinoza's psychology, sociology and political theory, is comparable with Matheron's book.

This book is a study of Spinoza's mature philosophy as a whole. My approach in it owes much to Pollock and Curley. However, since no student of Spinoza with whose work I am acquainted agrees with any other about all the major issues in interpreting him, nobody else presents the structure of his thought exactly as I do. Nevertheless, most of the components of my structure will be familiar from their use by others; and I do not think my use of them eccentric. My reconstruction of his revision of Descartes's theory of ideas was the only part of my work in which I seemed to be alone; but even there, my view of the theory of ideas as a whole was derived from Ian Hacking, and my dependence on the Cartesian studies of my former colleague, Alan Gewirth, left little room for personal oddity.

My primary object is to help philosophers who aspire to work out an adequate naturalism to learn from the the greatest of their naturalist predecessors. In the thirty-seven years during which I have been studying Spinoza, and especially in the last three years in which I have been doing so intensively, I often changed my mind about what he was teaching; and each change confirmed by later study led me to abandon some objection. Since I have little doubt that, as I continue to study him, I shall change my mind further, and in the same way, my hope is less to persuade others to agree with my interpretations, than to find the true ones I have not found.

In offering my approximation to an accurate twentieth-century exposition of Spinoza's philosophy as he himself left it to us, I believe that what it approximates could be brought up to date compatibly with twentieth-century science and logic, and with human experience. Such an up-to-date Spinozism would yield, like the original, an austere and tragic view of human life, but a decent one. Would it be true? In my opinion, it would not. It is an ancient philosophical delusion that the philosophy that is in fact true is the only one there is any reason to believe true. Like science, philosophy is better at falsifying than at verifying. Most philosophies, whatever their superficial attractions, are incoherent, and so impossible. Others, while not impossible, either gratuitously assume what there is no reason to believe, or deny what there is good reason to believe. Yet, whatever the true philosophy may be (I myself accept the supernaturalist one presupposed by the Jewish and Christian faiths Spinoza repudiated), it is not the only one which is possibly true, and which there is some reason to believe. Still, the number of possibly true philosophies there is some reason to believe is very small indeed, and the philosophical interest of every one of them is correspondingly great. Spinoza's is of that number.

Acknowledgements

Although particular debts of which I am conscious are acknowledged in the text or notes, some of my greatest debts are general, and many of them are of such long standing that I cannot remember to which of my innumerable philosophical creditors they are owed. I began to study Spinoza at Oxford in the fifties at Stuart Hampshire's seminar, because of reading his book in the Pelican series. Since leaving Oxford, I have taken whatever opportunities arose to discuss Spinoza with colleagues and to offer courses in which he could be studied. Wilfrid Sellars stands out among the former colleagues from whom I have learned about Spinoza; and over the years the scepticism of my students, among whom was Diane Steinberg, has prompted me to abandon a long succession of mistakes.

Marjorie Grene first persuaded me to publish my own interpretations of Spinoza, instead of grumbles about those of others. That I have learned from those who have been at pains to criticize those pieces in print, especially Jonathan Bennett, Edwin Curley, R.J. Delahunty, Joel Friedman, C.L. Hardin and George Kline, I hope will be evident. I do not refer to any of these earlier writings, not because I think that everything that was new in them is false, but because they do not express my present view of the fundamental structure of Spinoza's philosophy, which I arrived at in the course of writing this book. That view was shaped by criticism received at three conferences at which I presented papers on elements of it as they were being formed: one (on Spinoza's ethics) at the University of California at San Diego in 1986, where it was commented on by Paul Kashap; one (on Spinoza's theory of thought) at an international conference, on the theme 'Spinoza: Issues and Directions', held at the University of Illinois at Chicago, also in 1986; and a third (on Spinoza's theory of substance) in 1987, at the first of a series of conferences on Spinoza, this one on *Ethics* I, at the Hebrew University of Jerusalem. At the latter two of these conferences I was able to participate in discussions of Spinoza with a variety of European and Israeli philosophers, and learned that, among philosophers studying Spinoza, the only serious barriers to communication are linguistic. The papers I presented at these two conferences will be published at about the same time as this book, and comparison will, I hope, show that I benefited from discussion at them. I decided, with three exceptions recorded in my notes, to refer neither to papers presented at these conferences, which their authors might choose to revise, nor to forthcoming books that were mentioned. In consequence, I have referred neither to Professor Yirmiyahu Yovel's conference papers nor to his forthcoming book. When they appear, their influence on me will be evident; by my debt to Professor Yovel's conversation will not, and I wish to acknowledge it.

My greatest personal debt is to Edwin Curley. Not only did he furnish me (and many others) with a copy of his translation of the *Ethics* long before it appeared in print, and with an early version of his *Beyond the Geometrical Method*, but he has never failed to enlighten my ignorance on any of the numerous matters on which I have sought his help. In addition he was one those who, within the small group to whom I sent copies of my work in progress, responded not only with general encouragement, but with criticism of parts of it. The others were: Newton Garver, Marjorie Grene, Will Jones, Martha Kneale, William Kneale, and Diane Steinberg. The philosophers at Caltech while I was writing—Brian Barry, Jim Woodward, Bart Schultz, Randy Curren, Lee Rowen and Alan Strudler—also helpfully discussed my conference papers and parts of the text. And finally, I am indebted to Stephan Körner and to a reader whose name has not been divulged to me for encouragement, advice, and notice of embarrassing blunders.

Abbreviations

(A) Publications

AT   Adam, Charles, and Tannery, Paul (eds). *Oeuvres de Descartes*. 11 vols.

C   Curley, Edwin (ed. and tr.) *The Collected Works of Spinoza*. Vol. 1

G   Carl Gebhardt (ed.). *Spinoza Opera*. 4 vols.
Every reference to a passage in Spinoza's works gives: (1) the title of the work in which the passage is found, together with (2) the number(s) of the division and, where appropriate, the subdivision(s), all as given in G, and (3) the volume, page(s) and line(s) of G. Except for the first, in consecutive references to the same division or subdivision of the same work, only the volume, page(s), and line(s) of G are given.

PS   C.I. Gerhardt (ed.). *Die Philosophischen Schriften von G. W. Leibniz*. 7 vols. Since this abbreviation occurs in quotations, it is adopted, but only following the name 'Leibniz'.

W1   Wolf, A[braham] (tr.). *The Correspondence of Spinoza*.

Wr   Wernham, A.G. (ed. and tr.). *Spinoza: The Political Works. The* Tractatus Theologico-Politicus *in Part and the* Tractatus Politicus *in Full*.

(B) Titles of Spinoza's Writings

CM   *Cogitata Metaphysica: in quibus difficiliores, quae tam in parte Metaphysices generali, quam speciali occurrunt, quaestiones breviter explicantur.*

DPP	*Renati Des Cartes Principiorum Philosophiae Pars I et II, More Geometrico demonstratae.*
E	*Ethica, Ordine Geometrico demonstrata.*
Ep	*Epistulae.*
KV	*Korte Verhandeling van God, de Mensch en des zelfs Welstand.*
TdIE	*Tractatus de Intellectus Emendatione, et de via, qua optime in veram rerum cognitionem dirigitur.* [C.H. Bruder divided TdIE into sections in his edition (1843–6); the numbers of those in which passages referred to occur are given as in C.]
TP	*Tractatus Politicus.*
TT-P	*Tractatus Theologico-Politicus.*

(C) Subdivisions of DPP and E

a	Axiom.
c	Corollary.
d	(not following a reference to a proposition) Definition.
d	(following a reference to a proposition) Demonstration.
p	Proposition.
s	Scholium.
add	Addendum—whether labelled as such or (as with E2p13add) not.
ap	Appendix.
exp	Explication.
AD	Definition of an Affect (in E3add).
AGD	General Definition of the Affects (in E3add).
L	Lemma.
P	Postulate.

Thus, 'E2p13addL2' abbreviates '*Ethics* Part II, Lemma 2 in the addendum to Proposition 13'.

Commas are used to indicate that the subdivisions signified by the abbreviations on both sides of the comma are referred to. Thus 'E4p37,d,s2' refers to proposition 37 in E4, and to its demonstration, and to its second scholium.

1 Spinoza in Context

1.1 Spinoza's Writings

Except for a few letters recently discovered, the surviving writings of Baruch[1] de Spinoza are comfortably accommodated in the four generously printed and moderately sized volumes of Carl Gebhardt's edition.[2] Of those volumes, a third of the first is devoted to a *Compendium* of Hebrew grammar, and the remaining three and two-thirds to philosophical writings and correspondence. Although nothing philosophical Spinoza wrote and wished to preserve seems to have been lost, most of his writings had not been published when, on 21 February 1677, at a few months over the age of forty-four, he died. The *Ethics* (*Ethica Ordine Geometrico Demonstrata*) had been deliberately withheld (Ep68—G IV, 299/17-20). Two pieces were left incomplete: the early *Tractatus de Intellectus Emendatione*, and the late *Tractatus Politicus*. None of his philosophical and scientific correspondence had been printed, although part had been privately circulated.

In the year Spinoza died, his friends collected the writings he had intended for publication, all of them in Latin, and had them printed under the title *Opera Posthuma*. With these they included a selection of his correspondence, for which letters written in other languages were translated into Latin. In the same year, under the title of *De Nagelate Schriften*, they brought out a Dutch translation of this volume, omitting the *Compendium* of Hebrew grammar. At Spinoza's own request, his monogram, 'B.d.S', was printed instead of his name on the title-pages of both.[3]

The mature pieces in both collections are Spinoza's masterpiece, the *Ethics*, and his last work, the *Tractatus Politicus*, which, its editors inform us, his illness and untimely

1

death did not allow him to complete (G III, 272).

What the *Ethics* is about appears from the titles of the five Parts into which it is divided: 'On God', 'On the Nature and Origin of the Mind', 'On the Origin and Nature of the Affects', 'On Human Servitude, or the Power of the Affects', and 'On the Power of the Intellect, or on Human Freedom'. It is an ethics derived from a metaphysics: a theory of how human beings can live a free life, under the guidance of reason, in view of what they are, and of their place in the scheme of things. However, as Spinoza acknowledged in introducing Part II, no more metaphysics is supplied than his ethical purpose demands (G II, 84/8-12).

Since he held that the highest blessedness is attainable only in social life, in *Ethics* IV Spinoza worked out the fundamentals of a theory of politics; and in the unfinished *Tractatus Politicus* he set out to show, by reference to them, 'how Society must be organized, both where Monarchical Government exists and where Aristocrats govern, so that it may not degenerate into Tyranny, and so that the Peace and Liberty of the citizens may remain inviolate' (G III, 273).

Besides these mature writings, the *Opera Posthuma* includes seventy-five letters or excerpts from letters which Spinoza wrote or received, the earliest of which is dated August 1661, and the latest July 1676. One of them serves as preface to the *Tractatus Politicus*. The editors, incidentally disclosing their purpose in printing them, correctly described them as 'contributing not a little to the elucidation of his other works' (G IV, 3). Eleven further letters or fragments of letters came to light by the time Gebhardt prepared his edition, enabling him to print eighty-six: thirty-seven to Spinoza, and forty-nine from him. Since then, two more have been found.[4]

About a third of this correspondence consists of twenty-eight letters to or from Henry Oldenburg, who became joint Secretary of the Royal Society in 1662.[5] The rest, apart from five that I cannot usefully classify, fall into three groups: sixteen to or from members of Spinoza's circle of Dutch intimates—Pieter Balling (1), Johannes Bouwmeester (2), Simon de Vries (3), Jarig Jelles (7), and Lodewijk Meyer (3); nineteen to or from serious scientists and philosophers outside his own circle—J. Ludwig Fabritius (2), Gottfried Wilhelm

Leibniz (2), Nils Stensen (1), and Ehrenfried Walther von Tschirnhaus (14—Spinoza's intimate Georg Hermann Schuller being intermediary for five); and twenty to or from Dutch magnates with philosophical or theological interests—Hugo Boxel (6), Johannes Hudde (3), Willem van Blijenbergh (8), and Lambertus van Velthuysen (3—the Collegiant Jacob Ostens being the intermediary for two).[6]

The only other work included in the *Opera Posthuma* is entitled *Tractatus de Intellectus Emendatione*. It may well be the earliest of Spinoza's books,[7] and like the *Tractatus Politicus* it was never completed. The editors prefaced it with this statement:

> This *Tractatus* ..., which we give you ... in its unfinished state, was written by the author many years ago now. He always intended to finish it. But hindered by other occupations, and finally snatched away by death, he was unable to bring it to the desired conclusion. But since it contains many excellent and useful things ... we did not wish to deprive you of them. And so that you would be aware of, and find less difficult to excuse, the many things that are still obscure, rough, and unpolished, we wished to warn you of them. (G II, 4)

The treatment of cognition in this early *Tractatus* so differs from that in the *Ethics* that Spinoza could have completed it only by radically revising it.[8] Nevertheless, it throws light on how he arrived at his mature views.

Although Spinoza withheld the only philosophical work in his *Opera Posthuma* that he had completed, he did publish two philosophical books while he lived. The first, which appeared in 1663 under his own name, was printed in Amsterdam by a friend, Jan Rieuwertsz. It is made up of two pieces, the titles of which, translated into English, are: *Parts I and II of Descartes's* Principia Philosophiae *Demonstrated in the Geometric Manner* and *Metaphysical Thoughts* (Cogitata Metaphysica): *in which are Briefly Explained the more Difficult Problems which Arise both in the General and the Special Part of Metaphysics*. In the former, the first two parts of Descartes' *Principia* are restated in the *mos geometricus* adopted by Descartes himself in his *Responsio* to the second set of objections to his *Meditations* (AT VII, 160–70); and in the latter, various points in the metaphysics of the day are 'explicated', sometimes contrary to Descartes. A preface by Lodewijk Meyer, Spinoza's friend and physician, warns readers not to think that 'he is teaching here either his own opinions, or only those he approves of' (G I, 131).

The second book Spinoza published during his life, the *Tractatus Theologico-Politicus*, turned out to be the last. It first appeared in quarto in 1670. While its author is not named on its title-page, its printer is, but falsely, as Henricus Keunraht of Hamburg. It was thrice reprinted, its title-page remaining unchanged: once before 1674, when it was banned by the civil authorities; and twice after. Investigations by J.P.N. Land and Carl Gebhardt have established that these printings were by Spinoza's first publisher, Jan Rieuwertsz, in Amsterdam.[9] It is accurately described on its mendacious title-page as 'Containing several Discussions by which it is shown that Liberty of Philosophizing can be conceded without endangering Piety or the Peace of the Republic; but that it cannot be taken away without taking away Piety and the Peace of the Republic as well' (G III, 3).

In the year in which the *Tractatus Theologico-Politicus* was banned, a second anonymous edition of it appeared in octavo. without any indication of where or by whom it was printed. The title-page of this edition falsely advertises it as '*ab authore longe emendatior*'.

The remaining work included in Gebhardt's edition is entitled *Korte Verhandeling van God, de Mensch en deszelfs Welstand* (*Short Treatise on God, Man and his Well-Being*)– customarily referred to as the *Short Treatise*. It is described on its title-page as 'previously written in Latin by B.D.S. for the use of his pupils' (G I, 11). Most of those who have studied it have assumed in practice what its most recent editor, Filippo Mignini, has now demonstrated, that it 'constitutes the first systematic exposition of the Spinozist philosophy'.[10] Its argument is corrected and developed in the *Ethics*, but not fundamentally changed.[11]

Our text of the *Short Treatise* depends on two manuscripts in Dutch that came to light in the middle of the nineteenth century, one of which was written in the seventeenth century. Although there are several theories about how these manuscripts descend from the lost original, the most recent, Mignini's, is the most probable.

According to Mignini in the Introduction to his recent edition, towards the end of 1660, at the request of his friends, Spinoza composed, solely for their private use, a treatise in Latin setting out his unpublished ideas about metaphysics and ethics. His friends urged him to publish it, and begged for a Dutch translation. Spinoza so far complied as to correct the Latin text, adding dialogues and a note in reply to objections raised, and possibly an appendix. This was translated into Dutch, and furnished with the *notabilia* and internal references. About the time when he wrote Ep6 to Oldenburg (late in 1661, according to Mignini), Spinoza worked on this Dutch version, adding further notes, *notabilia* and references (cf. G IV, 36/10-25). Finally, late in 1661 or early in 1662, he decided to rework and rearrange this material, and wrote two series of numbers in the margin of his Dutch version as a guide to doing so. Our seventeenth-century manuscript is either a copy of that on which Spinoza wrote these numbers, or a copy of an intermediate copy.[12] The reworking became the *Ethics*.

1.2 Reconstructing Spinoza's Thought from his Writings

Spinoza expressed the core of his mature thought only in the *Ethics*. When he wrote the *Tractatus de Intellectus Emendatione* his theory of cognition was incomplete, as was his metaphysics when he wrote the *Short Treatise*. It would be impossible to infer from the *Tractatus Politicus* and the *Tractatus Theologico-Politicus* the fundamental philosophical ideas from which they ultimately derive. And the *Correspondence*, although indispensable as a commentary on his work as a whole, would often be unintelligible if the *Ethics* had perished. Yet comprehensive and systematic though the *Ethics* is, much in it perplexed those whom Spinoza permitted to have copies of the unpublished manuscript, and who wrote to him about it.

It is set out in geometrical order. Each of its five Parts purports to derive a set of theorems from a set of definitions and axioms, together with the definitions, axioms and theorems of the previous Parts. Up to a point this makes for clarity. It is true that some of his proofs do not satisfy the standards of rigour even of his own day: for example, those met by Newton's proofs in his *Principia*, published eleven years after Spinoza died. Every interpretation according to which the argument of the *Ethics* is consistent and well articulated, is therefore to some degree a correction. Since such interpretations have been produced, in which the corrections proposed are slight and not intrinsically implausible, they must be preferred to those that either fail to make its arguments coherent, or correct it more violently. Unfortunately, there are several of them; and which recaptures Spinoza's thought, if any does, cannot be determined by the twofold tests of coherence and fidelity to the text.

The *Ethics*, however, was not written in heaven. As Spinoza's correspondence shows, he planned his writings with certain kinds of readers in mind: readers acquainted with traditional theology and philosophy, but committed to the new science and philosophy of Bacon and Descartes, and willing to think freely about religious and political questions. He expected them to be alert. Consider the undefined words he uses in the definitions and axioms of the *Ethics*: for example, 'cause', 'essence', 'nature', 'conceive', 'constitute', 'infinite', 'necessary'. All are found in the writings of his philosophical contemporaries, yet no single usage of any was considered established. A variety of philosophical and scientific approaches were contending with one another, and advocates of each availed themselves of the right to adapt both traditional and new words to their own purposes, as did Spinoza. Much of the vocabulary of *Ethics* I and V is a modification of that of late scholastic philosophical theology, which itself had been modified by Descartes. Some of it is elucidated and further modified in the *Cogitata Metaphysica* which Spinoza appended to his exposition of the first two Parts of Descartes's *Principia*. And I shall try to show that the *Ethics* itself is designed to teach new ways of looking at things, and incidentally to confer new senses on a number of scholastic-Cartesian expressions.

The words Spinoza chose to use must therefore be considered in the context of the sentences in which they occur, those sentences in the context of his proofs and scholia, and they in turn in the context of the sorts of intellectual exchange of which specimens can be studied in his correspondence. Once tempting anachronisms have been discarded, the considerations that matter most come into view.

In his *Tractatus Theologico-Politicus*, for example, Spinoza elaborately examines the language of the Jewish scriptures, from which that of scholastic theology was in part derived, and works out general principles on which the claims of revealed religion, or 'prophecy', are to be approached in a scientifically enlightened age. Some common misunderstandings of the *Ethics* are obviated when its theological vocabulary is interpreted in the light of the *Tractatus*. For example, neo-Platonic and idealist interpretations become hard to maintain.

Again, the assumptions Spinoza shared with his contemporaries, which readers today no longer share, should be identified, although that is sometimes difficult. The most important example has to do with what Spinoza called 'cognition'. The text of the *Ethics* leaves no doubt that Spinoza embraced, with modifications, the theory of cognition that Locke was to call 'the new way of ideas'. It was originally developed by Descartes; but, disseminated by such manuals as the *Port Royal Logic*,[13] it rapidly became the common property of most advanced thinkers. When those who shared this conception wrote, they tended to assume that their readers shared it too, and seldom explained it except incidentally to proposing some modification of it. It is now so completely obsolete that few except historians heed Ian Hacking's warning that, unless it is mastered, no inquiry into seventeenth-century theories of cognition can prosper,[14] or recognize that it will not be mastered unless the authors who embraced it are studied as grappling with problems of their own day, not of ours.

Although in the latter half of *Ethics* II he succinctly expounds what is distinctive in his theory of cognition, Spinoza assumes that what he appropriates from Descartes's new way of ideas is common intellectual property. He has already employed most of it in Part I and the earlier half of Part II. The second, fourth, fifth and sixth axioms of Part I are no more intelligible to one who does not understand what

Spinoza thought an idea is, and what its fundamental relation to what he called its '*ideatum*' is, than Joseph Priestley's discovery of oxygen would be to somebody who does not understand the theory of phlogiston, and why Priestley thought of oxygen as 'dephlogisticated air'. Hence before *Ethics* I is tackled, the section on cognition in Part II should be studied; and, together with it, the pertinent portions of Descartes's own writings, of Spinoza's restatement of Descartes's *Principia*, and of the unfinished *Tractatus de Intellectus Emendatione*. Spinoza's theory of cognition can no more be expressed in terms of twentieth-century language-centred theories than Priestley's theory of kinds of air can be expressed in terms of Lavoisier's chemistry. To understand Spinoza, we must understand the theories with which he works; and even if some of them are false, it does not follow that everything he does with them is false. If Priestley could discover oxygen by working with the theory of phlogiston, until we have studied what Spinoza does by working with the theory of ideas, we should reserve judgement.

1.3 What Students of Spinoza's Thought Need to Know about his Life, and What They Need Not

In reconstructing Spinoza's thought from what he wrote, duly heeding subsidiary evidence about his studies and his scientific and philosophical exchanges with his contemporaries, little about other sides of his life need be taken into account. But that little includes something of the first importance: his relation to the religion and culture in which he was reared.

The *Tractatus Theologico-Politicus* and certain of Spinoza's letters[15] show that he was a Jew by birth and education, but had ceased to be a member of the Jewish community without subscribing, even outwardly, to any branch of Christianity. This would not have been possible, without special protection, except in the Netherlands. He was, perhaps, the first European to avow the secularization of intellectual life as an ideal, and to live it. Yet he did not idealize the reserve demanded by the life he had chosen. The surviving letters to him show that he found friends among the more independent-minded Dutch Protestants. But they also show that, while he inspired affection and in some devotion, as he did in de Vries (e.g. Ep8—G IV, 39/2–11), even to those with whom he was most intimate, he was always their teacher.

Why had he no acknowledged friends among his fellow Jews?

He was born on 24 November 1632, to Michael de Spinoza (or d'Espinoza) and his second wife, Hanna Deborah; and, as their first born son, although not his father's, he was named 'Baruch' in thanksgiving. His family were Marranos: Sephardic Portuguese Jews who, having been prohibited in Portugal from practising their faith, had outwardly embraced Roman Catholicism. His father, who was born about 1600 in Portugal, migrated to Amsterdam, where he is recorded as having married Rachel, his first wife, in 1620. The Jewish community in the Netherlands had been recognized a year before, by an ordinance of the States General, and its affairs regulated. It was prospering and securely established by the time Baruch was born.

He was educated in Hebrew, studying the Scriptures, the Talmud and the medieval Jewish classics. He was also taught Latin, in which he proceeded to advanced studies with an ex-Jesuit physician residing in Amsterdam, Frances van den Ende. Presumably it was while studying with van den Ende that he became acquainted with the new mechanistic science of nature, and with the philosophers who embraced it, above all with Descartes. By his early twenties, he had arrived at heterodox conclusions about the nature of God, and about the nature and content of divine revelation.

During the same period, the Marrano community in Amsterdam was striving to recover the full Jewish religious life it had been compelled in Portugal partly to abandon. It neither could find a place for a member who disavowed essentials of its faith, nor would continue in charity with an apostate. Yet Spinoza was committed, not only to the philosophical inquiry that had led him to abandon beliefs his community considered essential to membership, but also to the right of philosophers to communicate their results to whoever was fit to receive them. And so, on 27 July 1656, in the Amsterdam synagogue, he was solemnly expelled and cursed. Members of the Jewish community were forbidden to communicate with him in writing or speech, to render him any service or to approach within four cubits of him, or to read any of his writings.[16]

Although this ban severed overt communication between him and his fellow Jews, Spinoza did not renounce his Jewish heritage. Indeed, by composing his *Compendium* of Hebrew grammar, he did what he could to enable non-Jews to share it. As a rule he dissembled the contempt he confessed to Oldenburg for the Christian doctrine of divine incarnation, by pretending not to understand it (Ep73—G IV, 309/2-6; cf. TT-P, 1—G III, 21/13-5); but on one occasion he did not conceal his pride in the constancy of the Jews during a thousand years of insolence and persecution. A young former pupil, recently converted to Roman Catholicism, had been so ill-advised as to allude in a letter to the many Roman Catholics who had gone 'to meet martyrdom with alacrity and with the greatest joy' (Ep67—G IV, 290/4-5). Spinoza replied:

> [T]hat on which [Pharisees—i.e. orthodox Jews] most pride themselves is that they number far more martyrs than any other nation, and daily increase the number of those who with singular constancy of soul have suffered for the faith they profess. Nor is this a falsehood. I myself know, among others, of a certain Judah, whom they call 'the faithful', who in the midst of the flames, when he was believed to be already dead, began to sing the hymn that begins, *To thee, O God, I offer up my soul*, and so died singing. (Ep76—G IV, 321/17-18, 322/1-6)

No rejoinder has been preserved.

Except for his intellectual exchanges, the facts of Spinoza's life that students of his thought need to know have now been set out. He was born and reared as a Jew in a community of Marrano immigrants into the Netherlands; he was expelled from the Jewish community for heresy; he did not renounce his cultural heritage, but wished to communicate it to non-Jews; he was a respected, even a celebrated, member of the North European community of scientifically-minded philosophers; he refused to become a Christian; and he professed allegiance to the United Provinces of the Netherlands. Generally, his life was of a piece with what he wrote: discoveries about its details—apart from facts about his intellectual exchanges—bear dubiously on disputed questions about what he thought. While nobody who cares about his philosophy will be indifferent to how he applied it practically, the examples of Hobbes, Rousseau and Marx warn us that great theorists are not always great practitioners. It does not appear that any question about his political theories will be resolved by discovering what he did or said on issues of practical politics.

Notes

1. When he wrote in Latin, Spinoza used the Latin rendering of his name, 'Benedictus'.
2. None of the title-pages of the four volumes of G bears a date of publication. Most authors give its date as 1925. However, H.F. Hallett gives it as 1924 (Hallett (1957), p. xv), and A.G. Wernham gives it as 1924-26 (Wr, p. ix).
3. According to the editors' Preface to the *Opera Posthuma*. See Pollock (1880), p. 40.
4. The Dutch originals or Dutch translations of all eighty-eight may be found in F. Akkerman, H.G. Hubbeling and A.G. Westerbrink (eds), *Spinoza: Briefwisseling* (Amsterdam: Wereldbibliotheek, 1977), whose spelling of Dutch names I follow. Letters are numbered in chronological order, on a principle established by Gebhardt: namely, to adopt the numeration of J.V. van Vloten and J.P.N. Land in *Benedicti de Spinoza Opera quotquot reperta sunt* (The Hague: Nijhoff, 1882-3), for the eighty-four they knew; and to assign each subsequently discovered letter the number of the last earlier one in van Vloten and Land, with an alphabetical suffix. Thus Gebhardt assigned the number 48a to a newly discovered letter to Jarig Jelles, dated 19 April 1673, as written after Ep48 (dated 30 March 1673) and before Ep49 (dated 14 December 1673). Now that the letter from Jelles to which Spinoza's was a reply has been discovered, it is numbered 48a, and Spinoza's reply is renumbered 48b. See Wl, pp. 64-7; and C, pp. 159-62.
5. Wl, p. 34.
6. The fullest account of Spinoza's correspondents is in Meinsma (1983); but most of what one needs to know can be found in Wl, pp. 34-57.
7. C, pp. 3-6. Note particularly the references to Mignini.
8. See C, pp. 3-6; and cf. Joachim (1940), pp. 102-11.
9. G III, 363-82; cf. Wr, pp. 42-4.
10. Mignini (ed.) (1986), p. 97.
11. Mignini (ed.) (1986), *Introduzione*, esp. pp. 71-99. Cf. G I, 11: C, pp. 46-53.
12. Mignini (ed.) (1986), pp. 97-9; cf. C, 46-53.
13. Actually entitled *La Logique ou l'Art de Penser*, and written by Antoine

Arnauld and Pierre Nicole, whose first edition appeared in 1664, and whose fifth and last in 1685. It was much reprinted. A convenient modern edition, based on that of 1685, is Arnauld and Nicole (1970).

14 Hacking (1975), pp. 26-33, 43-9.
15 Esp. Ep76; cf. also Ep67, 67a, 71, 73-5, 77-8.
16 The biographical information in the preceding two paragraphs is derived from Meinsma (1983), esp. pp. 77-83 (notes 102-8), 118-25 (notes 139-45). Cf. Pollock (1880), pp. 1-21.

2 Judaism Naturalized

2.1 Searching the Scriptures: Interpretation and Criticism

In placing Spinoza under its solemn ban, the Amsterdam synagogue denounced him for having taught 'horrible heresies'; but it did not specify them.[1] Nor can we discover from his writings what they were; for he was only twenty-three, and nothing survives of what he had written by then. He put nothing into print that could be denounced as heresy until fourteen years later, in 1670, when he published his *Tractatus Theologico-Politicus*. However, a letter he wrote to Oldenburg[2] shows that he was at work on the *Tractatus* at least five years before he published it; and, lacking evidence that his religious opinions changed radically in the nine previous years, it may be inferred that what he published in 1670 was the fruition of what he thought in 1656.

To live according to Judaism is to observe the law revealed to Moses. That law is set forth in the Torah—the first five of the thirty-nine books recognized by Jews, since the third century of our era, as containing what God has revealed to them through their patriarchs and prophets. Problems about what the law requires in given cases are decided according to an oral tradition, from which collections of judgements have from time to time been put in writing. The Torah itself is now generally acknowledged to consist partly of early records of such rulings. The other thirty-four books recognized as canonical are traditionally classified either as 'Prophets' (including historical narratives of which reports of the doings and sayings of prophets are a part) or as 'Other Writings'.

Any study of the Jewish scriptures presupposes much about what can have happened, and what cannot. The *Tractatus Theologico-Politicus* differs from most such studies, then and now, because in it Spinoza states exactly what he presupposes.

Leo Strauss has tried to show that he should not be taken at his word. The *Tractatus*, he contends, is an esoteric work, written under religious persecution. It is opaque to those who do not recognize that writers in ages of persecution perfected a technique for concealing their meaning from the vulgar while disclosing it to the initiated.[3] They would safeguard themselves from charges of heresy by asserting what they did not believe, while directing the attention of a select few, by deliberate contradictions or paradoxes, to indirect signs in their texts from which what they intended to convey might be inferred.

It is true that Spinoza and Oldenburg exchanged letters about the malice of orthodox theologians, and their power to harass thinkers who were not circumspect in what they published (e.g. Ep30, 31). But harassment is not the sort of persecution that drives the heterodox to write esoterically. There was no inquisition in the Netherlands into the private beliefs of citizens. Nor was it unlawful either to disbelieve in Christianity in all its forms, or privately to circulate writings which the dominant religious group, the Calvinist Reformed Church, would have reprobated. While he was writing the *Tractatus*, Spinoza was privately circulating early drafts of the undeniably infidel *Ethics*. Publishing esoteric writings would have been a clumsy and inefficient way for him to have communicated his theological infidelities to the select few, and an utterly impracticable way of communicating them to anybody else. It is therefore a hypothesis of last resort that he wrote the *Tractatus* in the esoteric mode. Any plausible alternative must defeat it.

He himself offered such an alternative in his Preface. Although the *Tractatus* was written in Latin, he foresaw that some of its readers would belong to what he called the '*vulgus*', presumably having in mind coffee-house wits. Having them as disciples would not recommend his views to serious philosophers and scientists, and might frighten some of them into defending orthodoxy. He therefore expressed the hope that only the philosophically-minded would read the *Tractatus* at all. Among them, a few would be philosophers proper who would have nothing to learn from it, because they would already know its principles, and more. The majority, however, while accepting the new mechanical conception of nature, were still held back from following out its implications (from 'philosophizing freely') by their commitment to revealed theology. They, he wrote, were the readers he hoped to reach; and his purpose was to to persuade them that their new view of nature demanded a new view of revelation which, although unorthodox, citizens of the Netherlands could embrace loyally as well as lawfully (TT-P, Pref.—G III, 12/3-27).

It is true that the *Tractatus* contains things that tempt many readers today to doubt whether he believed them. Not only does he define revelation (or 'prophecy' as he prefers to call it) as 'sure cognition revealed by God to human beings' (TT-P, 1—G III, 15/5-6), but never questions that such revelations were received both by the Jewish patriarchs and prophets, and by Jesus. The questions he asks are, 'What did God reveal to them?' and 'How did he reveal it?' Strauss inferred that he was dissembling disbelief; but that is anachronistic. In his own day he was accused, not of disbelieving what he professed to believe, but of concealing the heretical implications of what he professed.

In judging his sincerity, two facts ought to be kept in mind. First, despite the synagogue's ban, he not only continued to study Hebrew literature, but, in writing his *Compendium* of Hebrew grammar, took pains to help non-Jews to study it. That literature consists of a purported record of divine revelation, and of reactions to it of a variety of literary kinds, composed over two millenia. No more than anybody else could Spinoza have admired it while condemning revelation as sheer superstition: he must have taken it seriously on unorthodox grounds, if he could not on orthodox ones. Secondly, his treatment of revelation was not *ad hoc*. Some non-religious phenomena, for example, ghosts and omens, are commonly held to be supernatural, yet he treated them exactly as he treated religious miracles and revelations in writing privately to friends, when he cannot plausibly be accused of disingenuously compromising with religious orthodoxy.

The principles he applied to scriptural reports of miracles appear in the letters he exchanged with Hugo Boxel about ghosts (Ep51-Ep56), a welcome comic interlude in his correspondence. Most ghostly phenomena, he told Boxel, are ill-authenticated and should be dismissed; and the few that are not can be explained without supposing that there are disembodied spirits. The more complex principles he applied to reports of revelation appear on his reply to a letter from Pieter Balling, the friend who had translated his restatement of Descartes's *Principia* into Dutch. After one of his children had died suddenly, Balling had written to Spinoza, disturbed at having heard, while the child was still well, sobbing like that which broke from him in his illness (Ep17—G IV, 76/15-17). Was the sobbing he had heard an omen? Spinoza replied that, while 'those sobs were nothing more than imagination' (G IV, 76/21-2), yet 'the effects of imagination, or images, which draw their origin from the constitution of the Mind, can be *omens* of some future event; because the Mind can confusedly feel in advance (*praesentire*) something that is future' (G IV, 77/24-6). As we shall see, except for those to Moses, he explains all revelations of the future to the Jewish prophets in just this way.

Scriptural texts, as Spinoza was among the first to demonstrate, do not disclose their meaning and purpose to those who bring to them only the ability to read and a tradition of pious interpretation. Much that students of the Scriptures need to know can be established only by scholarly methods: the history of the language in which the texts they study were written, how they were produced, and how they have been transmitted. Interpreting Scripture, he argued, is like interpreting natural phenomena:

> just as the method of interpreting nature chiefly consists in this, that a history of nature be put together (*concinnanda*), from which, as from established facts (*ex certis datis*), we infer definitions of natural things; so also, in order to interpret Scripture it is necessary to prepare (*adornare*) an honest history of it, and from that, as from established facts and principles, to make legitimate inferences about the mind of the authors of Scripture. (TT-P, 7—G III, 98/18-24)

What he meant by a 'history of nature' is clarified by his early correspondence with Oldenburg, who described his 'philosophical group' in London as devoting themselves 'to making experiments and observations, and ... putting together (*concinnandae*) a History of the Mechanical Arts' (Ep3—G IV, 12/1-3). According to Curley, Oldenburg's group was an 'informal gathering of scientists of Baconian inclinations' (C, 169 n. 10), and 'a history in the Baconian sense' is 'a collection of experimental data relating to some phenomenon' (C, 186 n. 46). Subsequent letters make plain that this group was representative of the philosophical readers whom Spinoza believed the *Tractatus* could benefit.[4]

Just as a Baconian 'history of the mechanical arts' would be a collection of experimental data about the various kinds of mechanism there are, so a Spinozist 'history' of the Jewish scriptures would be a collection of information of whatever sorts are pertinent to its interpretation. Spinoza listed three such sorts of information:

First of all, information about the nature and properties of the Hebrew language in which the Scriptures were written. Spinoza lamented that the Jewish nation retains only 'certain fragments of [its] language and of a few books' (TT-P, 7—G III, 108/22-3). Given this paucity of evidence, the peculiarities of Hebrew are such that 'so many ambiguities must arise that there is no method that can resolve them all' (G III, 108/35-109/3). Nevertheless, 'we are constrained to consider one Jewish tradition as uncorrupted, namely, that of the meanings of Hebrew words; ... for it could not be in anybody's power to change the meaning of any word from [that in common] use' (G III, 105/24-8). Students can recover what was meant by words in common use in a period, if the literature of that period contains enough specimens of their use; and for many words the biblical literature does.

Secondly, classificatory and comparative information. What topics are treated in each book? In what books is a given topic treated, and in what is it not? In what passages is a given topic treated? And which of those passages are ambiguous or obscure, and which contradict others (G III, 100/8-12)?

Thirdly, information about how each book was written, how its text was transmitted to the present, and how the canon of which it is a part was formed. With respect to how it was written, it must be ascertained who wrote it and what he was like, on what occasion he wrote it, in what period, and to whom (G III, 101/26-34).

Spinoza himself acknowledged that at least one medieval rabbi, Abraham Ibn Ezra, had partly anticipated his conception of a textual 'history' (TT-P, 8—G III, 118/20-120/31), which in turn partly anticipated techniques perfected in the nineteenth century. Yet he appears to have been the first to lay down, as 'the universal rule of interpreting Scripture', that we are 'to attribute nothing to [it] as its teaching that we may not hold as completely (*quam maxime*) evident from its history' (TT-P, 7—G III, 99/29-32). The results he obtained by following this rule shocked his contemporaries. He pointed out that the first twelve books in the Jewish canon (namely, the Pentateuch, Joshua, Judges, Ruth, Samuel I and II, and Kings I and II) have a single theme: 'the antiquities of the Jews from their origin to the first destruction of the City' (TT-P, 8—G III, 125/29-31); and he argued, in view of the connecting passages they contain, and other passages showing them to be 'apographs written many ages after the events', that they were put together after the return from Babylon by a single person, probably Ezra (G III, 126/25-30). Neither the arrangement nor all the matter of books so edited would have been divinely revealed.

He drew similar conclusions about the prophetic books. '[T]he prophecies which they contain were collected from other books,' he observed, 'and they neither are always set down in the same order as that in which they had been spoken or written by the prophets themselves, nor are they all even preserved, but only those which could be found here and there. That is why these books are nothing but fragments of the prophets' (TT-P, 10—G III, 142/15-20).

Defenders of orthodoxy, relying in part on the text, 'Thou shalt not follow a multitude to do evil; neither shalt thou bear witness in a cause to turn aside after a multitude to pervert justice' (Exodus 23:2), which they interpret by methods at variance with Spinoza's rule,[5] contend that the Torah itself empowers the rabbinate, as a court, to make binding rulings about its implications for cases about which it is not explicit. Spinoza rejected such rulings as merely human additions to Moses' teaching, and observed that a Baconian 'history' discloses that some of them have crept into the text of the Pentateuch itself (TT-P, 7—G III, 105/11-23).

Even so, the universal rule of interpretation furnishes no more than a fairly effective technique of authentication. It enables students to distinguish the original writings and reports preserved in scriptural texts from subsequent interpolations; but authentic originals, like authentic passports, may contain falsehoods. Having ascertained what the original writings and reports preserved in the scriptural texts are, it remains to determine whether what they contain was divinely revealed. Suppose that Exodus 11:1, 'The Lord said to Moses, Yet will I bring one plague more upon Pharaoh, and upon Egypt, afterwards he will let you go hence', can be shown to be an authentic original record. It would remain to ask whether the Lord said to Moses what he is authentically recorded as having said. To answer that, Spinoza saw that a further test is needed.

Secular historical sources seldom furnish the test of truth he sought, because they do not treat of the events which the Jewish and Christian Scriptures purport to narrate. He therefore turned to the new science of physical nature, which he credited to Bacon and Descartes (cf. Ep13—G IV, 66/33–67/12). That science had, he believed, brought to light 'the principles and notions upon which the whole of our natural cognition is erected' (TT-P, 1—G III, 28/24-5). According to it, nature is at bottom a system of extended material bodies, the fundamental laws of which are those of mechanics. Bacon and Descartes conceived nature's laws as deriving, not from matter, but from God, who imposed them on matter at the Creation, and has sustained them ever since. Descartes went further, and deduced from God's perfection what they must be—inferring, for example, from God's unchangeability that they must be such that the quantity of motion and rest he originally created is conserved. By thus accommodating their science to traditional theology, Spinoza considered that Bacon and Descartes partly spoiled it: the truth, he maintained, is that materiality (which, like Descartes, he identified with extension) is one among God's infinite attributes, and nature is God, not something created by him (TT-P, 6—G III, 83/34-5).

Of course, materiality is not nature's (or God's) only attribute—he must have infinitely many others; but since it is one of them, material nature must, being God, be unchangeable: not a mass in which everything is at rest, for according to the mechanical conception motion is a state and not a change of state, but rather a mass containing both rest and motion, its laws being such as to conserve a constant quantity of both. So conceived, the power of nature is 'itself the divine power and excellence (*virtus*)'; and the divine power is 'the very essence of God itself.' This power is revealed in nature's being as it is: a lawful self-caused system, whether as matter or as the infinite other things it is besides matter. Thus the intellect of God is God understanding himself completely; and the will of God is simply that he be as he understands himself to be (G III, 82/26–83/9).

This amendment of Bacon and Descartes was wholly Spinoza's: none of his contemporaries anticipated him, and none publicly acknowledged following him. That it is heretical was obvious. It immediately implies that God did not create the world out of nothing in six days, as Genesis narrates; for it was not created. And since God is not a supernatural being outside nature, it also follows that he does not intervene in the lawful course of natural events. Indeed, given Spinoza's conception of God, 'If ... anything happened in nature that was repugnant to its laws, it would necessarily also be repugnant to the [divine] decree, the [divine] intellect and the divine nature' (G III, 83/2–4).

Pierre Bayle, expressing what many must have thought, accused 'the Spinozists' of disingenuously begging the question against orthodoxy.

> Speak plainly and without equivocation [he adjured them]; say that the Laws of Nature have not been made by a free Legislator who knew what he made, but, being the action of a blind and necessary cause, nothing can come about that would be contrary to those Laws. You will then be stating against miracles your own Thesis: it would be a begging of the question; but at least you will be speaking frankly.[6]

Spinoza might fairly have rejoined that identifying nature with God implies, not that the cause of its laws is blind (it is thinking as well as extended), but that it is not supernatural. Yet that would not have sufficed for Spinoza's contemporaries, of whom most believed that physical nature needs a creator, as most of ours do not. Their seventeenth-century dogma is not refuted by anticipating a twentieth-century one; nor could Spinoza have refuted it without divulging the radical heresies of the *Ethics*.

Judaism Naturalized

Notwithstanding this, identifying nature with God yields a strong negative rule of truth: namely, that since God neither has created nature from outside, nor intervenes at will in its lawful course, any scriptural passage must be false that reports that he has done either, or has revealed that he has done or will do either. Yet, as Spinoza's own statement of it shows, following this rule is often difficult. It implies that

> if ... certain things are found in the Sacred Writings the causes of which we do not know, and which seem to have happened beyond or even contrary to the order of nature, they ought not to give us pause, but it is to be wholly believed that what really happened happened naturally. (TT-P, 6—G III 90/7–11)

That, however, leaves us with two options: either what is reported (whether revelation, or supernatural creation or intervention) did not really happen at all, and the passage reporting it is a pious fraud; or what is reported happened in the course of nature, but in ways that fall outside the present scope of human understanding. Between these options, since human beings are ignorant of much within the order of nature, the rule does not tell us how to decide.

2.2. Revelation as Practical, not Philosophical

If nature is God, then natural science is theology, at least in its fundamental principles; and God's essence is accessible to the natural light of human reason. Does this leave any room at all for revealed theology?

Spinoza agreed with the orthodox that God revealed to his prophets what is hidden from the wise, but not that he revealed answers to questions of speculative theology. If he had, then the Jews would have possessed more theological truth than their Greek contemporaries, which they did not:

> [I]f anybody reads through [Scripture] even cursorily, he sees clearly that the Jews outdid other nations in this alone, that they prosperously conducted affairs pertaining to their security of life, and overcame great dangers, and that above all by the outward help of God alone; in the rest of their affairs they were equal to others, and God was equally propitious to all. For it is plain that in respect of understanding (*intellectus*) they had

utterly common (*vulgares admodum*) thoughts about God and nature; and so they were not chosen by God before the others because of [their] understanding. (TT-P, 3—G III, 33/31-34/4)

The truths God reveals are of direct practical value; and the prophets to whom they are revealed grasp them in terms of their own beliefs about the world, which may be not only false, but grossly so.

The passage from Joshua which the Holy Office cited in condemning Galileo is an example. It relates that, when the Israelites were pursuing the Amorites after the battle of the five kings, Joshua 'said in the sight of Israel, Sun, stand thou still upon Gibeon. ... And the sun stood still ... until the people had avenged themselves upon their enemies. ... So the sun stood still in the midst of heaven, and hasted not to go down about a whole day' (10:12-13). This passage passes the tests for an authentic record of revelation laid down in Spinoza's universal rule, even though it is false that the sun ceased to move, either really (according to Ptolemy) or apparently (according to Copernicus). Does it follow that the scriptural record, although textually authentic, is false? Not at all, Spinoza answered:

> Are we ... bound to believe that the soldier Joshua was skilled at astronomy? And that a miracle could not be revealed to him, or that the light of the sun could not have been longer above the horizon than usual unless Joshua had understood the cause of it? (TT-P, 2—G III, 36/8-11)

God revealed to Joshua that daylight would last long enough for the Jews to complete their victory; and Joshua understood both revelation and miracle according to his pre-scientific beliefs. Believing that daylight could be prolonged only if the sun stood still, he believed that God had promised that it would stand still; and, when daylight was prolonged, he believed that it had done so. Yet the phenomenon revealed to him might have been caused naturally: perhaps the sunlight was refracted by ice in the air (G III, 36/16-18).

Not even Moses himself, the greatest of the prophets, rose above common opinion in his conception of God, although it was only to him that God spoke by means of a real voice (TT-P, 1—G III, 17/16-23). According to Spinoza, Moses did not fully grasp that God is omniscient, because on one occasion he expressed doubt whether the being who revealed things to him, whom he referred to as 'Jahweh', knew or cared whether the Israelites would believe what he was commanded to tell them (Exodus 4:1-8). Nor did he know that Jahweh exists necessarily and eternally; for he believed that he always has existed, exists, and will exist—that is, that his existence can be expressed by specifying the intervals of time it occupies. All he taught about Jahweh's nature was that he is merciful, benign and extremely jealous; that human beings are neither equal to depicting him by a visible image, nor strong enough to look at him; and that he is uniquely powerful (TT-P, 2—G III, 38/11-32). He was not even a strict monotheist; for he spoke of other gods than Jahweh, and although he asserted that they were subordinate, he left the question open whether they were created. Again, after narrating how Jahweh created the visible world out of chaos, he told how Jahweh chose a people for himself, and a territory for them to inhabit (which is why he is called the God of Israel, and the God of Jerusalem), leaving other peoples and territories to other gods (G III, 38/32-39/19).

Why did the prophets who received revelations make the mistakes they did about God's nature (TT-P, 1—G III, 16/26-31)? Natural cognition, although in a sense divine, is not revealed, because its foundations are intellectual: the idea of God or nature that every human being shares, however little most of them (the *vulgus*) make use of it (G III, 15/21-4, 16/7-19). Revelation, on the other hand, being 'sure cognition revealed by God to human beings' (G III, 15/5-6), is not intellectual. As reported in the Jewish scriptures, all revelations to the patriarchs and prophets were by words or what Spinoza called *figurae*—shapes or other sensible forms. Those words or *figurae* were either external physical realities which the recipient saw or heard, or imaginative representations which he may or may not have supposed to be externally real (G III, 17/9-15).

The Pentateuch tells us that the law was revealed to Moses in words uttered by a real voice, but not how those utterances were produced. And since it also tells us that 'there arose not a prophet since in Israel like unto Moses, whom the Lord knew face to face' (Deut. 34:10), Spinoza concluded that no other prophet received a revelation through a real voice, and that prophets like Samuel, who thought they really heard the voices through which they received revelations, in fact only imagined them. It is expressly recorded that revelations were made to other prophets through voices heard in dreams or *figurae* seen in visions (G III, 17/16-33; 20/13-32). Yet these differences do not matter. '[T]he Prophets perceived what God revealed only by means of imagination, that is, by mediating words or images, either real (*veris*) or imaginary' (G III, 28/3-5).

What is thus revealed has both the scope and the cognitive weakness of its imaginative medium. On the one hand, it is not confined to what can be grasped rationally; for imaginative ideas represent, although confusedly, things which unconfused natural cognition cannot represent at all (G III, 28/21-5). On the other, it is limited by the minds, cultivated or uncultivated, of the prophets to whom it is given: 'Prophecy', Spinoza observed, 'never made Prophets more learned (*doctiores*)' (TT-P, 2—G III, 30/8-9). Yet the prophets were well aware that imagining something is not a good reason for acting on it. All prophetic acts of imagination recorded in the Scriptures, as Spinoza points out, satisfy three conditions. First, the things imagined are vivid: as vivid as real objects affecting sight or hearing. Secondly, when a revelation is not confirmed by something already received as revelation (as Jeremiah's prophecies were), it is accompanied by what its recipient considers a sign of authenticity, whether or not that sign is expressly reported. Thirdly, and most important of all, the spirit of everybody to whom God reveals anything is directed solely to what is fair (*aequus*) and good (G III, 30/13-18; 31/23-32/17). Even so, Spinoza acknowledged, it does not 'mathematically' follow because an act of imagination satisfies these three conditions, that it is prophetic: that is, it 'does not follow from the necessity of the thing perceived or seen'. No prophet's assurance can be more than 'moral'; and what one prophet will act on, another will not (G III, 32/10-17). Part of the mystery of prophecy is that, however weak may be the grounds that convince a prophet that God is revealing something to him, 'God never deceives the pious and chosen' (G III, 31/15).

It does not follow, because God never deceives the pious, that he corrects the false general conceptions they already hold. The fundamental law of morality that human beings are to love God with their whole hearts and their neighbours as themselves, was revealed to Moses, and to many later prophets as well, along with its derivative precepts of justice and mercy. God did not deceive the prophets in revealing that law; for it is an eternal truth, not about how he acts, but about how it is rational for human beings to act. God is infinitely rational and infinitely good; but he cannot be 'the unique exemplar of human life', because he cannot coherently be conceived to love finite beings, or to be either just or unjust, merciful or unmerciful to them. Yet the prophets, believing that, as their creator, God had made human beings in his image, all taught that he is the exemplar of human life. Hence, when it was revealed to them that human beings are to love one another, they imagined it to imply the falsehood that God loves all men; and they could not distinguish that falsehood from what was revealed to them. Yet God did not deceive them: what he revealed to them was an eternal truth in the form of a commandment. The falsehood was the work of the prophets, which God tolerated because that truth could only be revealed through their defective imaginations (TT-P, 13—170/31–172/6).

Strauss reads this passage as saying both that God undeceitfully revealed that he is the unique exemplar of human life, loving and showing mercy to all human beings, and that it is a philosophical truth that what God thus revealed is false. He then takes this flat contradiction to be one sign among many that the *Tractatus* as a whole has an esoteric meaning; namely, that belief in revelation is superstitious; and that philosophy supplies all that the wise need for salvation.[7] That is perverse. Spinoza asserted, not that God revealed to the prophets that he is the pattern of human virtue, but that the prophets to whom God revealed the principle of charity believed it, and interpreted in terms of their belief the moral law God did reveal to them. It is true that, immediately after denying that 'human beings can ... imitate [God's] nature by a definite rule of life' (G III, 171/26-7), Spinoza also declared that God 'seeks nothing else from men than cognition of his divine justice and charity'. However, by adding that such cognition 'is not necessary for the sciences, but only for obedience', he intimated that the only part of that false cognition that God has revealed is the moral commandment implicit in it (TT-P, 13—G III, 172/26-9).

Although Spinoza reminded his readers that the Jewish Scriptures themselves bear witness that divine revelation is not confined to the Jews (for example, *Numbers* 22:5-24:25 narrates a revelation to the gentile Balaam—G III, 51/30-53/9), he recognized that they primarily record God's revelations to Jewish prophets. Those revelations are of two kinds: either commands that something be done, or useful information about what God would do. First, and fundamentally, the Jews received a law through Moses which, with ordinary luck, would have assured the prosperity of their state had it been observed with ordinary prudence. Secondly, despite their disobedience, imprudence, and occasional ill luck, the Jews were also granted a long series of revelations through prophets after Moses, which enabled their state at least to survive. Without this 'external help' from God, they could not 'have excelled other nations in successfully conducting their affairs as they concerned the security of life, and in surmounting great perils' (TT-P, 3—G III, 47/28-35).

2.3. Judaism and Christianity

By recognizing Jesus as the last authentic Jewish prophet Spinoza offended orthodox Jews; and by denying that he was more than a prophet he offended orthodox Christians. Because Spinoza recognized the prophetic mission of Jesus as unique, Hermann Cohen has denounced the publication of the *Tractatus* as a 'humanly incomprehensible act of treason' against Jews and Judaism,[8] and Strauss, while declining to go so far, has charged that it was 'amazingly unscrupulous' because it

> fights Christian prejudices by appealing to Christian prejudices; appealing to the Christian prejudice against Judaism, he exhorts the Christians to free essentially spiritual Christianity from all carnal Jewish relics (e.g. the belief in the resurrection of the body).[9]

This will astonish Christians. Exhortations to purify 'spiritual' Christianity from carnal doctrines such as the resurrection of the body appeal to a prejudice; but that prejudice is classical and humanist, as St Paul saw, not Christian. It offends orthodox Christians at least as much as orthodox Jews. And is it 'humanly incomprehensible' that a Jew who, although expelled by his own community for universalism, did not renounce his heritage should have thought of Jesus—not of Christians generally—as a forerunner?

Now and then Spinoza expresses as insults ideas about orthodox Jewish life that are not in themselves offensive. This is the worst example I have noticed:

> That [the Jews] have persisted [as a people] although for so many years dispersed and without power to govern (*imperium*) is not at all wonderful. For they have separated themselves from all other nations in such a way as to concentrate the hatred of all on themselves: and that not only by external rites contrary to the rites of all other nations, but by the sign of circumcision, which they preserve most religiously. That it is the hatred of the Nations that above all keeps them in existence [as a people] is something that experience has already taught. (TT-P, 3—G III, 56/20-6)

Singling out the rite of circumcision does seem to appeal to Christian prejudice; for that rite could not well arouse hatred of Jews in Muslims, who also practise it. And it is not impartial; for Spinoza will go on to explain distinctive Christian rites as instituted for the sake of the Church's integrity, without implying that it is partly because they inspire hatred in non-Christians, or insinuating that such hatred would be justified (TT-P, 5—G III, 76/15-17). While various explanations of these insults are to hand, evidence is wanting to decide which of them is true, if any is. Strauss's, however— that they are an unscrupulous device for turning Christian anti-Jewish prejudice against orthodox Christianity—seems false. They are too few and too unsystematic for that.

Spinoza's treatment of Christianity in the *Tractatus* was brief. Although he relied on the published work of Christian scholars instead of constructing his own 'history' of them, he decided that the Christian gospels qualify, according to his rule of interpretation, as authentic reports of divine revelation. Following the same rule, he concluded that if the gospel reports of revelations to Jesus were true, then Jesus received them, not by mediating 'words or visions', but 'immediately': so that 'God manifested himself through the mind of Christ to the Apostles as formerly to Moses by a mediating brazen voice' (TT-P, 1—G III, 21/6-8). The revelations made to Jesus were therefore, if the reports of them are true, a limiting case: he was 'not so much a Prophet as the mouth of God' (TT-P, 4—G III, 64/19). Hence what God revealed to him was not contaminated by his beliefs, as was what he revealed to earlier prophets:

> Like the angels, Christ perceived things truly, or understood them; for a thing is understood when it is perceived purely by the mind (*pura mente*) without words and images. And so Christ perceived revealed things truly and adequately. (G III, 64/34-65/2)

Because of this, Jesus could be sent to teach not only the Jews, but the whole human race, and he was.

What was revealed to Jesus was universal ethical truth, and it was received as such: that is, as a system of eternal truths about what makes for a good human life, and not as a set of commands to be obeyed under promises and threats. However, not even Jesus could teach what was revealed to him as it was revealed. Like the prophets before him, he could communicate to others only what they were capable of receiving. And so he adapted his teaching to the ignorance of those he taught, sometimes giving them commands, but more often telling them parables. That is why, like the earlier Jewish prophets, he and the Apostles publicly taught eternal truths about what human conduct is rational by presenting them as divine commands, which they are not, and by combining them with falsehoods, such as that God was loving, merciful and just. To 'those to whom it was given to know the mysteries of heaven', however, he taught eternal truths without disguise, and not as laws, 'and in this way freed them from the bondage of the law' (G III, 65/1-11).

When those that accepted the teaching of Jesus and the Apostles formed a society, the Church, they adopted rites which bound them together, as their ceremonial law bound the Jews. Yet, in Spinoza's judgement, the ceremonial practices Christians consider definitive of their religious life are in fact inessential, not only to any true religion, but to religion so far as it was revealed to Jesus.

> the Christian rites, Baptism, the Lord's Supper, feasts, public prayers, and such others as are, and always have been, common to the whole of Christianity—if they were ever instituted by Christ, or by the Apostles (which so far is not established to my satisfaction)—have been instituted only as external signs of the universal Church, and not at all as things which do anything for blessedness, or that may have any Sanctity in themselves. And so, while not for the sake of government (*imperii*), these rites nevertheless were instituted only for the sake of a Society's integrity. (TT-P, 5—G III, 76/8-16)

Nor, with one possible exception, does what Spinoza wrote about the content of what was revealed to Moses and Jesus either disparage one or idealize the other. It is no disparagement to say that what was revealed to Moses was, above all, a system of moral, civil and ceremonial law for a single people, along with appropriate conditional promises and threats; and that both before and after that law was revealed, practical directions for particular emergencies were also revealed to him, together with the information necessary for carrying them out.

With respect to morality, Spinoza discerned no substantial difference between what Moses taught the Jews to do, and what Jesus taught everybody to do. 'We perceive from Scripture itself without any difficulty or ambiguity that the highest [law] is to love God above all things, and [one's] neighbour as oneself' (TT-P, 12—G III, 165/11-13). We learn from the Jewish Scriptures not only the fundamentals which this law presupposes, such as 'that God exists, that he provides for all, that he is omnipotent, that by his decree it is well with the pious but ill with the wicked, and that our safety hangs on his grace alone', but also the specific precepts that follow from it, such as 'to maintain justice, to help the needy, to murder nobody, and to covet nothing of another's' (G III, 165/25-8, 31-3). By separating out its purely moral part, and teaching it to humanity at large, Jesus plainly did not invalidate the Mosaic Torah as the divinely revealed law of the Jewish state (TT-P, 5—G III, 56/34-57/5). And as the law of the Jewish state, Spinoza acknowledged no defect in the Torah, except for one reservation: that, after they had worshipped the golden calf, it was for vengeance, not for their security, that the Jews' sacred ministry was entrusted to the tribe of Levi, instead of to the first-born in all tribes (TT-P, 17—G III, 218/1–8). Partly owing to dissensions arising from this separation of powers, the affairs of the Jewish state in the end ceased to be well conducted, and it succumbed to Rome. Now there is no state in which God wills that anybody observe the law of the Jewish state, whether Jew or non-Jew: the Jews' belief that they are religiously bound to observe it in the Diaspora is mistaken. The moral provisions of the Torah indeed remain valid: but as eternal truths valid for everybody, not as the revealed law of a particular state.

The whole of what is needed for human 'salvation' (*salus*), Spinoza therefore concluded, was revealed by God to Moses. Far from adding to the Torah, Jesus omitted the part of it that provided for the special needs of the defunct Jewish state, and taught the remainder as a way of salvation for human beings of all nations. It is true that, unlike Moses, he received what was revealed to him without imaginative contamination. But, like Moses, he taught what was revealed to him, not what he grasped philosophically; and like Moses, he expressed it in a form designed to reach the imaginations of his audience. Jesus was a prophet, not a philosopher. The Jewish and the Christian Scriptures each record a genuine divine revelation of what is needed for human salvation; and, since every such revelation must have the same theological content, each furnishes philosophically-minded students with enough material for determining the essentials of the 'universal faith' that is the dogmatic content of all revelation.

A momentous political conclusion follows, as Spinoza pointed out. Since all genuine revelations have the same theological content, every good state ought to compel its citizens to profess a universal revealed faith, while defending their right to adopt any religious opinion, however controversial, that is not forbidden by it (TT-P, 14—G III, 173/34–174/4). The dogmas of this universal faith are seven, and no more, namely: (1) God, the supreme being, exists, and is the exemplar of human conduct; (2) God is one; (3) God is omnipresent and nothing is hidden from him; (4) God has supreme right and dominion, and is bound by no law; (5) the worship of God, and obedience to him, consists only in justice and charity, or love towards one's neighbour; (6) all who obey God by this way of living are saved, and only they; and (7) God condones the sins of the penitent (G III, 177/19–178/4). These dogmas, being elicited from records of divine revelation, are expressed in an imaginative form suited to the public at large. The philosophically-minded, understanding this, will profess them with appropriate reservations. The fifth dogma forbids any inquisition into those reservations; for it denies the right of the State to inquire into citizens' opinions except to determine whether they embrace practical precepts contrary to justice or charity. Spinoza believed that the best hope of bringing to an end the persecutions that had made Christianity infamous was not that the Christian churches would become enlightened, but that enlightened states would deprive them of the power to persecute.

Spinoza's Jewish critics acknowledge that the state he advocated would not favour Christians and disfavour Jews.[10] For example, it would be bound to suppress, as contrary to the fifth dogma, any attempt to compel Jews to acknowledge that Jesus was a true prophet. It would not forbid Christians to form private associations for celebrating their sacraments, or to exclude from those sacraments any who would not accept their superstitions about them; but neither would it forbid Jews to form private associations for observing the ceremonial precepts of the Torah, or to exclude from their rites any who believed those precepts to be valid only in a Jewish state. A state of the sort Spinoza approved would have permitted the Amsterdam synagogue to expel him, although not to punish its members for continuing in friendship with him.

Was Spinoza then sincere in asserting that God communicated with Jesus more directly than with Moses, and that what he communicated was addressed to all human beings, and not to the Jews only? If he lied when he claimed to believe that the Christian gospels report a genuine divine revelation as well as the Pentateuch, then he was not; and Cohen, with Strauss's endorsement, would have some ground for charging him with intending to disparage Moses and idealize Jesus.[11] But there is no evidence in the *Tractatus* or his other writings that he lied, except that to which Strauss drew attention, and of which I have tried to dispose.¹² And there is evidence that he did not. Alexandre Matheron has shown how Spinoza could reasonably have considered the revelation to Jesus, made at a time when the western world was unified by the Roman Empire, as necessary to the diffusion of the ideas on which liberal Protestants would draw, and which would reconcile Jews and Christians.¹³

2.4. The New Science as the Key to True Religion

Unlike the agnostics and atheists today, Spinoza refused to identify either Judaism or Christianity with their orthodox forms. He thought it evident that most human beings cannot do without religion; and also that, despite the superstitions of the orthodox, Judaism and Christianity both teach their faithful much that is true. Useful truth is not only acquired scientifically. Classical and modern history confirms the teaching of the Jewish Scriptures that men like Moses and Alexander the Great have divined, without the benefit of science, not only what institutional arrangements would work, but what risks to take. These powers were natural, although they were often superstitiously believed to be supernatural. The philosophically-minded should not exaggerate the practical scope of science: they should acknowledge that there is practically useful cognition that is not scientific, and develop a theory of it. Revelation, as it has occurred in Jewish and Christian history, is such a form of cognition. To understand that history, a theory of superstition as error produced by fear (cf. TT-P pref.—G III, 5-7) is not enough. A theory of revelation as non-scientific cognition is also needed: a theory that does not deny it, but naturalizes it.

As the researches of Richard Popkin and others have shown, Spinoza's view of revelation, although unique as a whole, had much in common with others contemporary with it.¹⁴ Oldenburg's letters make plain that many in the scientific movement believed that much in orthodox Christianity was superstitious accretion, and would entertain speculations about purer forms of it; and among Protestants, many Anabaptists and Quakers believed the same on purely religious grounds. Total scepticism about both Judaism and Christianity was, however, rare; and no thinker adopted it whose surviving writings are of any value. Spinoza was separated from his liberal contemporaries less because he repudiated orthodox dogmas they wished to retain than because of his interpretation of those on which they agreed.

The Christians whom he vainly tried to persuade—among his correspondents, Oldenburg, van Blijenbergh, and van Velthuysen—all wished to liberalize Christianity; and some hoped for a reconciliation with Judaism. Oldenburg at one period might have accepted Spinoza's conception of a universal religion, taken as revealed to Jesus and the Jewish propehets; and after Spinoza's death, Newton reached one very like his, which other secret Arians in the English establishment appear to have shared. But neither Oldenburg nor Newton had any doubt at all that nature was supernaturally created by a supernatural God; or that God has supernaturally intervened in the course of nature, whether in revelations to prophets or in producing physical events that would not have occurred in the ordinary course of nature (that is, in miracles). What divided Spinoza from these liberal Christians was his conception of nature.

Like them, he believed that the Jewish and Christian Scriptures authoritatively reported on a single body of actions of God in nature, whether revelations or miracles, that elude human capacities of scientific explanation; but unlike them, he believed that the new mechanical conception of nature furnishes a critical principle by which to distinguish what in an authentic scriptural record of a purported revelation or miracle is true from what is false. He could not understand how anybody who embraced the mechanical conception of nature could fail to analyse in terms of it all scriptural passages about God he accepted as true. According to that conception, nature has some of the properties possessed only by God: for example, self-existence and infinity. And nature certainly exists. So, he argued, it follows that nature must be God, and that the supernatural God of the theologians is a relic of the imaginations of the ignorant prophets to whom God revealed himself. Since 'no sound reason entices [us] to attribute to nature a limited power and virtue, and to lay down that its laws are apt for certain things only, and not for everything', neither can there by any sound reason for distinguishing between 'laws and rules of nature and decrees of God', or for scrupling to believe that 'the power of nature is infinite, and extends itself to all things that are conceived, even by the divine intellect itself' (TT-P, 6—G III, 83/18-24).

The naturalization of God that makes Spinoza's theology unique also makes his philosophy unique. Strauss was justified, although not for the reason he gave, in describing the *Tractatus* as 'Spinoza's introduction to philosophy'.[15] It is the royal road to understanding his use in the *Ethics* of the language of theology. It is true that, by distinguishing nature's infinity from God's, his contemporaries reconciled their continued adherence to the doctrine of creation with the new conception of nature as infinite. Spinoza disdained to pretend that superstition could be rescued by what seemed to him a quibble. While Descartes before him and Leibniz after were trying to synthesize traditional theology with the new science, he was trying to naturalize it; and if we read him as we read Descartes and Leibniz, we shall misunderstand him as most of his contemporaries did. He did not foresee that interpreters would one day make his *Ethics* safe, if not for superstition, then for a kindred neo-Platonism, by restoring to its theological terms the pre-naturalized senses of which he strove to rid them.

Notes

[1] Meinsma (1983), p. 124; cf. Pollock (1880) 17-19.
[2] Ep30,—G IV, 166/20-9). Although Ep30 (a fragment preserved in the *Opera Posthuma*) is undated, Gebhardt quotes a letter of Oldenburg's dated 10 October 1665, in which it is quoted, and described as 'very lately written' (G II, 404).
[3] This is the opinion of Leo Strauss in Strauss (1952), pp. 142-201, and in the introduction to Strauss (1965).
[4] For what Spinoza took a 'philosophical reader' to be, see the following passages in the first four letters he exchanged with Oldenburg: G IV, 5/25-6/3, 8/18-31, 12/1-9, 25/5-9.
[5] See J.H. Hertz (ed.) *The Pentateuch and Haftorahs* (2nd edn, London: Soncino Press, 1978), p. 316, where the words 'pervert justice' are glossed as follows: 'The Rabbis disregarded the literal meaning of the last three Hebrew words, and took them to imply that, except when it is "to do

evil", one should follow the majority' (ibid.). Izhak Englard, 'Majority Decision and Individual Truth', *Tradition* 15 (1975), pp. 137–52, movingly defends the orthodox position.

6   Bayle (1720), III, p. 2642 (Article on Spinoza, Note R—Popkin (1965), p. 319).
7   Errol E. Harris lists eight such signs which Strauss claims to detect, this being the third; and shows all to be spurious (Harris (1978), pp. 6–8, 13–14). They are Strauss's principal evidence (Harris (1978), p. 8) that 'Spinoza's critique is directed against the whole body of authoritative teachings and rules known in Spinoza's time as Judaism' (Strauss (1965), pp. 27–28).
8   According to Strauss (1965), p. 19.
9   Strauss (1965), pp. 19–20.
10 E.g. 'The liberal society with a view to which Spinoza composed the *Treatise* is then a society of which Jews and Christians can be equal members. For such a society he wished to provide' (Strauss (1965), p. 20).
11 Strauss (1965), p. 19.
12 According to Strauss, even Cohen conceded that 'Spinoza had a genuine reverence for Jesus' teachings' (Strauss (1965), p. 19).
13 See Matheron (1971), esp. chs. 1 and 7.
14 Popkin (1979), esp. chs. 11 and 12; and Popkin (1987), pp. 38–43. Despite pervasive debts, I do not accept Popkin's opinion that 'Spinoza did not merely doubt the truth claims of Scripture, he denied them except for a moral message' (Popkin (1979), p. 238). Cf. Matheron (1971), ch. 6.
15 Strauss (1965), p. 28.

3 Cogitatio

3.1. The New Way of Ideas

Throughout his writings, Spinoza treats it as an evident truth that human beings think (*cogitant*). In *Ethics* II he enunciates it as an axiom (a2); and in the axiom that follows, he announces his acceptance of a theory of thinking and its place in mental life that his contemporaries would have recognized as Cartesian. Every mental state, whether cognitive (such as believing something, doubting it, or supposing it) or affective (such as enjoying something or being saddened by it, loving it or hating it) is, he declares, a mode of thinking (*modus cogitandi*); and the most primitive mode of thinking, present in every other, is having what is called an 'idea' of something. 'There are no modes of thinking, such as love, ... unless there is in the same Individual the idea of the thing loved. ... But there can be an idea, even though there is no other mode of thinking' (E2a3).

Descartes introduced this theory of mind to the philosophical world in 1641, in his *Meditations on First Philosophy*. Locke was later to name it 'the new way of ideas'. It perplexed some acute readers, as the *Objections* of Caterus and Hobbes included in later editions of the *Meditations* disclose (AT VII, 92, 102–5, 179–81).[1] Yet neither its novelty nor its difficulty repelled others. It was adopted by the authors of the *Port Royal Logic*,[2] and its acceptance by advanced thinkers as common doctrine may be dated from the success of that work, the first chapter of which begins: 'The word *idea* is of the number of those that are so clear that one cannot explain them by others, because there are none more clear and more simple.'[3] Although it is now held by nobody, Ian Hacking has rightly warned that if this theory is forgotten as well as abandoned, late seventeenth-century philosophy will become unintelligible.[4] Unfortunately, except in name, it is now largely forgotten.

Descartes arrived at it by reflecting on the doctrine of his Jesuit teachers, which descended from Aristotle's *De Anima*.[5] According to that doctrine, two cognitive functions are found in the souls of animals: sensation together with sensory imagination, and thinking. In both, something is represented in the soul. In sensation, the sensible 'forms' of physical objects—their shapes, sizes, motions, colours, smells and tastes—come to exist in the matter of the organs of sense. Animals see round shapes because those shapes in distinguishable colours come to exist in the matter of their eyes. And in thinking, without benefit of any organ, the intelligible 'forms' of objects generally—their 'universal' qualities and relations—come to exist in the immaterial being of the receptive intellect. A rational animal thinks of roundness because, in some way appropriate to its immateriality, roundness comes to be in it.

The scholastic Aristotelians invented a terminology for this that remains in use. As it exists in a penny, they called the being or reality of its roundness 'natural' (*esse naturale*). Descartes preferred Suarez's name 'formal'; and he thought of formal being or reality as having degrees: pennies having more of it than their shapes. On the other hand, as it exists in the sense organs and intellect of an animal who sees a penny's shape and thinks of it, the Aristotelians called the being of its roundness 'intentional' (*esse intentionale*).[6] Here again Descartes chose to follow Suarez, and named it 'objective'. In setting out part of the argument of his *Meditations* in geometrical order, he gave this definition of the 'objective reality of an idea':

> D3. By the *objective reality of an idea* I understand the being of the thing represented by the idea, insofar as it is in the idea (*Resp. ad Obj.* II—AT VII, 161/4-6).[7]

Spinoza reproduced this definition in his geometrical version of the *Principia* (G I, 150/1-2).

While Descartes did not quarrel with the Aristotelians' description of what happens in sensation and thought, he ridiculed it as theory. Through the mediation of light, a penny indeed causes the retina of your eye to receive its shape with its colour; but a mirror reflecting it does as much, and yet sees nothing. Just so, should the sight of a penny cause you to receive in some non-physical receptor its dematerialized and universalized shape, you would not thereby be anything more than an immaterial mirror. Descartes did not deny that, as far as they went, the Aristotelians were largely right: every sensory or intellectual representation has a double being—its formal or natural being as something that can in turn be represented in thought, and its objective or intentional being as representing something else. His complaint was that they did not go far enough. They did not perceive that a reproduction of a thing in the sense organs or intellect of a rational animal does not *per se* have this double being. Such reproductions therefore do not explain the representativeness of sensation and thought, even if they play a part in it.

Physical reproductions, Descartes reasoned, are representative derivatively, by being viewed as such. Representativeness is therefore a fundamental non-physical property. Nothing physical, for example a picture, can possess it except by the mediation of representations that represent immediately or in their own right. Such representations must be more than replicas, even non-physical ones, caused in thinking beings by whatever is represented. Descartes's name for these postulated representations was 'ideas'; for, as he explained to Arnauld, 'idea' was 'the standard philosophical term used to refer to the forms of perception belonging to the divine mind' (AT VII, 181/10-12). God represents things to himself without the mediation of anything that is not representative in its own right.[8] Since human animals must have a similar power, their representations may also be called by the name we give to God's.

A human animal's idea of something, although it is not physical, is a 'mode' of that animal, which can itself be represented just as bodily 'modes' can. Since all ideas are modes of thinking of the same kind, Descartes inferred that none has more formal being than any other. Yet an idea differs radically from from a bodily mode like a cramp in a leg muscle, because, being a representation, its being is not only formal, but also 'objective' or 'intentional'. Although equal in their formal being, ideas differ in objective being; for each has as much objective being as what it represents has formal being. Thus, since a substance has more formal being than its modes, the idea of a substance has more objective being than the idea of one of that substance's modes.

Because it seemed evident to him that nobody can have an idea without being aware of it—that is, without having an idea of it—Descartes concluded that all ideas must have the recursive property of being identical with ideas of themselves.[9] Accordingly, in his reply to Bourdin, he wrote:

> The initial thought by means of which we become aware of something does not differ from the second thought by means of which we become aware that we were aware of it, any more than this second thought differs from the third thought by means of which we become aware that we were aware. (AT VII, 599/16-20)

'[T]his', Gueroult points out, 'amounts to saying that there is no real difference between a thought and a thought of a thought, but only a difference of reason.'[10] That is a mistake: there is more than a difference of reason. Even if it followed from the nature of ideas that every idea is accompanied by an idea of itself, since an idea and an idea of it differ in objective reality—in what they are ideas of—none of the infinitely many ideas of ideas that accompany a given idea can be identical either with it or with every other.

Although for the most part Descartes expounds his theory of ideas clearly, he has perplexed many readers by formulating some of its parts sloppily. The worst such formulation is his definition of '*cogitatio*' in the geometrical restatement of the argument of his *Meditations* in *Resp. Obj.* II, which he echoes several times, and which Spinoza reproduces:

> D1. Under the word *thought* I include everything which is in us and of which we are immediately conscious. (AT VII, 160/7-8; cf. G I, 149/18-19)

As it stands, this implies that, when you think of something, your left hand say, you are 'immediately conscious' of your idea of your left hand, but not of your left hand. That is misleading, because it implies that the only things ideas can immediately represent are other ideas, even though it is fundamental to Descartes's concept of an idea that, whatever it represents, it represents immediately. No harm is done, however, as long as it is remembered that such remarks are equivalent to: 'Under the word *thought* I include everything of which we can become conscious in such a way that there is no room for doubt whether what we are conscious of exists.' We all have ideas of some of our bodily states. Although it is possible to imagine that a malign genius created us as disembodied minds, and hence that nothing outside our minds corresponds to what our ideas of our bodily states represent, it is impossible to imagine that it created us as minds perpetually deluded about what our ideas represent; for, like a painting containing a painting of a painting, a representation of another representation contains a representation of what that representation represents. It cannot be denied that a painting of the artist exists if a painting of his studio depicts it as containing a painting of him; for a painting of a painting of him is also a painting of him.

Having decided that no analysis can reduce the objective being of ideas to physical properties (cf. AT VII, 78/8-20), Descartes concluded that materiality and mentality are really distinct. Spinoza, as we shall see, follows him not only in this, but in a further conclusion. Since modes of thinking cannot be analysed in terms of physical properties, thinking cannot be illuminated by investigating either the meanings of spoken and written utterances, or the causes and effects of physcial changes in the organs of sense. Fruitful investigation must go in the opposite direction.

Philosophers influenced by Wittgenstein are apt to object that, having failed to describe representation in intelligible terms, Descartes postulated a magical mental realm that does not have to be described intelligibly. That is unjust. Descartes was not confronted with physical phenomena which, because he could not understand how they are produced, he declared to be produced by mental magic. He drew attention to a familiar phenomenon—representation—which nobody has ever seriously denied occurs. He did not offer it as the explanation of anything. If it is presupposed that every intelligible phenomenon must be reducible to a physical one, it is undeniably mysterious how representation can be so reduced; but there is no good reason to presuppose it. Far from postulating a magical realm to explain representation, Descartes did not attempt to explain it, he reminded us that it occurs, and that it is irreducible.

3.2 The Structure of Representative Ideas: Descartes's Examples

Descartes's occasional remarks about ideas in general add little to our understanding of what it is for an idea to represent something. Yet one is often quoted for the simile it contains:

> [A]lthough one idea may perhaps originate from another, there cannot be an infinite regress here; eventually one will reach a primary idea, the cause of which will be like an archetype which contains formally all the reality which is present only objectively in the idea. So it is clear to me by the natural light that ideas in me are as it were images (*quasi imagines*) which can easily fall short of the perfection of the things from which they are taken, but which cannot contain anything greater or more perfect. (AT VII, 42/6-15)

At first sight, this may appear to imply that ideas are likenesses taken from what they are ideas of, as portraits are likenesses taken from their sitters. Yet Descartes cannot have intended that. According to his theory of mind, portrait painters produce painted likenesses of individual sitters because they have visual ideas of them; but they do not produce their visual ideas because they have yet other ideas. An idea is like a painting painted without an intervening idea.

Although Descartes's treatment of particular examples of ideas throws a light on their internal nature which his general statements about them do not, Alan Gewirth was the first systematically to investigate it, in a series of articles published more than forty years ago.[11] Gewirth drew particular attention to the treatment of ideas of pain in *Principia* I, 68, which brings out that what is commonly mistaken for Descartes's idea of pain is no more than a component of two different ideas of it. One is clear and distinct. In it, 'pain ... is regarded (*spectantur*) merely as (*tantummodo ut*) [a] sensation (*sensus*) or thought' (AT VIII-1, 33/10-12). The other, expressed by speaking of pains as in the body, is confused:

> If someone says he ... feels pain in a limb, this amounts to saying that he ... feels something there of which he is wholly ignorant.... Admittedly, if he fails to pay sufficient attention, he may easily convince himself that he has some knowledge of what he ... feels, because he may suppose it is something similar to the sensation of ... pain which he experiences (*experitur*) within himself. But if he examines what it is which that sensation of ... pain represents as existing in the paining part (*tanquam ... in parte dolente existens, repraesentet*)—he will realize that he is wholly ignorant of it. (AT VIII-1, 33/15-25)

Since Descartes describes the former as clear and the latter as obscure (AT VII-1, 33/8), he regards them as two and not one. And, since what he 'experiences within himself' is the same in both, he does not consider it to be more than a component of either.

In speaking of what the person in question 'experiences within himself', Descartes makes it plain that he is referring, not to a corporeal sensation of the sort which human beings share with brute animals, but a mental accompaniment of it. That mental accompaniment is presented in both ideas, but in each it is presented differently: in the former as something regarded as caused by an unknown state of a limb; in the latter as something in that limb. Both are representations, not because either is an image of any sort, but because each is a specific mental act: a *regarding* of what is presented *as* something formally real. Gewirth therefore distinguishes three 'factors' in an idea's structure: something immediately present to the mind, a regarding of what is thus present as something, and what it is regarded as. He calls the first of these elements the 'direct content' of the idea, and the third its 'interpretive content'.[12]

The most obscure of these factors is the third. Fortunately, Descartes throws some light on what he had in mind by remarking, in his third *Meditation*, that ideas may be 'materially' false; and giving as his reason that, since 'there can be no ideas except of things (*nisi tanquam rerum*)' (AT VII, 44/34), they are materially false when they 'represent a nonthing as a thing (*non rem tanquam rem*)' (AT VII, 43/29-30).

The idea of a pain in a limb as something mental which the person experiencing it has a propensity to regard as caused by a state of that limb, while recognizing that he is ignorant of that state, is therefore materially true: for that mental thing is formally real—a thing—and is represented as being so. By contrast, the idea of a pain in a limb as something mental in that limb is materially false; for a physical thing with a mental mode can no more be formally real than an angry apple, and to regard it as formally real represents a non-thing as a thing.

Pains in limbs, like the states of those limbs that cause them, are actual existents, having effects on other actual existents. But, as Descartes pointed out in the following passage from *Meditation* V, there are formally real things that are not actual existents, even though ideas of them are neither invented nor dependent on anyone's mind:

> When, for example, I imagine a triangle, even if no such figure exists, or ever has existed, anywhere outside my thought, there is still a determinate nature, or essence, or form of the triangle which is immutable and eternal, and not invented by me or dependent on my mind. This is clear from the fact that various properties can be demonstrated of the triangle, for example, that its three angles equal two right angles. (AT VII, 64/11–20)

Such determinate natures or essences are possible individuals, although their possibility is neither invented nor dependent on minds, but an eternal truth. As possible individuals they are abstract: a triangle, as an essence, has only those properties that are implied in being a triangle, such as having sides each of some length or other, but not those implied in being an actually existing triangle, such as having sides each of a certain particular length.

Not all ideas, however, are of formally real existents or essences: there are ideas we simply make up (Descartes referred to those he himself made up as '*ideae a me ipso factae*'—AT VII, 38/1) which represent non-existents or non-essences: for example, winged horses or rhombuses inscribed in circles. These ideas are materially false; for they represent non-things as things.

Spinoza not only adopted Descartes's conception of ideas as modes of thinking that are representative in their own right, of which those who have them are conscious, but treated their structure similarly. His analysis of the popular idea of free agency is a good example, because it resembles Descartes's analysis of the confused popular idea of pain. When most people think of themselves as acting freely, he points out, they have no more in their minds than

> that they are conscious of their actions and ignorant of the causes by which they are determined. This, then, is their idea of freedom—that they do not cognize any cause of their actions. They say, of course, that human actions depend on the will, but these are only words for which they have no idea. (E2p35s—G II, 117/14-18)

Their idea of freedom, in short, consists in presenting their actions to themselves as physical events without physical causes, and regarding them, so presented, as real things. It is materially false, because real physical things necessarily have physical causes.

Descartes's doctrine that ideas are materially false if they represent non-things as things is effectively endorsed by Spinoza in an axiom in *Ethics* I, 'A true idea must agree with its ideatum' (E1a6). The Latin name, *'ideatum'*, which he gave to what the thing or non-thing presented in an idea is regarded as, is scholastic.[13] He first used it in his early *Tractatus de Intellectus Emendatione*, when laying down a general principle which (see 3.1) Descartes at best acknowledged tacitly: that

> A true idea (for we have a true idea) is a different thing from its ideatum: for the one is [for example] a circle, the other the idea of a circle. The idea of a circle is not something having a periphery and a centre, as [does] a circle.[14] (TdIE, 33—G II, 14/13-16)

Since there must be more than a distinction of reason between an idea and what it is an idea of, no idea can be identical with an idea of itself.

That Spinoza often expresses ideas by sentences shows that having an idea, as he conceived it, resembles propounding a proposition; yet he did not confound them. A simple idea, for example the materially true idea of a pain, is the regarding of a presented individual as something formally real. Three operations can be distinguished in it: thinking of or referring to a world of formally real things, thinking of an individual or presenting it to yourself, and regarding an individual thus presented as a thing in the formally real world to which you refer. Its structure can be expressed in the verbal formula (not to be read as an irregularly formed open sentence)

(1) P regarded as some i,

where 'P' stands for a presentation to yourself of a pain you feel, 'i' for a variable ranging over the formally real objects you think of or refer to, and 'regarded as some i' for an act by whoever presents to himself the individual named by the expression to its left, in which he regards that individual as identical with something formally real.

Every idea has a propositional counterpart: that is, a proposition that would be true if and only if the idea were materially true. The propositional counterpart of (1) is expressible by the sentence 'Something is a [bodily] pain', the elements of which are a quantified variable, ranging over a domain of formally real objects, usually symbolized by 'x', and the predicate 'is a pain', which may be symbolized by 'is F'. The structure of that counterpart is therefore displayed by the open sentence.

(2) For some x, x is F.

Plainly, (1) expresses a materially true idea if and only if (2) expresses a true proposition.

While a simple proposition is true if and only if its predicate is true of whatever it is predicated as true of, propounding a proposition is not the same thing as affirming it.[15] Although in our society it is a convention that uttering a sentence expressing a simple proposition, in the absence of express signs to the contrary, is an affirmation of its truth, affirmation is not confined to simple propositions. Since any proposition, say 'p', can be false, it is possible to form a further proposition to that effect, which is expressed by means of the operator 'It is false that ... ', yet uttering the sentence 'It is false that p' obviously does not affirm that p, although it propounds it. Again, given any ordered pair of propositions, p and q, it is possible to form a variety of compound propositions from them by means of appropriate connectives: for example that both are true (by the connective 'and'), that at least one of them is true (by the connective 'or'), and that it is false that the former is true and the latter false (by the connective 'if ... then ...'). The formation of negative and compound propositions is possible because it can be affirmed of any proposition that it has one of the two truth-values, true and false.

It may at first appear that, since ideas are either materially true or false, negative and compound ideas can be formed from simple ones in similar ways. Yet they cannot, because what is presented in an idea, unlike what is propounded in a proposition, is always positive. Yet, as Spinoza saw, no account of thinking in terms of ideas is possible unless in the realm of ideas there are counterparts of negative propositions.

3.3. Ideas as Affirmations: Spinoza Emends Descartes

In *Meditation* IV Descartes attempted to solve the problems of negation and error in thought together, by distinguishing two powers possessed by thinking beings: intellect, which forms simple and compound ideas; and will, which affirms or denies the material truth of the ideas so formed (AT VII, 56–60). Seeing more deeply into the implications of the theory of ideas than its creator, Spinoza flatly rejects this. 'In the mind', he declares, 'there is no ... affirmation ... except that which the idea involves insofar as it is an idea' (E2p49). His attempt to prove it, however, is one of his rare aberrations: he argues that, since every idea, for example the idea of a Euclidean triangle, 'involves' every truth that can be derived from its definition and Euclid's axioms, it is impossible to have that idea without affirming those truths. This is invalid, because you can have the idea of a triangle as expressed in its definition and the related axioms without affirming any of the theorems that are 'involved in' (i.e. that follow from) it. In addition, the proof is so carelessly formulated that, as Curley has pointed out, the proposition to be proved is assumed in it as given (G II, 130/29–30)![16]

It is not in his proof that every idea is an affirmation that Spinoza's insight appears, but in his treatment of examples, many of which are of compound ideas in which component ideas are linked either by conjunction (forming several together) or by exclusion (forming one that excludes another already formed). Negation arises from the exclusion of one idea by another.

The core of his theory of linkage is found in his analysis of one of his own experiences.[17] Replying to some questions about premonitions in a letter from his friend Pieter Balling, Spinoza remembered awaking from a troubling dream the previous winter, and finding that an image in the dream of a scabby Brazilian he had never seen before remained as vividly before his eyes as if he were seeing something real. He would have regarded that image as caused by a scabby Brazilian actually present, had it not vanished as soon as he fixed his eyes on objects that were really in his bedroom, and in time become fainter even when he lapsed into inattentiveness (Ep17—G IV, 76/26–77/6). His explanation of this was partly physiological. Visual ideas in waking life are as a rule more or less true representations of external things that cause physiological 'images' in us—motions in the fluid parts of the organs of sight. Visual ideas in dreams, on the other hand, are as a rule false ideas of the causes of those 'images', when they are in fact caused, during sleep, by changes in the softer solid parts of the brain. If those changes persist after you wake, the idea in your dream will persist, along with your waking visual ideas. Since waking ideas are normally true representations, you will regard each such idea as a true representation of an external cause affecting your body, unless other ideas you have exclude its being so (E2p 17cd—G II, 105/5–20).

Spinoza regarded experiences like this as phenomenological evidence that affirming the material truth of an idea you have depends on your power to form ideas, and not on a power of will independent of it. Before he fixed his eyes on real objects in his bedroom, he was unable to refuse assent to his false idea that a scabby Brazilian was present; after he did so, he did refuse assent to it, not because of an exercise of will independently of his ideas, but simply because his true ideas made his false one fade.

How, according to Spinoza, did his idea of the furniture of his bedroom exclude that of a scabby Brazilian? Although he does not answer this question, it can be answered for him. To the extent that he could tell whether his idea of a closet in a certain position in his bedroom had an ideatum—that is, was materially true, he could also tell that its ideatum, if it had one, could not also be the ideatum of his idea of a scabby Brazilian.

Just as understanding a sentence is understanding its truth-conditions, so having an idea is understanding what it would be for it to have an ideatum; and understanding what it would be for two of your ideas to have ideata is, in some cases at least, understanding whether they can have the same ideatum or not. A further conclusion follows. According to Spinoza's Cartesian physics, bodies occupying the same place at the same time are one and the same body. Hence, if a single substantial body part of which is now occupying a region of your bedroom three feet in front of you is a closet, and another single substantial body part of which is now occupying that region is a scabby Brazilian, then those two substantial bodies are one and the same. Now, if having ideas of those two single substantial bodies involves understanding that whatever is the ideatum of one cannot be that of the other, then you cannot simultaneously have both. If one has an ideatum, then it is excluded that the other has: that is, if one is materially true, then the other is materially false. Each will tend to exclude the other, although you can vacillate between them. (cf. E2p49s—G II, 134/16–20)

An application of exclusion of some theoretical interest is that in which an idea is composed of simpler ideas, each excluding the ideatum of the other as its ideatum. 'The very nature of a square circle', Spinoza observes, 'indicates why it does not exist' (E1p11d—G II, 53/3–4). The idea of a square has as a component the idea of a figure bounded by straight lines; and the idea of a straight line has as a component the idea of a line which excludes that its ideatum be that of an idea of a line having more than two points equidistant from a given point. On the other hand, the idea of a circle is that of a figure bounded by a line all the infinity of points on which are equidistant from a single point: that is, by a line the idea of which excludes that its ideatum be that of an idea excluding as its ideatum a line on which more than two points are equidistant from a given point. Because each of its component ideas excludes the ideatum of the other as its ideatum, the idea of a square circle is such that it cannot have an ideatum.

As Spinoza goes on to make plain, the concept of the exclusion by one idea of of another's having an ideatum is fundamental to his theory of cognition:

[T]he imaginations of the Mind contain error, not regarded in themselves, ... but only insofar as [the Mind] is considered to lack an idea that excludes the existence of the things that it imagines to be present to it. For if the Mind, while it imagines non-existent things as present to it, at the same time knew (*sciret*) that those things do not really exist, it would, of course, attribute this power to a virtue of its nature, not to a vice. (E2p 17s—G II, 106/12-18)

According to Spinoza, being in error is not merely affirming a false idea, as Descartes believed; for having it is affirming it. Rather, it is not affirming (that is, not having) other ideas that 'exclude' the material truth of the false idea, which may linger as a suppressed tendency to make an affirmation. This correction of Descartes is indispensable if the theory of ideas is to contain a coherent theory of their linkage rich enough to furnish counterparts of the logical operations of negation and the formation of compound propositions.

3.4. Ideas and Words

Spinoza warned his readers 'to distinguish between ideas and the words by which we signify things' (E2p49s—G II, 131/32-3). We signify things by words mediately, through ideas; but ideas represent things immediately, in their own right. Does this, as David Savan has argued, separate words from ideas 'so sharply ... that it is difficult to make out for language any useful philosophical function at all?'[18] Although the respects in which Savan found Spinoza to separate words from ideas are, with one exception, not logical, and although Parkinson has shown that the non-logical ones do not justify the dire inferences he draws,[19] the logical one calls for further probing: namely, that 'whereas ideas and their *ideata* are singular and unique, words are inherently general and applicable to an indefinite multitude'.[20]

For reasons we shall go into in 7.3-4, Spinoza divides ideas into those that are inadequate and so partly false, and those that are adequate and true. Most words that express ideas of both kinds—verbs, general nouns, adjectives, and adverbs—are predicative: that is, they are applicable to an indefinite number of things. Spinoza treats predicative terms by which inadequate ideas are expressed separately from those by which adequate ones are; and he will be misunderstood if his distinction is not kept in mind.

He further classifies the predicative words that stand for inadequate ideas as either 'terms called *Transcendental* ... like Being, Thing and something', or terms standing for 'notions they call *Universal*, like Man, Horse, Dog, &c.' (E2p40s1—G II, 120/28-9, 121/13-14)—and he treats the two classes differently. Terms of the first class, he says,

> like Being, Thing and something ... arise from the fact that the human Body, being limited, is capable of forming distinctly only a certain number of images at the same time. ... [W]hen the images in the body are completely confused, the Mind also will imagine all the bodies confusedly, without any distinction, and comprehend them as if under one attribute, viz. under the attribute of Being, Thing, &c. (E2p40s1—G II, 120/28-121/7)

Tracing the presence of transcendental terms in language to the confused idea of an essence that is common to everything, and utterly general—the most comprehensive of all universals—Spinoza points out that this confused idea is materially false: that there is no such essence. What in adequate thinking corresponds to the confused idea of being in general is not a distinct idea, but a component in all ideas, namely, the operation of referring to an ideatum. Lacking the modern logical concept of a variable, he of course has no notion that the syntactical oddities of transcendental terms can be explained by their doing the work of variables.[21]

Terms of the second class—those standing for notions called 'universal'—originate in a similar confused way, but the confusion is less radical. Thus the idea of a man is formed

> because so many images (... of men) are formed at one time in the human Body that they surpass the power of imagining—not entirely, of course, but still to the point where the Mind can imagine neither the individual differences of the singulars (such as the colour and size of each one, &c.) nor their determinate number, and imagines distinctly only what they all agree in, so far as it affects the body. ... And it expresses this by the word *man*, and predicates of it infinitely many singulars. (E2p40s1—G II, 121/13-22)

Unlike the ideas corresponding to transcendental terms, which confound an operation involved in all ideas with attributes allegedly shared by everything, universal notions formed in this way identify, although inadequately, certain sets of things in the world: namely, those sets the members of which cause distinctly recognizable images in human bodies of what they agree in. Since some medieval nominalists maintained that all predicative terms are derived from just such images, Spinoza is sometimes considered to be a nominalist. That is a mistake.

As Parkinson correctly protests, there are predicative expressions whose use Spinoza did not explain in this way.[22] When he discusses geometrical terms, he treats the ideas for which they stand as analysable by means of what he calls 'common notions': notions of what all things agree in, and without which they cannot be adequately thought of (E2p38c). Taking the idea of a triangle as exemplifying all ideas that can be analysed into common notions, he also says that 'the definition of the triangle expresses nothing but the simple nature of the triangle, but not any certain number of triangles' (E1p8s2—G II, 50/27). Natures or essences, as we have seen, are individual. But, as is shown by a remark in the early *Tractatus de Intellectus Emendatione*, to which H.G. Hubbeling has drawn attention, Spinoza saw that they discharge some of the functions assigned to universals. It runs:

> [T]hese fixed and eternal [things], individual [things] though they be, nevertheless on account of their presence everywhere, and their very extensive power, will be for us as universals or the genera in the definitions of individual changeable things. ... [23] (TdIE, 101—G II, 37/5-9)

As Hubbeling reminds us, what is regarded in a Cartesian or Spinozist idea as a thing is always an individual essence.[24] Yet unless it is infinite, such an essence, while not a universal, can function as one. For although the essence of a triangle can be identified neither with any actual triangle as distinct from any other, nor with the set of all of them, it is the essence of every one of them; and in that respect it can function as a universal.

Spinoza therefore holds that universal terms in language are sometimes used to express confused ideas formed from perceiving a multitude of individuals, and sometimes to express ideas of natures or essences, which, although they are individual, may function as universals. In the former case they express inadequate ideas, in the latter, adequate ones. As Bennett succinctly sums up: he offers 'not a metaphysical view about all general terms, but only an aetiology and criticism of some of them', and hence 'not nominalism, but rather a rejection for theoretical purposes of sense-based universality'.[25]

Ideas of different sorts, adequate and inadequate, correspond to the different sorts of universal term, and an operation involved in every idea corresponds to the traditional 'transcendentals'. However, as we have seen in 3.3, ideas are affirmations; and what corresponds to negation and to other logical operations on their unaffirmed propositional counterparts is their linkage, which may take several forms.

In the realm of ideas, the counterpart of negation, as has been shown in 3.3, is exclusion. Of the other forms of linkage, the counterpart of conjunction is the simplest. Since every idea is an affirmation, having several ideas in mind together is the same thing as affirming them all. Such a compresence of ideas is the counterpart of the sentence formed by conjoining the sentences that are the counterparts of each of them. And just as in propositional logic the remaining sentential connectives can be defined in terms of negation and conjunction, so in the realm of ideas, their counterparts can be analysed in terms of exclusion and compresence. Thus the connective 'if ... then ...' can be defined in terms of conjunction and negation, and its counterpart in the realm of ideas is the exclusion of the compresence of one idea with the exclusion of another.

Those who embraced the theory of ideas distrusted words, because of the tedious complication of putting into words exclusions of ideas by ideas that most children learning elementary geometry perceive at once from diagrams. It must not be forgotten that seventeenth-century logical theory could not explain why elementary pieces of arithmetical and geometrical reasoning are sound. Crude though the concepts of the compresence of ideas and the exclusion of one idea by another may be, they seemed to Spinoza to make it possible to elucidate what sound thinking is, and to distinguish it from unsound—including the comparatively trivial part of thinking for the expression of which the logicians of his time possessed rules.

3.5 The linkage of Ideas: Behind the Geometrical Method

Spinoza was never persuaded by Descartes's conception of philosophical method: that of emptying your mind of its ideas, as you empty a basket of apples of which you suspect some are rotten, and readmitting only those that, on careful inspection, satisfy some intuitively evident criterion of certainty. On the contrary, in his earliest work, the abandoned *Tractatus de Intellectus Emendatione*, he had maintained that

> just as men, in the beginning, were able to make the easiest things with the tools they were born with (however laboriously and imperfectly), and once these had been made,... proceeding gradually from the simplest works to tools, and from tools to other works and tools, reached the point where they accomplished so many and so difficult things with little labour, in the same way the intellect, by its inborn power, makes intellectual tools for itself, by which it acquires other powers for other intellectual works, and from these works still other tools, or the power of searching further, and so proceeds by stages, until it reaches the pinnacle of wisdom. (TdIE, 31—G II, 13/30–14/7)

There is no intuitive criterion of certainty. You must make do with the ideas you have, most of which even Descartes acknowledged to be materially true, and judge those you doubt by those you believe true (TdIE, 38—G II, 15/30–16/4).

Success is not assured. If you take a false idea as your standard, as the superstitious do, you will discard your true ideas instead of your false ones. Yet neither it is impossible. The evidence of success, like the evidence that you are improving your tools, will be that your power to solve intellectual problems increases. Here too, there is no absolute assurance. The superstitious may be satisfied that their power to solve problems increases the more they follow some superstitious rule. That is not your problem. They will not claim to be following the same procedure as you, but one which you cannot reconcile with ideas you have; and the ideas you have are the only ones by which you can judge any ideas at all.[26]

Constructing a philosophical system, according to Spinoza, is forming a comprehensive complex idea of what there is. In expressing that idea in words, its author should be aware that he is not re-enacting the process by which he himself formed it. He has several styles of exposition from which to choose. Like Descartes in his *Meditations*, he may set out a sequence of reflections as intellectual exercises by performing which the reader will arrive at the idea to be conveyed. Or, like Spinoza in the *Short Treatise*, he may construct that idea by reminding his readers of ideas familiar from his predecessors, and criticizing them. Many contemporary scientists, however, among them Thomas Hobbes,[27] were captivated by the method of Euclid's *Elements*, in which everything asserted was deduced, by steps the reader would accept as self-evident, from a set of expressly enunciated axioms that were also accepted as self-evident. Descartes himself experimented with it in his *Responsiones* to the second set of objections to *Meditations*.

Although Euclid's *Elements* is not rigorous by today's standards, the standards it satisfies are high. Yet Spinoza knew, from restating the first two Parts of Descartes's *Principia* in geometrical order, that philosophical works demonstrated in that order will not have axioms that everybody will accept as self-evident. His editor implicitly warned readers that he did not accept all the axioms he attributed to Descartes; and he could not have deceived himself that his own axioms in the *Ethics* would be accepted by all its readers as self-evident. Echoing Wolfson's question, what lies behind his adoption of the geometrical order?[28]

It would be a gross anachronism to suppose that, like Leibniz, he sought axioms the contradictories of which could be shown to be self-contradictory, by either a finite or an infinite process; and an even grosser one to imagine that he anticipated Frege, and proffered his axioms either as laws of logic, or as reducible to them by formulable rules of inference. He nowhere betrays any sign of conceiving such projects. However, his experience in putting Descartes's *Principia* into geometrical order may well have suggested to him that no other style of exposition exhibits more clearly the linkages between the elements of the complex idea of nature he was trying to express. He would have learned that he could present that idea geometrically in a number of ways. Did it also occur to him that he could most effectively teach his readers to form that idea for themselves by presenting the counterparts of its more palatable components as axioms, and proving those of the less palatable components as theorems? Whether it did or not, his approach is less shocking and more seductive in the *Ethics* than in the *Tractatus Theologico-Politicus*.

Notes

1 For an illuminating discussion of Caterus's objection see Grene (1985), pp. 124–7.
2 Arnauld and Nicole (1970) (see ch. 1, n.13). Cf. Hacking (1975), pp. 28, 33; and, on Port Royal and Descartes, Grene (1985), pp. 180–91.
3 Arnauld and Nicole (1970), p. 65.
4 Hacking (1975), pp. 15–18, 26–33.
5 The largely unargued view of Descartes's theory of ideas presented in this chapter is mine, although everything in it is derived from somebody else. My chief debt is to a series of three articles by Alan Gewirth: 'Experience and the Non-Mathematical in the Cartesian Method' (*Journal of the History of Ideas* 2 (1941): 183–210); 'The Cartesian Circle' (*Philosophical Review* 50 (1940–1): 368–95); and Gewirth (1943). These articles have coloured much of what I have taken from others: in particular, from E.M. Curley, Marjorie Grene, Martial Gueroult, Anthony Kenny, and Margaret Wilson.
6 Cf. Aristotle, *De Anima*, II, 416 b32–418 b2; 424 a17–424 b3 (on sensation); and III, 427 a18–430 a25 (on imagination and thought). Aquinas, *Summa Theologiae* Ia 85, 1–2, explains the distinction between how what is thought of exists in nature and in the intellect.
7 Cf. Gueroult (1984), p. 61.
8 Thus the *Port Royal Logic* attacks Hobbes for treating words as being representative without the mediation of ideas, which represent in their own right (Arnauld and Nicole (1970), pp. 68–9).
9 In this passage Descartes reminded Arnauld that he had defined an idea as whatever is immediately perceived by the mind (AT VII, 181/5–10). However, the innovation Descartes wished to mark by his new terminology was not that human thinkers can immediately perceive their own thoughts (few had ever denied that they do), but that their thoughts by themselves, without mediation, represent whatever they represent.
10 Here and in the sequel, when Spinoza in DPP reproduces Descartes's wording, I follow Curley's translations rather than Cottingham's.
11 Gewirth (1943), esp. pp. 257–66. Cf. Kenny (1967), pp. 244–9. While withholding judgement, Willis Doney gives a decisive reason for preferring Gewirth's interpretation to Kenny's, unless relevant texts can be found directly contradicting it (as far as I know, none has been): if it is adopted,

it can be explained how Descartes distinguished ideas that are clear and distinct from those that are not; but if Kenny's is, it cannot be (Doney, (ed.) (1967), p. 20).

12. Gewirth (1943), pp. 258-9.
13. According to Parkinson, 'For the Scholastics an *ideatum* was something produced by God as a copy of the idea which he himself had' (Parkinson (1953), p. 112 n.1). Curley translates '*ideatum*' as 'object'. I follow Eisenberg in leaving it untranslated (Eisenberg (ed.) (1977), p. 42), partly because it is a term of art equally intelligible in both languages, and partly because Curley's 'object' also renders '*objectum*'. See '*Ideatum*' in Curley's Glossary (C, 681).
14. The translation is Eisenberg's (Eisenberg (ed.) (1977), p. 38).
15. Curley asserts that 'if we regard the idea as a sort of thought which might be expressed by a proposition ... we can no longer say that the idea itself involves neither an affirmation nor a denial ... ' (Curley (1975), p. 173). But most logicians, from Frege to the present, say that a proposition in itself involves neither.
16. Curley (1975), p. 169.
17. In criticizing a forerunner of this chapter presented at the 1986 Chicago conference, Étienne Balibar objected that I did not give enough weight to what Spinoza says about linkage in the formation of complex ideas. I found that he was right.
18. Savan (1958), p. 63.
19. Parkinson (1969), pp. 78-92.
20. Savan (1958), pp. 62-3.
21. For a different interpretation see Parkinson (1969), p. 82.
22. Parkinson (1969), pp. 82-3.
23. The translation is Eisenberg's (Eisenberg (ed.) (1977), p. 100). Some make bold to confine these '*fixa et aeterna*' to the attributes.
24. Hubbeling (1966), pp. 22-3, esp. 22.
25. Bennett (1984), p. 40.
26. On the concept of truth in *TdIE* see Garrett (1986), and on the relation between the concepts of method in *TdIE* and in *KV* see Mignini (1986).
27. See Kneale and Kneale (1984), p. 311 (on Hobbes—citing John Aubrey, *Brief Lives* (ed. Clark), vol. 1, pp. 332 and 336), and pp. 379-81 (on the Euclidean ideal in seventeenth-century philosophy).
28. The title 'Behind the Geometrical Method', originally chosen by Wolfson for ch. 1 of Wolfson (1934), has also been adopted by Curley for Curley (1988). Important recent treatments of the *mos geometricus* in Spinoza's *Ethics* are: Macherey (1979), pp. 55-94; Curley (1986); and Klever (1986).

4 The Elements of the Idea of Nature as God

4.1. Reinterpreting Necessary Existence

Spinoza gave notice in the *Tractatus Theologico-Politicus* that the theology of the *Ethics*, early drafts of which he was circulating among friends, would be a naturalized one. God would not be regarded as a supernatural being who has created nature and established its laws by an act of will, but rather *as* nature; and nature's laws would be presented as expressing God's essence, not as something he could have made otherwise. Most of his contemporaries tenaciously resisted this naturalization. They were convinced that, while the physcial world exists precariously, God exists necessarily and in his own right. Of course no physicist, Aristotelian or Cartesian, doubted that the physical world was stable; but most of them held that this stability was at God's pleasure, and would not continue forever.

This view of things was formally expressed in the medieval doctrine that, while in created things existence and essence (also called 'nature' and 'quiddity') are distinct, in God they are identical. Maimonides's version of it is representative:

> Existence ... is something that is superadded to the quiddity of what exists. This is clear and necessary with regard to everything the existence of which has a cause ... As for that which has no cause for its existence, there is only God, may he be magnified and glorified, who is like that. For this is the meaning of our saying about Him, may He be exalted, that His existence is necessary. Accordingly, his existence is identical with His essence and His true reality, and His essence is his existence.[1]

Although this conception of necessary existence was shared by most Muslim, Jewish and Christian philosophers in the Middle Ages, nobody who accepted the Cartesian theory of ideas could accept it as it stood. Like Descartes himself, they could agree that God's essence is absolute perfection, and that in some sense the existence of an absolutely perfect being is necessary; but they could not escape distinguishing the ideas of the attributes that follow from God's absolute perfection both from one another and from the idea of existence.

Descartes therefore revised the traditional doctrine in the light of his theory. Recognizing existence as a nature along with the other natures included in the divine essence, he declared that, although existence is not identical with the divine essence, it is inseparable from it.

> Since I have been accustomed to distinguish between existence (*existentia*) and essence in everything else [he wrote], I find it easy to persuade myself that existence can be separated from the essence of God, and hence that God can be thought of as not existing. But when I concentrate more carefully, it is quite evident that existence can no more be separated from the essence of God than the fact that its three angles equal two right angles can be separated from the essence of a triangle. ... (AT VII, 66/4–11)

The reason why existence cannot be denied of God, Descartes concludes, is not that it is identical with his essence, but rather that the idea of the divine essence excludes the exclusion from itself of the idea of existence, just as the idea of a triangle excludes the exclusion from itself of the idea of having interior angles equal to anything but two right angles.

As we have seen in 3.2, Spinoza follows Descartes in conceiving an essence, whether of a triangle or of God, as a 'determinate nature' which, whether it exists or not, is 'not invented by me or dependent on my mind' (AT VII, 64/16–7). Such natures are individual—but individuals whose existence need not be more than possible, given the laws of nature. They are also abstract—they have no properties that do not follow from what they are. Thus the essence of a triangle is a possible individual that is either equilateral or isosceles or scalene; but there is no question which of the three it is, as there is for any actually existing triangle (cf. 3.2). Again, a finite essence does not as such have any particular number of actualizations: what their number is, whether zero or any other, depends on causes other than itself (E1p8s2—G II, 50/24–8). Although some commentators on Spinoza appear to be unfamiliar with this

The Elements of the Idea of Nature as God 59

concept of essence,[2] I shall assume that it is not unintelligible, and that it demonstrably is Spinoza's concept, as well as Descartes's.[3]

Jonathan Bennett has expressed astonishment that although Spinoza uses the term 'essence' freely in the *Ethics*, beginning with the first definition of Part I, he does not define it until Part II.[4] That is a muddle. He uses it as an undefined primitive term throughout the *Ethics*, because its sense was commonly understood. What he defines in Part II is not the expression 'essence', but the expression 'belonging to' (*pertinere*) as it applies to an essence. The definition runs:

> to the essence of any thing belongs that which, being given, the thing is necessarily posited and which, being taken away, the thing is necessarily taken away; or that without which the thing can neither be nor be conceived, and which can neither be nor be conceived without the thing. (E2d2)

In other words, for y to belong (*pertinere*) to the essence of x, it must be true both that if y is given then x is posited (that is, if x is taken away then y is too), and also that if x is given then y is posited (that is, if y is taken away then x is too). Spinoza speaks of an essence as 'given' when it, a possible individual, is accepted as actually existing. It is therefore a truism that, when the essence of x is given, the thing x is posited—that is, its actual existence is (implicitly) affirmed. To think of an essence, however, is not the same as to accept it as given (cf. 3.3). When a child is first told that there are winged horses, he accepts that essence as 'given', in the sense that he regards winged horses as actually existing; yet it will be 'taken away'—that is, he will regard their actual existence as excluded—as soon as he acquires a rudimentary stock of zoological ideas. Inquiry would be crippled if ideas of essences of individuals in the order of nature could not be formed and then perceived to represent non-things as things; that is, if those essences could not be thought of first as 'given', and then as 'taken away'.

In the definition in *Ethics* II, as Gueroult and others have pointed out,[5] Spinoza is correcting a doctrine about what 'constitutes' an essence which, in expounding the *Principia*, he ascribed to Descartes: namely, that

> If something can be removed from a thing, while that thing remains intact, it does not constitute the thing's essence; but if something, on being taken away, takes the thing away, it does constitute the thing's essence. (G I, 183/30-4)

His objection is that Descartes's doctrine implies 'either that the nature of God belongs to the essence of [what are commonly considered] created things, or that [those] things can be or be conceived without God' (E2p10s—G II, 93/27-9).

Spinoza's analysis of transcendental terms like 'being', as we have seen in 3.4, implicitly excludes existence as a presented determinate nature or essence that can be regarded as formally real and not made up. As he points out, if such terms (among which is 'existent') are treated as universals abstracted from our experience of things, they have no place in serious thinking (E2p40s1—G II, 120/29-121/12). Nor do they correspond to anything he expressly recognizes as a common notion. Rather, they are counterparts, not of any idea, but of an operation involved in every idea, namely that of referring to the domain of formally real things that provides their ideata. While the ideatum of a materially true idea is always something having formal reality, the expression 'something having formal reality' no more stands for a nature or individual essence than does the quantified variable that is its sentential counterpart.

Spinoza therefore has reason to reject both the traditional scholastic conception of God's necessary existence and Descartes's amendment of it. Yet he wished to distinguish the existence of his naturalized God from that of all the finite things existing in him, and to express that distinction, as far as possible, in traditional theological terms. To do so, he had to seek a naturalized sense of 'exists necessarily'.

4.2. Causation: Immanent and Transient

Spinoza's first step in developing the conception he needed is on its face regressive. It is a definition

> By cause of itself [he writes] I understand that whose essence involves existence, or that whose nature cannot be conceived except as existing. (E1d1)

In definitions such as this, which stipulate that an expression to be defined stands for the same thing as a defining expression, what the defining expression stands for is assumed to be shared information. Yet, as we have seen in 4.1, Spinoza's readers would have found his putative defining expression uselessly equivocal; for they were familiar with two distinct senses of 'that whose essence involves existence', the Maimonidean one and the Cartesian one. It is true that Wolfson informs us that the phrase 'cause of itself' had 'already been in use in the philosophical literature' in the Maimonidean sense, as standing for a being who needed no cause, and so was 'primarily nothing but a negation, meaning causelessness',[6] but no reader acquainted with the *Tractatus* could assume that Spinoza would respect medieval usage, and no reader of *Ethics* II would expect him to stipulate a sense for 'cause of itself' that was inconsistent with his emendation of the new way of ideas.

However his early readers resolved this initial perplexity, as they read on they were confronted with another. The word 'cause', unaccompanied by 'of itself' is used three times in the axioms of *Ethics* I (in a3 and a4), and is nowhere defined. It therefore signifies a fundamental primitive idea—and one important enough for the word to be used sixty-six times in Part I in the nominative singular alone.[7] Readers were therefore expected to understand it without the help of a definition. And if they had provisionally assumed that 'cause', when accompanied by 'of itself', has a sense unrelated to its sense as a primitive term, they would have found themselves corrected in the scholium to proposition 25, from which they would learn that 'in that sense in which God is called cause of himself, he must also be called cause of all things' (E1p25s—G II, 68/6–8).[8] If God is cause of himself in the sense in which he is cause of all things, then 'cause of itself' cannot mean 'causeless'.

The generic sense in which Spinoza uses the word can be gathered without difficulty from the *Tractatus Theologico-Politicus*, where it is laid down that, since 'the universal laws of nature are nothing but decrees of God, which follow from the necessity and perfection of the divine nature' (TT-P, 6—G III, 82/35–83/2), whatever happens 'comes about through the will and eternal decree of God' (G III, 83/12-13). Since what comes about through the will of God and what is caused by God are the same, it follows that the open sentence 'God causes x' is equivalent to 'God is such that it is a law of nature that if God exists then x exists or occurs, or will do so'.

At first sight, this makes the sentence 'God is cause of himself' senseless; for what sense can be made of the saying that God is such that it is a law of nature that if he exists then he exists or will do so? The answer is found in a distinction between two kinds of laws of nature that corresponds to a distinction Spinoza goes on to draw between two kinds of causes: transient[9] and immanent. Although he uses the term 'immanent' only twice, the second time alluding to the first,[10] its scientific sense is plain. According to the mechanical conception of nature, the things in the physical universe that come into being and pass away are not ultimate, but come to be and pass away in something that neither comes to be nor passes away. The atomists conceived this ultimate thing as a collection of atoms in an infinite void, and the things that come to be and pass away as configurations in the motions of those atoms. Spinoza preferred an alternative proposed by Descartes: that the ultimate thing is an infinite extended plenum, in which various motions occur; and that the finite things that come to be and pass away are either simple bodies or persisting configurations of bodies distinguishable within that ultimate plenum by their states of motion and rest relative to one another. According to both versions of the mechanical conception, it is a law of nature that what is ultimate neither came into being nor will cease to be. It can, therefore, be truly described as 'cause of itself', as Spinoza understood the word 'cause'.

It is a law of nature that everything except the ultimate plenum exists as distinguishable within that plenum by virtue of its internal motion. Once introduced, that quantity of motion is conserved, and within the infinite plenum, which complex state of rest and motion succeeds which is determined by laws of motion according to which finite things at rest or in motion relative to one another either remain in those states, or communicate them to the other finite things contiguous to them (E1p28). The laws of motion, as Spinoza conceived them, are laws of transient causation. Yet motion and rest, as they are conserved in nature, are not introduced into it by the free action of something supernatural, but are caused according to laws of immanent causation constituting nature's essence (E1p25c). The laws of immanent causation therefore determine not only God's being, but also his essence; and the laws of transient causation that determine the succession of finite states of motion and rest are derivative from them.

Transient causes cause the happening of their effects. Since the causes of finite happenings are themselves happenings, every transient cause is itself an effect of another transient cause, as the laws of transient causation show by their form; for they all imply that, for every effect that has a transient cause, there is an infinite series of temporally prior transient causes and effects (E1p28). It is otherwise with immanent causes. A thing such that it is a law of nature that it is conserved is immanently caused by itself, and not by anything else. What is conserved or self-caused may immanently cause other things besides itself, when processes going on in it are such as to enable individuals to be distinguished in it. However, no further process going on in the individuals thus caused can make them in turn immanent causes; for every process in an immanently caused individual is also a process in its immanent cause. Not only are self-caused things immanent causes, but nothing except what is self-caused can be an immanent cause. Except for itself, no effect of an immanent cause can be an immanent cause.

If from the beginning of *Ethics* I Spinoza had made plain that his definition of 'cause of itself' is really a definition of 'that whose essence involves existence', and had defined both 'immanent' and 'transient', his intention to naturalize the concept of the relation between God's essence and his existence would have been unmistakable. He did neither, presumably because in setting out he chose not to disclose his ultimate destination. Since he had to introduce the concept of an immanent cause, because his argument depends on God's being the immanent cause of himself and of everything else, he did so without explanation by means of the verb phrase 'to be in'; and he allowed it to emerge that being in something is the same as being immanently caused by it only after demonstrating the necessary existence of his naturalized God (E1p18d—G II, 64/2-7). His discretion, unfortunately, disorders his proofs: some of them go through only if what he withholds is assumed.

4.3. Cognition, Conception and Causation

Spinoza uses the verb '*cognoscere*' and its cognate noun '*cognitio*' to stand for the process of intellectually grasping something by forming an idea of it. It is used almost interchangeably with the verb '*concipere*' and its cognate noun '*conceptus*', except that the latter are usually used for ideas formed and retained, while the former extend to the derivation of one idea from another by linkage. Since much of the *cognitio* we have is confused and inadequate, *cognitio* is not the same as knowledge. I therefore render it and its cognate verb '*cognoscere*' by their now uncommon English descendants, 'cognition' and 'cognize'.

Although conception and cognition can both be erroneous, when Spinoza instructs his readers how to cognize or conceive something, or lays down axioms about what cognition depends on, or how things can be conceived, he is of course telling them how to cognize or conceive truly. In some cases it is idle to point this out. Nobody fails to see that, when he lays down the axiom that 'cognition of an effect depends on, and involves, cognition of its cause' (E1a4), he does not mean that possibly false cognition of an effect is thus dependent. But, as we shall see in 4.5, there is an exception.

In his earliest surviving work, the *Tractatus de Intellectus Emendatione*, Spinoza had disparaged Aristotelian definitions by genus and differentia, and contended that a true idea of a thing must disclose its inmost essence, and hence what causes it to exist, if it exists (TdIE, 95—G II, 34/29-35/9); and he inferred that, while a definition of a created thing must include its proximate causes, that of an uncreated thing must exclude every cause (TdIE, 96-7—G II, 35/12-16, 28-30). Once he decided that what is confusedly conceived as uncreated is truly conceived as immanently self-caused, however, he saw that it follows that nothing can be truly conceived except through its cause. As he wrote to von Tschirnhaus, 'I make only one observation about how I might know (*scire*) from which of many ideas of a thing all its properties as subject could be deduced, that that idea or definition of the thing should express its efficient cause' (Ep60—G IV, 270/20-3).

4.4. The Fundamental Disjunctions

Although it is fundamental to the argument of the *Ethics* that 'cognition of an effect depends on, and involves, cognition of its cause' (E1a4), Spinoza does not make it plain by laying it down as an axiom 'that there must be, for each existing thing, a certain cause on account of which it exists': he divulges it, as something 'to be noted', in a scholium to a theorem (E1p8s—G II, 50/28-9). Nor does he disclose that both of the disjunctive axioms he does lay down depend on the concept of immanent causation. The first of those axioms is: 'Whatever is, is either in itself or in another' (E1a1)—that is, either is its own immanent cause or is immanently caused by another.

The first clause of this axiom ('Whatever is') is neither hypothetical ('If anything is') nor categorical ('Something is'). It leaves completely open the question whether there is anything at all—whether the universe is empty. True, Spinoza does not think it is open. Anybody who asks whether there is anything is entitled to answer it affirmatively, as Descartes showed in his second *Meditation*. Hence no student of the *Ethics* will be in any doubt that, if Spinoza's axiom is true, at least one thing is either in itself or in something else. Yet he does not formally enunciate it, although he now and then implies it, until in *Ethics* II he lays down two empirical axioms: 'Man thinks' (E2a2) and 'We feel that a certain body is affected in many ways' (E2a4). His lack of doubt that the axioms of *Ethics* I are about really existing things appears only when he illustrates his propositions by examples from the physical world and from human thought.

Since Spinoza nowhere claims that there is any self-contradiction in the idea of a perishable universe, consisting solely of things that merely happen to be, and are not immanently caused at all, he does not offer it as a logical truth; nor is it one. He expected his chosen readers, those who embraced the new mechanical conception of nature, to accept it as presupposed by that conception; and he confined his attention to them, because only they would grasp that all fundamental principles must be justified as the principles of the mechanical conception are. How he justifies those principles can be learned from his treatment of any of them; for example, from his treatment of Descartes's law of inertia. That law is:

> Each and every thing, in so far as it can, always continues in the same state; and thus what is once in motion always continues to move. (*Princ. Phil.* II, 37—AT VIII, 62; cf. DPP II, p14c)

Every seventeenth-century scientist was aware that this law contradicts the conception of motion fundamental to Aristotelian physics, which none of them claimed to be self-contradictory. Yet most of them, like Spinoza, found 'the reasoning of ... Descartes' conclusive (cf. Ep13—G IV, 67/7-8).

Descartes sets those reasonings out in *Principia* II, 37-8, as Spinoza remarks in his restatement (DPP II, p14cd—G I, 202/5-6). He begins by asserting generally that 'each thing, in so far as it is simple and undivided, always remains in the same state, as far as it can, and never changes except as a result of external causes' (AT VIII, 62/10-13). This, of course, does not tell us what a 'state' is. Aristotle thought of a thing's position at an instant as one of its states. If he was right, it would follow, according to Descartes, that its motion from one position to another must have an external cause. Descartes therefore excludes Aristotle's view by declaring motion a state: 'nor is there any ... reason, if [a thing] moves, to think that it will ever lose its motion of its own accord' (AT VIII, 62/17-20).

Here Descartes himself confesses that popular opinion sides with Aristotle: 'we tend to believe that what we have apparently experienced in many cases holds good in all cases— namely that it is of the very nature of motion to come to an end' (AT VIII, 62/27-63/1). He therefore gave reasons why this popular belief is mistaken; and although the first of them (see AT VIII, 63/3-5) must be rejected as assuming what it purports to prove,[11] his second reason, which in fact persuaded his contemporaries of the truth of his law, is of a different order. It runs:

> [O]ur everyday experience of projectiles completely confirms this [law]. ... For there is no other reason why a projectile should persist in motion for some time after it leaves the hand that throws it, except that what is once in motion continues to move until it is slowed down by bodies that are in its way. (AT VIII, 63/6-11)

Here it must be remembered that the motion of projectiles is not in itself incompatible with Aristotle's idea of motion as needing a cause to sustain it, any more than the motion of a boat being pulled up a beach, which stops as soon as those who are pulling it stop, is incompatible with Descartes's. Nor does Descartes imply that it is. In terms of the theory of ideas, he and Aristotle both presuppose that a materially true idea of motion must represent any motion, without leaving its properties unaccounted for. Rather, he contends that, while his idea accounts for the fact that a boat being pulled up a beach stops when the pulling stops by a cause that Aristotle himself acknowledges, namely friction, no cause by which the motion of projectiles has been accounted for in Aristotelian physics satisfies Aristotelians themselves.

Those who developed the mechanical conception of nature tacitly recognized a characteristic of thinking which Pierre Duhem first made explicit, and on the importance of which W.V. Quine has memorably dwelt: its holism.[12] Since no general belief can be tested by observation or experiment except in company with a whole body of others, both general and specific, it is always possible to uphold the truth of any general belief by abandoning others. The internal organization of each person's beliefs determines which he will thus treat as invulnerable to empirical falsification, that is, as true a priori. The principles of Aristotle's conception of motion were long received as true a priori, because without them the whole of his physics would have collapsed, and no acceptable alternative had been proposed. When an acceptable alternative appeared, which solved problems Aristotle's could not, and did not leave unsolved any which his solved, some of those principles were abandoned.

The philosophically controversial axioms of the *Ethics* are Spinoza's generalizations of the principles of the new physics.[13] Thus the axiom 'Whatever is, is in itself or in another' (E1a1), generalizes its principle of conservation, that whatever is either is ultimate and so conserved, or is in what is ultimate by virtue of some process internal to it. From that axiom, Spinoza at once passes to its epistemic counterpart, that 'whatever cannot be conceived through itself must be conceived through another' (E1a2). Given his fundamental axiom of cognition, that 'cognition of an effect depends upon, and involves, cognition of its cause' (E1a4), it should not be an axiom at all; for it can be proved as a theorem as soon as being in something is explicitly defined as being immanently caused by it.

Spinoza proceeds in *Ethics* I as though he has two disjunctive principles about whatever is: that it is either in itself (is its own immanent cause), or in another (is immanently caused by another) (E1a1); and that it is conceived either through itself, or through another that is conceived through itself (a stronger version of E1a2). Given that being in something is identical with being immanently caused by it, it follows (by E1a4) that whatever satisfies either member of either of these disjunctions, satisfies the corresponding member of the other. What is in itself must be conceived through itself, and what is in another must be conceived through that other, and conversely, what is conceived through itself must be in itself, and what is conceived through another must be in that other.

The analysis of immanent causation in 4.2, according to which nothing that is the effect of an immanent cause can itself be an immanent cause, yields a further result. If everything is immanently caused by itself or by another, then everything is either immanently self-caused or is caused by something that is immanently self-caused. And from that, together with Spinoza's definitions of a substance as 'that which is in itself, and is conceived through itself' (E1d3), and of a mode as an affection of substance, or 'that which is in another through which it is conceived' (E1d4), it follows that whatever is either is a substance or is an affection of substance—a mode. Spinoza asserts this in his proof of *Ethics* I, 4 (G II, 47/28–9); but he does not prove it.

4.5. Substances in General

The first eight propositions of *Ethics* I form a theory of substance, the scope of which is disputed. Perhaps the greatest of Spinoza's commentators, Martial Gueroult, contends that they are only about substances of one attribute.[14] There are obvious objections to this. First, nothing in the propositions themselves, or in their proofs, with one questionable exception, indicates that they are so restricted. Their wording is perfectly general. Secondly, two of them serve as steps in proofs of theorems about a substance with more than one attribute—God. To defend the demonstrability of these theorems, Gueroult has to find alternative implicit proofs. Of course, that is not fatal: on no interpretation of *Ethics* I are all Spinoza's proofs sound as they stand. Yet, while nobody willingly jettisons what cannot independently be shown to be defective, Gueroult's interpretation constrains him to replace arguments that have no intrinsic fault with alternatives that have fairly been described as 'labyrinthine'.[15] I hope to show that his complexities can be avoided without accepting others even more contrived.

Spinoza's theory is summed up in four propositions of *Ethics* I: namely, 5, 6c, 7 and 8. The first is that 'In nature there cannot be two or more substances of the same nature or attribute' (E1p5). A 'nature or attribute' is defined in terms of the theory of ideas, as 'what the intellect perceives of substance, as constituting its essence' (E1d4). Spinoza uses both the words 'perceive' and 'conceive' for forming an idea, although he will later define an idea as a 'concept (*conceptus*) of the mind' rather than as a perception (*perceptio*), because

> the word 'perception' seems to indicate that the mind is acted upon by the object. But 'concept' seems to express an action of the Mind. (E2d3exp)

An attribute is therefore that by which the intellect forms an idea of the essence of a substance. And since, as we have seen in 3.2–3, an idea of X is the regarding of some presented individual X as something formally real, an attribute is a presented essence of a substance that really is as it is presented. Finally, since the essence of a substance is an individual, attributes as Spinoza conceives them are not properties, but individuals.

A surprising number of competent commentators, reading the words 'what the intellect perceives' in Spinoza's definition of attribute as equivalent to 'what the intellect (possibly) falsely perceives', have denied that the definition implies that the essence of a substance is in fact constituted by its attributes. Since it is now commonly acknowledged that Gueroult, in a magisterial Appendix,[16] has demolished this reading, it suffices to remark that Spinoza himself treats his definition as implying that attributes really are what the intellect perceives them to be. For example, he describes the attributes of a substance as 'hav[ing] always been in it together ... each express[ing] the reality or being (*esse*) of substance' (E1p10s—G II, 52/6-8).

He begins his proof that there cannot be two or more substances of the same nature or attribute by pointing out that, since they cannot differ in their modes without some prior difference in their essences, which are constituted by their attributes, differences of modes can be set aside as wholly dependent on differences of attributes (E1p5d—G II, 48/10-12). He then correctly infers that, except by diversity of attributes, 'one [substance] cannot be conceived to be distinguished from the other' (G II, 48/13-14). It would be legitimate to write 'QED.' here, as Spinoza does, if the theorem were only about substances of one attribute; but not if it is about substances generally, as his subsequent use of it suggests. He has shown that two substances cannot be distinct if the essences of both are constituted by the same attributes; but not that they cannot be if they differ in one attribute while sharing others. Gueroult credits this objection to Leibniz.[17]

The supplement Spinoza's proof needs to dispose of this objection is ready to hand. If the essences of two substances differ because one is constituted by all the attributes that constitute the other, and by one more which the other lacks, then each of the attributes they have in common must constitute two different essences. However, the very idea of an attribute constituting really distinct essences seems unintelligible; and if it is, then Leibniz's objection fails. As we shall see, Spinoza holds that an essence may be constituted by really distinct attributes, but nobody has seriously ascribed to him the inverse, that an attribute may constitute really distinct essences.

That 'A substance cannot be produced by anything else' (E1p6c) is the second proposition of Spinoza's theory. For some reason I have not fathomed, Spinoza presents it as a corollary to a special case of itself, although he also proves it independently. It is theologically momentous; for it implies that no substance can be created, even by a super-substance. Its proof is neat: namely, that 'if a substance could be produced by something else, cognition of it would have to depend on cognition of its cause (by a4); and so, (by d3) it would not be a substance' (G II, 48/31-3). Yet, despite its theological importance, this theorem is superfluous; for it would better have been presented as a negative corollary of the third proposition of the theory: that 'it pertains to the nature of substance to exist' (E1p7). This is commonly misunderstood as equivalent to:

(1) It is necessary that, for some x, x is a substance.

That this is a mistake is shown by its proof, which is by way of the definition of a cause of itself as that whose essence involves existence. As has been argued in 4.2, the force of this definition is that it is a law of nature that anything whose essence involves existence is conserved, neither coming into existence nor passing away. And that is equivalent to:

(2) For all x, if x is a substance, it is necessary that x is conserved.

Plainly, (2) does not entail (1). It does not follow, because all substances necessarily exist, that there necessarily exists some substance. What Spinoza offers to prove is that all existing substances must, by their very nature, be conserved, not that all logically possible substances must, by their very nature, be actual.

As it stands, the proof he offers is invalid, because he cannot directly infer from his definition of substance that substances must be causes of themselves. He vainly tries to derive it from the second proposition of his theory, arguing as follows:

> A substance cannot be produced by anything else (by p6c); therefore it will be the cause of itself, i.e. (by d1) its essence necessarily involves existence, or it pertains to its essence to exist. (G II, 49/4-6)

This fails, because it has nowhere been made explicit that what is not produced by anything else must have a cause. It is, of course, implicit in its first axiom, that whatever is either is in itself or is in another; but to make that plain, Spinoza would have to acknowledge that by 'to be in' he means 'to be immanently caused by'.

The fourth and final proposition of Spinoza's theory is that 'every substance is necessarily infinite' (E1p8). A substance can be said to be infinite in two senses: either 'absolutely infinite', or consisting of infinitely many attributes, each expressing an infinite essence (cf. E1d6); or else 'infinite in its kind', that is, not limited by another of the same nature (CF. E1d2).[18] That in this theorem 'infinite' is used in the second of these senses is evident from the way Spinoza proves it; for he is content to show that any arbitrary substance of one attribute must be infinite. A substance of one attribute can only be infinite in its kind. But if a substance of one attribute must be infinite in its kind, it will follow that a substance of more than one attribute will be infinite in as many kinds as it has attributes.

That an arbitrary substance of one attribute is such that it cannot be limited by anything else of the same nature, that is, constituted by the same attribute, is easily shown. Since no attribute can be common to two substances, there can be no substance of the same nature to limit it, and hence nothing to limit it (for a substance's own modes only limit each other). QED. Apart from treating the irrelevance of a substance's modes as evident, this is the nerve of Spinoza's own proof (Ep8d—G II, 49/13–16); and it suffices. Unfortunately, in stating it, he makes a point of mentioning the irrelevancy that, as substances, both putative limiter and putative limited must necessarily exist (G II, 49/11–16).

Having now established what substances in general are, Spinoza has all the elements of a naturalized theology. Whatever is, consists of substances; for nothing exists except substances and modes, and modes, being immanently caused by substances, have no being apart from them. Substances are self-caused, and are conceived through themselves: that is, their essences are such that their existence is conserved according to laws of nature, and hence is conceived through their essences. In this naturalized sense, they exist necessarily.

The Elements of the Idea of Nature as God 73

None therefore can be brought into existence or destroyed by anything else, not even by another substance. Each of them is unique in its kind: that is, none has any attribute in common with any other. And finally, each is infinite in its kind; for there is nothing in its kind to limit it. It remains only to show that whatever is consists, not of a plurality of independent substances, each infinite in its kind or kinds, but of one absolutely infinite substance, which engrosses all the kinds there are, and leaves room for nothing else.

4.6. Necessity: a Note on Spinoza's Rationalism

Spinoza often speaks of ideas as following *necessarily* from other ideas, meaning by it, as we have seen, that one idea can be linked with another because the exclusion of its ideatum is excluded by it (see 3.4). Today's logicians explain this linkage by the laws or fundamental truths of logic: ideas are simply mental equivalents of their propositional counterparts; and one idea I_q follows from another I_p when their propositional counterparts q and p are such that it is logically necessary that *If p then q*, that is, that the conjunction of p and *It is false that q* can be shown, by purely logical steps, to be the negation of some logical truth. Commentators influenced by today's logic are prone to credit Spinoza with thinking of the linkages of ideas on which philosophy and the natural sciences depend as necessary in this logicist way: that is, as having propositional counterparts that are either logical truths, or are reducible to them by purely logical steps.

The doctrine that, for any true proposition, there is a reason why it is true, which Bennett, in ascribing it to Spinoza, has named 'explanatory rationalism', is often taken as equivalent to this logicism.[19] Since a certain non-empty possible world is actual, and not some other possible world (including an empty one), explanatory rationalists must hold that there is a reason why it is actual, and it appears that the only consideration that could count as a reason for it would be that it is logically impossible that any other possible world be actual. Spinoza is therefore said to believe that it is logically impossible that there should exist any possible world other than the one that does.

So far, I have implicitly argue that there is no reason to believe that he is an explanatory rationalist in this sense. He does believe that the world necessarily exists, in the sense that it is a law of nature that the substances that compose it cannot be created or destroyed; but he nowhere says or implies that it is logically impossible that the world be other than it is.

I do not deny that Spinoza could have anticipated the twentieth-century concept of logical necessity, and employed it in his metaphysics, as Leibniz did.[20] But I contend that we cannot assume that he did unless there is evidence of it in his writings, or in reliable reports of the opinions he expressed; and there is none. About logic as a discipline he makes only one remark, which echoes Descartes: namely, that it 'serve[s] only to train the memory', but does 'not serve to train the intellect' (CM, I—G I, 233/10–14).[21] If he ever speculated whether traditional logic could be developed in a more fruitful way, no record of it has survived.

If he is not an explanatory rationalist, is he a rationalist of any other sort? Bennett notes that there are philosophers who deny that 'logical (or absolute)' necessity is distinct from 'causal necessity'; and for that reason conclude that it is logically or absolutely impossible that anything should happen contrary to the laws of nature.[22] He calls them 'causal rationalists', and decides that 'Spinoza seems to have accepted causal rationalism' because he held that a cause is related to its effect as a premiss is to a conclusion that follows from it.[23] Certainly, Spinoza described the effect of a determinate cause as *necessarily* following from it (E1a3), presumably meaning that a proposition correctly describing a cause in the language of physics, say

(1) Two bodies, A and B, absolutely equal, move in a straight line towards each other with equal speed, and meet is related to a similar one describing its effect, say

(2) A and B will each be reflected in the opposite direction without losing speed,

as the premise is to a conclusion that follows from it. Yet since it is transparently false that (2) follows from (1) according to any truth of logic, traditional or modern, he may also be presumed to mean no more than that it follows given some principle like the Cartesian Rule he enunciates as Proposition

24 in his restatement of Descartes's *Principia* II (G I, 211/12–15). That, however, implies no failure to distinguish causal from logical necessity. Like Descartes before him and all physicists after him, Spinoza believed that, *given a law of nature*, a statement of an effect worded in terms of that law will logically follow from a similarly worded statement of its cause. If he is a causal rationalist, it is in a sense that will offend few philosophers of science.

Notes

1. *The Guide of the Perplexed*, I, 57. Cf. Wolfson (1934), I, p. 115.
2. Bennett (1984), pp. 61–2.
3. The clearest elucidation of what Spinoza means by an essence in the *Ethics* is in Matheron (1969), esp. pp. 9–12, 18–21, 55–7. Gueroult's '*Distinction entre plusieurs sens du mot essence*' brings out the crucial distinction between an individual's essence as an individual, and as belonging to a species (Gueroult (1974), Appendix 3, sect. 2—pp. 548–9). Wolfson usefully surveys the history of the question of the relation of essence to existence (Wolfson (1934) I, pp. 121–32), but his conclusions about Spinoza are vitiated by his assumption that 'while Spinoza differs from his [Aristotelian] predecessors as to the nature of a definition, he does not differ from them as to the meaning of the term essence'—that is, that an individual's essence is the essence of its species, defined *per genus et differentiam* (I, pp. 383–4). Mason (1986), pp. 332–9 is helpful.
4. Bennett (1984), p. 61.
5. Gueroult (1974), pp. 20–21, 26–28; cf. C, 447 n.l.
6. Wolfson (1934), I, p. 127.
7. Gueret, Robinet and Tombeur (1977), pp. 52–3; instances of '*causa*' in other cases, or in the plural, are less frequent but still numerous (pp. 53–6).
8. Curley points out that in TdIE, 97 (G II, 35/28–30), Spinoza did treat a cause of itself as causeless, although he changed his mind (C, 40, n.64).
9. In Spinoza's Latin, '*transiens*'. Because 'transient' connotes much that is alien to what Spinoza means by '*causa transiens*', Curley renders it by 'transitive'. But since what Spinoza has in mind in calling a causal relation '*transiens*' is not that it is 'transitive' in today's logical sense, I reluctantly prefer 'transient'.
10. In E1p18,d—G II, 63/33, 64/7, and Ep73—G IV, 307/5–6. See entry '**Causa**, (5) *Causa immanens*', in Giancotti (1970), p. 135; and cf. Gueret, Robinet and Tombeur (1977), p. 174.
11. Spinoza himself, in *Ethics* II, 13add., employs a question-begging argument like Descartes's (G II, 99/1–7). But his use of a bad argument in conjunction with a good one (as here) does not show that the bad one is primary in his thought.

12. Pierre Duhem (tr. Philip P. Wiener), *The Aim and Structure of Physical Theory* (New York: Atheneum, 1962), pp. 180–218; cf. W.V. Quine, *From a Logical Point of View* (2nd edn, Cambridge, Mass.: Harvard University Press, 1961), pp. 40–2.
13. Cf. Curley (1969) ch. 3, esp. pp. 99–101. We converge on Quinian holism: he showing that experimental scientists like Galileo appealed to a priori arguments, I that 'rationalist' ones like Descartes did not neglect observed phenomena.
14. Gueroult (1968), ch. 3 *passim*.
15. Gueroult (1968), pp. 185–6, 225–6. I owe much in my comment, as well as the epithet 'labyrinthine', to a paper presented by Willis Doney to a conference in Chicago in September 1986.
16. '*La Controverse sur l'Attribut*', Appendix 3 to Gueroult (1968), pp. 428–61. The treatment in English most cited is Haserot (1953).
17. Leibniz's treatment of this objection (Gueroult (1968), pp. 120–1) may be profitably compared with Bennett (1984), pp. 69–70).
18. Kline (1977), pp. 342–7.
19. Bennett (1984), p. 29. The logicizing of Spinoza's view of modality is criticized in Mason (1986), of whose brilliant treatment I would have made more use had my chapters on Spinoza's metaphysics not been drafted before I had read it. Cf. also Klever (1986), pp. 185–9.
20. The senses in which Leibniz was and was not a rationalist are lucidly sorted out in Brown (1984), pp. 3–5, 43–7, 187–9, 203–6.
21. Cf. Descartes, *Discours de la Methode* II (AT VI, 17). According to Giancotti and Curley, Spinoza uses the Latin word '*logica*' only once: in E2 pref (G II, 277/12–16). What he means by it—it is not logicians' logic—is explored in de Dijn (1986).
22. Bennett (1984), pp. 29–30.
23. Bennett (1984), pp. 29–30.

5 God as Absolutely Infinite Substance

5.1. Spinoza's Principle of Plenitude

Spinoza must now investigate what substances make up whatever is, considering them both as causes and as effects. He begins with substances as causes. Are they many, or not? If they are many, are they equal or unequal?

Different substances have been shown to have no attribute in common (E1p5). An exclusionary principle follows: namely, that whether substances are many or few, equal or unequal, no substance has a rival in its own kind. What rivals are excluded, however, depends on what actual substances there are; and that, Spinoza declares, is determined by a principle that is 'known through itself' (*'per se notum'*), namely, 'to be able not to exist is to lack power, and conversely, that to be able to exist is to have power' (E1p11d—G II, 53/29–31). Although its truth is not evident to me, his idea is plain enough:[1] that the more powerful a thing is, the less its existence needs explanation, and the less powerful it is, the less its non-existence needs one. Given that idea, since he equates power with what he calls 'quantity of reality or being', he has a principle determining the nature of at least one substance included in whatever is: namely, that it possess the fullness of being or reality—the greatest possible quantity of it. It is a principle of plenitude; and self-evident or not, it deserves serious consideration.[2]

Spinoza assumes that his readers will need no explanation to understand the phrase 'the quantity of reality or being (*esse*) of a thing R'. As far as I can tell, he thought of it as standing for how much would be added to whatever is if R came into existence after not existing, or how much would be subtracted from whatever is if, after existing, R ceased to exist. What would be added or subtracted would be a certain essence of a substance. (The modes of a substance, it must be remembered, are involved in its essence.) Now as we have seen (in 4.5), the essence of a substance is truly conceived by the intellect as constituted by each of its attributes (E1d4); and, as the essences of substances constituted by one attribute alone would each be infinite in their kinds (E1p8), such essences may be presumed to be equal in quantity of reality. Spinoza appears to have concluded from this that the only way in which any substance can have more reality or being than another is to have more attributes than it. 'The more reality or being (*esse*) each thing has, the more attributes belong to it' (E1p9).

This theorem would be useless if the ideas of attribute and essence excluded the existence of an essence constituted by more than one attribute; but Spinoza argues that they do not. 'Each attribute of a substance must be conceived through itself' (E1p10); for if it were not so conceived, then what is truly perceived as constituting the essence of a substance would lack something which, by definition, that essence has (E1p10d). So far, so good. He adds, in a scholium, that 'From these propositions it is evident that although two really distinct attributes may be conceived,[3] i.e. one may be conceived without the aid of the other, we still cannot infer from that that they constitute two beings, or two different substances' (E1p10s—G II, 52/2-5). This puzzled a group in Amsterdam studying *Ethics* I in an early draft, and they inquired what propositions he had in mind as making this evident (Ep8—G IV, 41/1-14). Spinoza replied:

> You say that I have not demonstrated that a substance (or being) can have more attributes than one. Perhaps you have neglected to pay attention to my demonstrations. For I have used two: *first* that nothing is more evident than that we conceive each being under some attribute, and that the more reality or being a being has, the more attributes must be attributed to it; ... *second*, and the one I judge best, is that the more attributes I attribute to a being, the more I am compelled to attribute existence to it; that is, the more I conceive it as true. It would be quite the contrary if I had formed the idea of (*finxissem*) a Chimaera, or something like that (Ep9 — G IV, 44/34-5, 45/18-25).

Neither of these 'demonstrations', however, will do at all.

The first makes use of two propositions: (1) that each substance can be conceived under some attribute, and (2) that the more reality a being has, the more attributes must be attributed to it. But it does not follow from (1) and (2) alone that one substance can have more attributes than another: it must also be assumed that one substance can have more reality than another. It may be true that *if* a substance has more reality than another *then* it has more attributes (that is what (2) amounts to); and yet false that any substance can have more reality than another. The second demonstration does no better. It is true that *if* forming the idea of a substance having more than one attribute is not like forming an idea of a chimaera, *then* the greater the number of attributes conceived to belong to a substance, the nearer the idea of it must be to the idea of something containing the greatest possible quantity of reality, and hence to the idea of something that, according to Spinoza's principle of plenitude, must be contained in whatever is. But the group in Amsterdam suspected that forming such an idea is like forming the idea of a chimaera.

In its final version, the scholium of *Ethics* I, 10 is much subtler than this reply to de Vries. The propositions it offers as making it evident that a substance may have more than one attribute are: first, that each attribute constitutes whatever essence it does independently of the others; and hence, secondly, that if the essence of a substance were to be constituted by several attributes they would likewise constitute it independently.

> [I]t is of the nature of a substance [he writes] that each of its attributes is conceived through itself, since all the attributes it has have always been in it together, and one could not be produced by another, but each expresses the reality, or being of a substance (G II, 52/5-8; cf. Ep8—G IV, 41/5-7).

This amounts to arguing that, since each is conceived without the help of any other, there is no way any attribute can exclude any other from the same substance. In other words: in the absence of a specific intrinsic reason why one attribute should exclude another from expressing the same essence, the independence of the attributes entitles us to presume that none can be given.[4]

If the difficulty of the Amsterdam group was that a

plurality of attributes in the same substance would exclude one another, then it collapses; for to sustain it, they had to show that independently conceived attributes can exclude one another, and they were not able to do it. Spinoza has therefore established his right to presume that a substance can have more than one attribute, and then, invoking his criterion of quality of reality, to apply his principle of plenitude.

5.2. What the Proofs of *Ethics* I, 11 Prove

Spinoza applies his principle of plenitude in the third and last of his three proofs of *Ethics* I, 11 (G II, 53/29–36), thereby proving that whatever is includes an absolutely infinite substance;[5] but what he offers it as proving is the very different proposition that an absolutely infinite being necessarily exists. If an absolutely infinite substance in fact exists, demonstrating that it necessarily exists is trivial; for, as Spinoza points out in the first of his proofs of *Ethics* I, 11, every substance necessarily exists (by E1p7), in the naturalized sense explained in 4.5 (cf. G II, 52/27–9). However, it cannot be assumed that what is true of every substance is true of an absolutely infinite one until it has been shown that there is an absolutely infinite one.

Did Spinoza fail to see that the first and third of his proofs of *Ethics* I, 11 prove two different propositions, or did he deliberately leave it to his more attentive readers to perceive it? While either explanation may be true, I incline to the latter. It is consistent with the strategy discernible in his not making explicit that to be in something is to be immanently caused by it: the strategy of presenting a naturalized theology in traditional words, incidentally teaching his readers to give new meanings to those words. Whichever is true, the third of the proofs in *Ethics* I, 11 proves the more fundamental proposition, that whatever is includes an absolutely infinite substance. It is presented in two forms. The first runs: since to be able to exist is to have power, and to be able not to exist is to lack power, if finite beings are able to exist and an absolutely infinite being is not, then finite beings would be more powerful than an absolutely infinite being; but that is absurd (E1p11d—G II, 53/29-32). The second runs: the more attributes a thing has, the more reality or being it has (E1p9), and 'the more reality belongs to the nature [i.e. the essence] of a thing, the more power it has, of itself, to exist'—the conclusion being obvious (G II, 54/5-7).

The best commentary on these proofs is a paper, '*De Rerum Originatione Radicali*', which Leibniz wrote twenty-one years after meeting Spinoza in 1676.[6] In the following passage from it, he states a principle of plenitude more general than that employed by Spinoza in both forms of his proof.

> [F]irst, from the fact that something exists rather than nothing, we must acknowledge that there is a certain exigency (*exigentia*) to existence in possible things or in possibility itself or essence, or (let me say) a *praetensio* towards existing. Put briefly, essence *per se* tends to existence. Whence it follows in turn that all *possibilia* or [things] expressing essence or possible reality, tend to existence with a right (*jure*) proportional to [their] quantity of essence or reality, or to the grade of perfection which they involve; for perfection is nothing but quantity of essence.
>
> Hence, as manifestly as can be, it is understood that, out of the infinite combinations of *possibilia* and possible series, that exists through which the greatest quantity of essence or possibility is brought into existence.[7]

As Leibniz describes it, combinations of *possibilia* differing in strength struggle to exist, and the strongest prevails—that is, the combination having the greatest quantity of essence. Although Spinoza was more reticent, his proof, if taken literally, implies what Leibniz makes explicit. Yet is is repugnant to the naturalism of the *Tractatus Theologico-Politicus* to think of non-existent possibilities as doing anything at all, much less as struggling against a more powerful enemy.

Benson Mates raises the same questions about Leibniz's generalization of Spinoza's proof. '[T]alk of possible things,' he observes, 'although it permeates the Leibnizian writings, is, if taken literally, productive of paradox and quite foreign in spirit to his metaphysical outlook.'[8] Non-existent logically possible beings can make no difference to actual existing ones. Only actual existents can actually cause anything. These truisms were as obvious to Spinoza and Leibniz as they are to philosophers now. And so, as Mates argues, it would be absurd to take literally Leibniz's oft-repeated principle that all the possibles 'strive for existence' (see *PS* VII, p. 195). In the context of his philosophy this obviously means that whatever is compossible with what exists, exists—i.e., if God could create x, then he would do so unless the creation of other things prevents it.[9]

A parallel line of thought holds for Spinoza. Essences, i.e. *possibilia*, do not fight among themselves, the winner being rewarded with actuality. When Spinoza says things that imply that they so fight, they should be construed as figurative if they can be.

Can they be? In a letter to Johannes Hudde, Spinoza described his God in a way that points to a naturalistic sense that might underlie his talk about the striving of *possibilia*.

> [S]ince the nature of God [that is, of an absolutely infinite being] does not consist in a certain kind of being [he wrote], but in Being, which is absolutely unlimited (*indeterminatum*), his nature also demands (*exigit*) everything which perfectly expresses τὸ *esse*;[10] because otherwise his nature would be limited and deficient (Ep36—G IV, 185/29-32).

This implies, not that a possible absolutely infinite being defeats the other *possibilia* in a struggle for existence, but that the nature of an actual absolutely infinite being 'demands' that it consist of every attribute expressing an eternal and infinite essence. According to the view of things Spinoza put forward in the *Tractatus Theologico-Politicus*, passages about what an absolutely infinite being's nature demands should be construed as being about what, according to the laws of nature, it must be. Nor would it be contrary to that general view that it be a law of nature that any essence of a substance that is constituted by an attribute expressing an infinite essence is also constituted by every other such attribute.

If two substances cannot have any attributes in common, and if there are n attributes, then an actual substance whose essence is constituted by n attributes may well be said, for the sake of vividness, to prevent substances with fewer than n attributes from existing. And from that it is a short step to imagining possible substances as engaged in a struggle for existence, in which one having n attributes will always defeat one with fewer than n. As long as it is remembered that speaking so is figurative, it does no harm. There is no reason to suppose that Spinoza ever forgot it, although he saw no reason to disturb the orthodox by reminding them of it. Hence when he writes that 'the more reality belongs to the nature of a thing, the more powers it has, of itself, to exist' (G II, 54/5-7), he should be read as figuratively declaring that, however many attributes there may be, the more nearly the number of an imagined substance's attributes approaches that number, the less it falls short of a maximally real substance that must be included in whatever is. And, since every attribute whatever independently constitutes the essence of a maximally real substance, his principle of plenitude may be formulated nonfiguratively as what I shall call 'the principle of substance plenitude': namely, that any essence that is constituted by some attribute, as the essence of every substance is, must be constituted by every attribute.

As I have interpreted them, both Spinoza's third proof of *Ethics* I, 11 and his argument to Hudde are formally unobjectionable. If it is a law of nature that no essence can be constituted by any given attribute of substance unless it is also constituted by every other attribute, then 'a being absolutely infinite, that is, a substance consisting of infinite attributes,[11] of which each one expresses an eternal and infinite essence' must be included in whatever is; and Spinoza defines God as just such a being (E1d6). George Kline has pointed out that, in so defining God, Spinoza uses the adjective *'infinitus'* in two distinct but related systematic senses. In the first, it is equivalent to 'perfect without limitation'; and in the second to 'all without exception'.[12] God, as defined, is therefore a being perfect without limitation (he is 'infinite' in sense i), consisting of all attributes without exception (the number of his attributes is 'infinite' in sense ii), of which each expresses an essence that is eternal and perfect without limitation (each is infinite in sense i).[13] How many attributes God has will therefore depend upon how many there are. There is no implication that their number must be enormous.

Ethics I, 11 would also be demonstrated by its second proof if that proof were not, unlike the third, simply invalid. Postulating that there must be a cause why anything whose existence is intrinsically possible, as a divine substance's is, must exist unless its existence is excluded by the existence of something of the same nature, Spinoza infers that a being of the same nature as God, i.e. God, must exist. Alas, the phrase 'of the same nature' is equivocal: it can mean having all attributes in common; but, in Spinoza's systematic sense, it means sharing at least one attribute. Lacking a principle to the contrary, such as the principle of plenitude used in the third proof, a being having one but not all of God's attributes is intrinsically possible; and, if it were actual, would extrinsically exclude God's existence.

5.3. The Rejection of Monadism

Is Spinoza's principle of substance plenitude true? By proposing an alternative, Simon de Vries, the spokesman of the Amsterdam group that did not at first understand why he held that a substance can have more than one attribute, indirectly argued that it is not. Rather than say that one substance has every attribute, he suggested the following:

> if I should say that each substance has only one attribute, and if I had the idea of two different attributes, I could rightly conclude that where there are two different attributes, there are two different substances. (Ep8—G IV, 41/9–13)

This proposal raises two deep questions.

First, does not a world in which every attribute constitutes a substance, but no substance is constituted by more than one, contain as much reality as one containing a single substance constituted by every attribute? Secondly, if attributes are really distinct from one another and totally independent, would a world in which no substance is constituted by more than one attribute differ in any way from one in which those attributes all constitute the same substance? In other words, how does a substance constituted by really distinct attributes differ from a mere aggregation of substances of one attribute.

As Leibniz was to show in '*De Rerum Originatione Radicali*', criteria of plenitude strictly apply to worlds—'combinations of *possibilia* and possible series'—and not to things in worlds. By Spinoza's own criterion of quantity of reality, the quantity of reality of possible worlds is proportional to the number of attributes actualized in them. That number remains the same, whether the attributes actualized constitute a single substance, as in Spinoza's scheme, or are distributed over as many substances as there are attributes, as in de Vries's; and it would remain the same if they were irregularly distributed among unequal substances.[14] Hence Spinoza's principle of substance plenitude cannot be justified, as he seems to have believed, solely by his criterion of quantity of reality. Something more than that criterion is needed.

A de Vriesian world would consist of an infinite extended substance as described in Descartes's physics, an infinite thinking substance completely independent of the extended one, and along with them, a series of further infinite non-thinking substances, each constituted by distinct attributes of which we have no conception. It could only by accident be the world which, in a fragmentary way, human beings conceive, employing materials drawn from their experience of what happens in their bodies. In such a world, it would be an accident if the infinite thinking substance thought about any other substances at all; and if it did, it would be a further accident if it thought about them as they are. Why should the infinite thinking substance think about other substances which cannot affect it or be affected by it? And if it does, why should it think of them as they are, or care about whether it does?

A passage in the *Short Treatise* reveals that such considerations were in Spinoza's mind when he put forward his principle of substance plenitude. Why, he asks, do we believe that 'all these attributes which are in Nature are only one, single being, and by no means different ones (though we can clearly and distinctly understand the one without the other)' (KV I, 2—G I, 23/15-17)? After vainly appealing to his criterion of plenitude, he answered that it is 'Because of the unity which we see everywhere in Nature; if there were different beings in Nature, the one could not possibly unite with the other' (G I, 23/18-29). That is, the attributes we see everywhere are everywhere seen as united. Yet we see only two: extension and thought. What did he mean when he wrote that we see them everywhere as united?

Something I submit, like the following. The primary objects

of the thinking of all human beings are happenings in their own bodies, many of which they attribute to happenings in the world at large. They construct conceptions of the world in the light of these primary objects; and, even though they are far from adequate, those conceptions continue for the most part to cohere with the changes they constantly experience in those objects. Given the theory of substances in general (see 4.5), the thoughts of all human beings must be finite modes of an infinite thinking substance, and their ideas of their bodies and of their physical environment are either true or false representations of finite modes in the infinite extended substance. The coherence of those ideas with one another, and the fact that those who have them can regard them as both generally true and corrigible by reference to the new ideas of their bodies and their environment they constantly receive, suggests that they are as they are regarded. In that case, the whole system of ideas in the infinite thinking substance of which human minds are finite modes can reasonably be supposed to be a materially true representation of the whole system of finite bodies in the actual infinite substance constituted by extension.

The grounds of Spinoza's specific principle of substance plenitude are therefore two. First, by his criterion of quantity of being, the world with the greatest possible quantity of being is that in which every attribute is actualized. And secondly, because the world is experienced as a unity, the attributes actualized in it cannot constitute a number of distinct substances.

5.4. The Constitution of God's Essence

The second question implicit in de Vries's letter was: How would a substance of infinite really distinct attributes differ from an infinite aggregate of substances of one attribute? Because of the experienced unity of the attributes, it is impossible to believe that our world is de Vriesian, made up of windowless substances of one attribute. In our world, as Spinoza reminds us in the scholium to *Ethics* II, 7, the modes constituted by the really distinct attributes we think of, extension and thought, have the same order and connection. Attributes constitute the essence of the same substance if and only if it is a law of nature that the order and connection of the modes they constitute are the same; otherwise, they constitute the essences of different substances.

Since the essences of a substance and of its modes are conceived only through its attributes, the order and connection of its modes cannot be specified independently of its attributes. Whether they are identical or not can therefore only be discerned by comparing them as separately conceived through each attribute. Every substance, no matter by what attributes it is constituted, immanently causes both itself and its modes. Immanent causation is therefore a 'trans-attribute' relation: that is, it relates a substance both to itself and to its modes no matter what attributes constitute them.[15] Yet, like its relata, immanent causation can only be understood through some attribute. 'The modes of each attribute', Spinoza says, 'have God for their cause only insofar as they are considered under the attribute of which they are modes' (E2p6). The internal process by which a substance's modes are caused is determined, for each of its attributes, by a set of laws of immanent causation conceived through that attribute. If any such set of laws is given, the modes of the substance follow, along with the laws of transient causation governing their interaction. What it is for the modes under two attributes to have the same order and connection can be understood only by considering the sets of such laws, one for each attribute, by which that process is determined in each case. The order and connection of the modes conceived under both attributes will be the same, as Spinoza understands it, if and only if both sets of laws are each projections of the other (cf. E2p7). Equipped with the rule of that projection, a sufficiently powerful mind who truly conceived one of these sets would be able to form a true conception of the other.[16]

Although the causation by which modes are related to their substance and to one another is a trans-attribute relation, it cannot be conceived except through one or another of the attributes constituting the essence of the substance in which those modes are. Neither modes nor substances have any trans-attribute character through which the identity of their order and connection can be defined. Actual substances constituted by two really distinct attributes are therefore identical if and only if the set of laws of immanent causation of either is such that is is a projection of the set of laws of immanent causation of the other.[17]

When thought is one of the attributes, a further consequence follows. In a substance S, constituted by thought and some arbitrary attribute A, its modes as thought are not a projection of its modes as A without regard to what they represent. One of the sets of thoughts in S must represent it and its modes as A. The modes of S as a thinking substance having the same order and connection as its modes as an A substance will be thoughts of its modes as an A substance, and not merely a string of thoughts about something or other. And since what is true of an arbitrary member of a class is true of all its members, whatever exists formally in God as constituted by any attribute other than thought must exist objectively in him as constituted by thought. 'God's power of thinking is equal to his power of acting' (E2p7c).

It is now possible to state generally what Spinoza means both when he says that an attribute 'constitutes' the essence of a substance, and when he says that two really distinct attributes 'constitute' the same essence. A single attribute constitutes the essence of a substance if and only if it is a law of nature that whatever has that attribute can neither be created nor destroyed, that it immanently causes modes in a certain order and with certain interconnections, and that it is of a certain kind. Two or more attributes constitute the essence of the same substance if an only if it is a law of nature that whatever has either can neither be created nor destroyed, and that it immanently causes modes both in the same order as whatever has the other, and with the same interconnections, although insofar as it is constituted by one, its kind is distinct from what is insofar as it is constituted by the other. A substance of two attributes would therefore be trans-attributively the same as a substance of only one of them, but it would be of two kinds, not of one.

What constitutes an essence may be identical with that essence, and so with its substance, but it need not be. The attribute constituting the essence of a substance of one attribute is identical with it; for it determines not only the being of that substance, but also its kind. No attribute of a substance of more than one attribute, however, can be identical with its essence, because, although it determines its being, it determines only one of its kinds, and not those determined by its other attributes. Spinoza speaks of each of the attributes of a substance not only as 'constituting' its essence, but also as 'expressing' that essence. The relation to which he refers when he uses the two phrases is the same; but he tends to use 'express' when he particularly has in mind the kind to which the attribute assigns the substance, and 'constitute' when he has not.[18]

God or nature, as Spinoza conceives him or her, is therefore a substance as analysed in his theory of substances in general (see 4.5), but one such that, for every attribute that constitutes its essence, it is a law of nature that the essence it constitutes is also constituted by every other attribute that constitutes the essence of any substance. In other words, God or nature is a substance whose essence exemplifies the principle of substance plenitude.

5.5. Panentheism

Spinoza's definition of God, like all definitions of individual things, is of him as an essence, not as an existent. Strictly, what it defines is *a* divine being (an essence whose actualizations are indeterminate in number), and not the unique divine being; for no essence involves any particular number of individuals (cf. E1p8s2—G II, 50/22-5). Hence in proving that whatever is includes a divine being, Spinoza has not shown that there is only one such being. The proof, however, is elementary: 'if there were any substance except God, it would have to be explained through some attribute of God, and so two substances of the same attribute would exist, which (by p5) is absurd' (E1p14d).

What else can be proved of this divine being? Traditional theologians, whether Jewish, Christian or Muslim, provoked Spinoza's scorn by their confessed inability to offer more than negations and remote analogies (KV I, 7—G I, 44/4-7, 45/1-

32). In *Ethics* II he formally identifies extension and thought, of each of which every human being can form an adequate, non-analogical idea (E1p15c2), as divine attributes. But before investigating them, he takes time to distinguish what is true from what is false in traditional theology's negations and analogies about God's trans-attribute properties.

Traditional theology had held that God is simple in the sense that the various attributes ascribed to him represent merely negative or figurative ways of conceiving an essence that admits no real distinction within it, and hence that he is indivisible. Although Spinoza cannot agree that God is simple in this sense, because he refuses to confound his really distinct attributes, he does agree that God cannot be divided into parts, whether of the same kind or attribute (E1p12), or of different kinds or attributes (E1p13). As Gueroult has seen, he confronts the thesis of divisibility with a dilemma: if a substance could be divided into parts, those parts would either be substances or not,[19] and they can be neither; for if they were substances, one substance would have produced another; and if they were not, something that necessarily exists would have dissolved. Orthodox theology has gone astray in inferring that, because bodies are divisible, God cannot be spatially extended. It ought to have inferred, according to Spinoza, that no divisible extended body can be more than a mode of an extended substance: 'no corporeal substance, insofar as it is a substance, is divisible' (E1p13s).

Since whatever is either is a substance or is a mode of substance, and since God is the unique substance, whatever is must be either God, or a mode of God; and since a substance is in itself and its modes are in it, it follows that whatever is must be in God. Furthermore, since whatever is must be conceived through what it is in, it also follows that 'without God, nothing can be or be conceived' (E1p15,d). It does not follow from this that the totality of finite things is God; for since finite modes are not self-caused, their totality cannot be self-caused either. Spinoza is not a pantheist. Yet if everything that is not God is in God, there is no gulf between anything and God. God is not a transcendent being whose nature we dimly apprehend through negations and analogies with sensible things. On the contrary, sensible things can be truly cognized only as modes under truly conceived divine attributes. Although Spinoza is not a process theologian, he is a 'panentheist' in the sense in which process theologians understand that word.[20]

Things other than God, the modes, are in God by virtue of being immanently caused by him. And since God has infinite attributes (that is, every attribute there is), each of them infinite in its kind, Spinoza argues that from the necessity of the divine nature 'must follow ... infinite things in infinite modes (*infinita infinitis modis ... necessario sequi debent*)' (E1p16—G II, 60/17-19): that is, infinitely many attributes (all of them without exception), with infinitely many modes under each. Not content with citing the definition of God, Spinoza both reminds us of the principle of substance plenitude, according to which there must be a substance constituted by all the attributes without exception (*infinita*), and for good measure points out that the modes under each attribute must realize everything an infinite intellect can conceive as falling under it, because every substance is infinite in its kind (E1p16d—G II, 60/21-30).

The necessity by which infinite attributes in infinite modes follow from the necessity of the divine nature is of course logical; but the necessity of the divine nature is that of laws of nature: primarily, the law underlying the naturalized principle of plenitude; and secondarily, the laws governing the processes in the infinite substance by virtue of which it immanently causes its modes. It is widely believed that Spinoza held that the modes of the infinite substance under each of its attributes are directly deducible from the definition of that attribute, and hence that all the modes of infinite substance as extended are deducible from the definition of extension (presumably, from the definition of an infinite Euclidean solid). Yet not only is that position absurd; it is not affirmed in the theorem under discussion.

Three corollaries, however, do follow from it: namely, (c1) 'that God is the efficient cause of all things which can fall under a divine intellect'—that is, a cause that makes happen, and not merely the matter from which something comes, or the end towards which it is directed; (c2) 'that God is a cause *per se* and not *per accidens*—that is, that his making something happen does not depend on anything else; and (c3) 'that God is absolutely the first cause'—that is, that he does not depend on any prior cause. Later (in E1p18), Spinoza will expressly distinguish the causal relation between God and his modes from that between one mode and another, as we have already been obliged to do in order to explain what being in something is.

Not only is God the absolutely first efficient cause, and is so *per se*, he 'acts solely by the laws of his nature, and is compelled (*coactus*) by nobody' (E1p17). This follows obviously from the immediately preceding propositions, and could easily be demonstrated from the axioms. And it, too, has corollaries deserving of notice: in particular, (c1) that it is only the perfection of his nature, and not an extrinsic or intrinsic cause, that incites him to act, and (c2) that he alone is a free cause—that is, a cause that acts as he exists, solely from the necessity of his nature (cf. E1d7).

Two other theological commonplaces which Spinoza reaffirms acquire a non-traditional sense when interpreted according to his axioms: namely, that 'God, or all God's attributes, are eternal' (E1p19), and that 'God's existence and his essence are one and the same' (E1p20). The traditional sense of the latter is that God as a possible existent is identical with the fact that he exists; and in that sense, as has been argued in 4.1, Spinoza considers it absurd; but in his proof he treats it as meaning that the same attributes which unfold (*explicant*) or constitute the eternal essence of God also unfold or constitute his eternal (that is, his intrinsically necessary) existence (E1p20d—G II, 64/33–65/1). A necessary existent, by its very nature, can only be the unique divine being; and a divine being can only, by its very nature, be the unique necessary being. Both are constituted by the same infinite attributes. Given Spinoza's axioms, there is nothing absurd about this, but it is not what traditional theologians meant when they said that God's essence is identical with his existence.

If 'eternal' is used in its usual theological sense, in which it is a synonym for 'timeless' in its customary philosophical sense, so that being eternal excludes being in temporal relations, then Spinoza, as we shall see in 6.2, would be compelled to deny that God is eternal; for he holds that it is by motions within substance as infinitely extended that finite extended modes are immanently caused. Here too, instead of denying that God is eternal, he reinterprets 'eternity' in a way more congenial to Jewish prophets than to scholastic theologians, and defines it as 'existence itself' insofar as it is conceived to follow necessarily from the definition alone of an eternal thing' (E1d8). He accompanies this radical innovation in defining 'eternity' with a parallel innovation by which 'duration' is defined in terms of contingent existence; and then he restricts the sens of the word 'time' to that of an interval of time. These innovations enable him to assert that God is 'eternal', but not in the sense in which traditional theologians asserted it.

Some scholastic theologians had described God the creator as '*Natura naturans*', or 'Nature naturing', and created nature as '*Natura naturata*', or 'Nature natured'. Spinoza eagerly seized on these locutions; for they apply to his God literally, and not figuratively. As he intimated in the *Short Treatise*, it was not accurate for the Thomists to describe 'a being beyond all [natural] substances' as '*Natura naturans*' (KV I, 8—G I, 47/26-7). By contrast, a being which immanently causes everything, including itself, by virtue of laws of nature, may as well be called '*Natura*' as '*Deus*'; for both God's necessary existence and his actions are a matter of nature being herself— of Nature 'naturing'. And since the effects of God's immanent causation are not external to him, they may with strict propriety be described as nature '*naturata*' or 'natured'. Spinoza therefore declares that 'from the preceding ... it is already established that by *Natura naturans* we must understand what is in itself and is conceived through itself, or such attributes as express an eternal and infinite essence, i.e. (by p14c1 and p17c2), God' (E1p29s).

Notes

[1] Despite its plainess, some commentators have failed to see it, and have even resorted to textual emendation. Curley's note is admirable (C, 418 n.28).

[2] Spinoza's implicit use of a principle of plenitude in E1p11 was pointed out to me by Martha Kneale, who remarked on the neglect of it by most commentators except Matheron and Delahunty. On the principle in Leibniz, see Brown (1984), p. 181.

3 Here Curley translates 'although two attributes may be conceived to be really distinct'.
4 Spinoza thus at least in part appreciated the criticism of Descartes which Leibniz presented to him (*PS* VII, 261–2). See Brown (1984), pp. 61–2.
5 The proofs of *Ethics* I, 11, are among the most intensively studied passages in Spinoza's *oeuvre*. My radical treatment, which I have no space to defend in detail, stands or falls with the argument in chs. 2 and 4 that Spinoza is using the language of scholastic theology in a new naturalized way. Cf. Wolfson (1934) I, pp. 158–213, and the papers by Bar-On (1983) and Marcus (1983) it inspired; Hubbeling (1964), pp. 86–102 (a complete survey and analysis of all Spinoza's proofs of God's existence); Gueroult (1968), pp. 177–204 (a meticulous commentary on E1p11d); and Harris (1973), pp. 33–47 (the most attractive conservative commentary in English). I have found Joel Friedman's formalizations of *Ethics* I suggestive: see Friedman (1977).
6 Cf. Ep70—G IV, 302/33–303/20; Ep72—G IV, 305/17–24. In 1676, the year after these letters were written, Leibniz visited the Hague, conversed with Spinoza often and at length, and was allowed to read the *Ethics* (W1, 47). Cf. Brown (1984), pp. 54, 61.
7 Leibniz, *PS* VII, p. 303 (emending '*ad essentiam tendere*' to '*ad existentiam tendere*', according to the obvious sense of the passage and to other variations on the same formula—e.g. '*ad existendum tendunt*' on p. 304).
8 Mates (1986), p. 73.
9 Mates (1986), p. 73, n.25.
10 Here Spinoza places the Greek 'τό' before the Latin '*esse*' so that '*esse*' can be preceded by a definite article, which Latin lacks.
11 Kline (1977), pp. 341–7, 351–2. Kline acknowledges debts to Joachim (1901), pp. 23, 28, 41 and Wolf (1927), p. 26; and demolishes Hallett's objections (pp. 351–2).
12 Kline (1977), pp. 342–3.
13 Curley renders '*infinita attributa*' in two ways: in d1, as 'an infinity of attributes', and in E1p11 as 'infinite attributes'. I prefer the latter throughout.
14 Leibniz, *PS* VII, p. 303.
15 I owe the expression 'trans-attribute' to Bennett (Bennett (1984), pp. 41–7).
16 Although his approach differs from mine, I find Macherey's treatment of God's constitution 'in diverse real attributes' illuminating (Macherey (1979), pp. 107–33).
17 Bennett has argued that the same substance cannot be said to have two really distinct attributes unless it can be identified through a third attribute that, although really distinct from both, cannot be conceived in abstraction from either (Bennett (1983), pp. 144–5).
18 What is said here applies only to 'express an essence' when said of an attribute: Spinoza uses 'express' in other ways. Cf. Deleuze (1968), pp. 9–11.

God as Absolutely Infinite Substance 95

[19] Gueroult lucidly analyses the differences between p12 and p13 and between their demonstrations (Gueroult (1968), pp. 207–11); but those differences do not presuppose, as he maintains, that God is a union of substances of one attribute. Cf. Macherey (1979), pp. 110–23.

[20] See Gueroult (1968), pp. 222–3. Roughly, a *pantheist* holds that everything is God, a *panentheist* that everything is in God.

6 God as Cause and as Effect

6.1. Perfection Naturalized

Having demonstrated that whatever is can only be a unique absolutely infinite substance, God, the immanent cause of itself and whatever else there is, Spinoza remarks, in a scholium, that the nature of such a substance 'excludes all imperfection, and involves absolute perfection'(E1p11s—G II, 54/31-2). Introducing the concept of perfection in this way was an innovation, although an unobtrusive one; for perfection, as Descartes understood it, is an essence of which we have an innate idea, about which we ask whether anything outside our minds corresponds to it. As Spinoza introduces it, 'perfection' is simply our name for what our idea of an absolutely infinite essence involves, and 'imperfection' our name for what it excludes. Instead of possessing an innate idea of what a perfect being would be, to which we can prove that the actual absolutely infinite being must correspond, we must reconcile ourselves to acclaiming as absolutely perfect whatever that being turns out to be. An ideal supernatural property has been supplanted by an actual natural one.

God's (or nature's) perfection, therefore, cannot be used as a premise in determining what he (or she) is like. That will depend both on God's trans-attribute properties, especially his causality, and on his attributes. The remainder of *Ethics* I is devoted largely to God's causality, from the points of view both of God as cause and of God as effect.[1] Although propositions about God's causality can only be proved by purely trans-attribute considerations, to anybody who had no idea of any attribute they would be so abstract as to be almost vacuous. Hence Spinoza accompanies his abstract proofs by illustrations, mostly in his scholia, from the attributes of

God as Cause and as Effect

extension and thought, the two attributes of nature cognized by human beings. The few illustrations in his proofs are from the attribute of thought (e.g. in E1p21d); but those in his scholia from the attribute of extension tell us more.

Most of his contemporaries, whether theologians or scientists, were convinced that extension cannot express an infinite essence because everything extended is divisible into parts.[2] In a long scholium to *Ethics* I, 15, Spinoza argued that this is a prejudice founded on imaginative confusion.

> [W]e are, by nature, ... inclined to divide quantity [he observed], ... [because] we conceive quantity in two ways, abstractly, or superficially, as we imagine it, or as substance, which is done by the intellect alone. So if we attend to quantity as it is in the imagination, ... it will be found to be finite, divisible, and composed of parts; but if we attend to it as it is in the intellect, and conceive it insofar as it is a substance, ... then, as we have already sufficiently demonstrated, it will be found to be infinite, unique, and indivisible.
>
> This will be sufficiently plain to anyone who knows how to distinguish between the intellect and the imagination—particularly if it is also noted that matter is everywhere the same, and that parts are distinguished in it only insofar as we conceive matter to be affected in different ways, so that its parts are distinguished only modally, but not really. (E1p15s—G II, 59/20-35)

Although his line of argument is plain, the latter part of this passage is opaque to most readers today, because it is addressed to his contemporaries, for whom up-to-date physics was Cartesian physics.

By those who 'distinguish between the intellect and the imagination', he meant those who followed Descartes in distinguishing what the intellect clearly and distinctly perceives from what is believed on grounds of sensory experience; for it was they who accepted Cartesian physics, and believed that finite bodies cannot be separated by empty space, but are distinguished in an infinite extended plenum by reference to motions occurring in it—the various 'ways' in which it is affected.[3] Because of these motions, they held that finite parts of the plenum, or bodies, can be distinguished as internally at rest, but as moving relative to the bodies they immediately touch, and as either at rest or in motion relative to more remote bodies. Bodies consist of nothing but extension, and so are indistinguishable from the space they occupy; but they are not empty, for two bodies cannot share the same space. They all remain at rest or in uniform rectilinear motion relative to others unless they collide with them; and when they do, their resultant states of relative motion and rest are determined by laws. (The part of Cartesian physics first perceived to call for revision was its laws of motion.) Bodies only act on one another by impact: there is no action at a distance. And, except for the interventions of its supernatural creator, the physical world is causally a closed system.[4]

To readers today, brought up on Newtonian and post-Newtonian dynamics, this is almost as quaint as Aristotle. Bennett, for example, imagines that, in using 'body' and 'matter' to mean ' what is extended', Descartes thinks of what is extended as dividing into what has mass and what lacks mass, where 'mass' stands for whatever makes the difference between vacuum and occupied space. And he proceeds to charge him with stupidly drawing physical conclusions from his eccentric definition.[5] Yet Descartes's view of matter was subtle and coherent. It rests on two simple ideas: first, that since extension is an attribute of substance, whatever is extended must be a substance; and secondly, that since distinct extended substances or portions of an extended substance must be external to one another, they must be impenetrable by one another. Given these ideas, as Descartes saw, it follows that at any given time, a body (a finite extended substance or part of one) cannot be distinguished from the space it occupies. The body's position, however, is not the space it occupies; for it is not a thing at all, but an *ens rationis*, determined by reference to co-ordinates. The perceived differences between what is at a position at different times all depend solely on the shape and size of the bodies that occupy it, and on their motions. No position is empty. Every motion is a displacement. A body can move only as a fish moves in a bowl of water, by displacing other bodies. Such displacements are therefore vortical and simultaneous, the last body displaced occupying the position vacated by the first.[6]

Nothing Spinoza wrote is inconsistent with his harbouring this view of matter, and even Bennett concedes that much he wrote is inconsistent with any other.[7] Yet Spinoza did not endorse everything in Cartesian physics. He recognized it as what it was: the physics that largely set the agenda of the European scientific community in the third quarter of the seventeenth century. The studies of Spinoza as a scientist recently collected by Marjorie Grene and Debra Nails in *Spinoza and the Sciences*[8] confirm the impression his published correspondence leaves upon most readers, that, as David Savan has put it, 'although [he] was thoroughly competent and acquainted with some of the best [scientific] work of his time, he contributed little of importance to research and theory'.[9] He was a 'normal-scientist', not a revolutionary one; and the science he recognized as normal was Cartesian.[10] To quote Savan again, he was 'by and large a follower of Descartes and Huygens'.[11] While he would correct accepted opinion on particular points as his own work required, he neither addressed himself to the deeper problems of Cartesian physics, nor was his confidence in it undermined by them. Powerful scientific theories are abandoned, not because of what they cannot do, but because of what their rivals can.

According to Spinoza's physics, God or nature as extended immanently causes the finite bodies that are its modes as extended, not by dividing into parts, but by its internal state of motion and rest. A difficult problem for that physics is how that internal state, so far as it is a motion, is caused. Ehrenfried von Tschirnhaus, the German scientist, inventor, and entrepreneur who elicited from Spinoza in the last three years of his life some of the most informative of his letters, asked him to explain how an extended plenum that is wholly self-caused can be anything but internally at rest. Descartes had held that of itself an infinite extended plenum would remain 'quiescent' unless a cause external to it were to produce motion in it (Ep 82—G IV, 333/6-13). The problem is acute for Spinoza, because he insists that everything falling under an infinite intellect must follow from the necessity of the divine nature (E1p16). Many commentators read this as a declaration that every mode of God conceived through any attribute must be such that it follows from the fact that God has that attribute that he has that mode. If they are right, then Spinoza cannot admit any internal motion in God as extended unless it would follow from the nature of extension itself that there would be that motion in him; and if he is committed to that, then his theory of nature as extended must collapse.

Fortunately, both in the *Ethics* itself and, more emphatically, in writing to von Tschirnhaus, he denied that he is so committed.

> What you ask [he replied], whether the variety of things can be demonstrated a priori solely from the concept of Extension, I believe myself already to have shown clearly enough—it is impossible. Hence matter is badly defined by Descartes in terms of (*per*) extension; and it must instead necessarily be explicated in terms of (*per*) an attribute which expresses an eternal and infinite essence. (Ep83—G IV, 334/22-6)

By translating '*per*' as 'as', Wolf reached the impossible conclusion that Spinoza was repudiating Descartes's analysis of matter as extension.[12] He was not: his objection to Descartes was that, having correctly identified one of Nature's infinite attributes, Descartes spoiled his achievement by thinking of extension as an abstractly conceivable property, and not as expressing an eternal and infinite essence—which, according to the principle of substance plenitude, is the essence of the unique absolutely infinite substance. Having dissociated himself from Descartes's mistake, he explained to von Tschirnhaus that much more follows from the proposition 'Nature is constituted by extension, which expresses an eternal and infinite essence' than from 'Nature is extended':

> What, however, you add, that from the definition of each thing, considered in itself, we are entitled (*valere*) to deduce only a single property, perhaps has validity for the simplest things, or for entities of reason (among which I count figures), but not for real things (*realibus*). For from this alone, that I define God as a being to whose essence pertains existence, I infer several of his properties.... (G IV, 335/1-6)

As was his wont, the inference he offered as example was simpler than the one that troubled his correspondent. Nor was it taken from the *Ethics*, although *Ethics* I could easily be reconstructed with a definition of a divine being as one whose essence involves existence. Yet the point he was trying to make is discernible.

What von Tschirnhaus had written is true of definitions of entities of reason—that is, of entities represented by ideas of the sort Descartes described as '*a me ipso factae*' (see 3.2). In conceiving them, we get out of our ideas what we put in, no more. When we consider real essences, however, and even more, when we consider actually existing things, there is no such restriction. Thus, when we define God as a being to whose essence pertains existence, that is, as something self-caused, we are entitled to employ, in our inferences from it, whatever eternal truths we cognize about whatever is. And since among those truths is that beings like ourselves, finite minds and bodies, can only exist as modes immanently caused by a unique infinite substance that immanently causes itself, we can deduce from our definition two real properties of God that eluded the entire body of traditional theologians: that God is extended and that our thoughts are his.

By reminding von Tschirnhaus of how he established God's real attributes, Spinoza shows us how he thinks he is entitled to establish what God as extended immanently causes. Our bodies are finite modes of God, and there are states of motion and rest both within our bodies and outside them. The essence of God as expressed by the attribute of extension is therefore such as immanently to cause motion and rest in himself. This is fully consistent with *Ethics* I, 16. That God thus causes motion in himself, while it does not follow from the concept of extension considered abstractly, does follow from the necessity of his divine nature as extended.

The implications of Spinoza's naturalization of the concept of perfection are now a little clearer. A perfect being is what God is. And, although it has not been formally demonstrated, it has been made evident that God, as extended, is the infinite plenum of the physical universe, viewed both as cause (*Natura naturans*) and as effect (*Natura naturata*). If we ask Spinoza what a perfect being is, he refers us, first of all, to physics. Nature is infinite, and indifferent to us:

> [M]any are accustomed to arguing in this way: if all things have followed from the necessity of God's most perfect nature, why are there so many imperfections in nature? why are things corrupt to the point where they stink? so ugly that they produce nausea? why is there confusion, evil, and sin? ... [T]hose who argue in this way are easily answered. For the perfection of things is to be judged solely from their nature and power; things are not more or less perfect because they delight or offend men's

senses, or because they agree with (*conducunt*) human nature or are repugnant to it. (E1ap—G II, 83/17-26)

6.2. The Modal System and its Causation

The example of extension shows how Spinoza conceived God's immanent causation of modes as constituted by every attribute. The divine substance, he held, immanently causes within itself, but without dividing itself, a process that makes it possible to distinguish finite things within it. That process, like the substance itself, must be constituted by every attribute, and the order and connection of the finite modes it immanently causes must be the same, no matter by what attribute they are constituted. Hence each set of finite modes as conceived through a given attribute can be put in one-one correspondence with each set of them as conceived through another; and each member of every set will be identical with the member of every other that is in one-one correspondence with it, although it will be expressed and conceived differently.

While the immanent causing of an effect is instantaneous, stages can be distinguished within effects as conceived. Certain things, Spinoza tells us, follow immediately from each of God's attributes, that is, 'from [their] absolute nature', and those things 'have always had to exist (*semper existere debuerunt*) and be infinite, or are, through the same attribute, eternal and infinite' (E1p21): he calls them 'immediate' infinite modes of Nature under the attribute in question. Other things follow from each of God's attributes, not immediately, but insofar as each 'is modified by a modification that thus exists necessarily and is infinite', and they too 'must exist necessarily and be infinite' (E1p22): them he calls 'mediate' infinite modes (E1p23d—G II, 67/6-9). No mode can exist necessarily and be infinite unless it follows, immediately or mediately, from some attribute (E1p23).

Along with these infinite and necessarily existent (or eternal) modes, there are other modes that follow neither immediately nor mediately from any attribute. They are 'singular', that is, they 'have a finite and determinate existence'. And they have causes of a special kind: they can be determined neither to exist nor to produce effects (*ad operandum*) except by causes that in turn have a finite and determinate existence (E1p28).

The proofs of these propositions all depend on the proof that whatever follows from the absolute nature of any attribute of an absolutely infinite being must exist necessarily and be infinite (E1p21d). Although the proof is not elegant, the idea underlying it is simple (cf. G II, 65/16–33). A finite thing can be limited only by some other finite thing of the same attribute (E1d2). But if a finite thing should follow from the absolute nature of some attribute, its finiteness or limitedness would have to follow from that absolute nature, which has been shown to be infinite (E1p10s). Yet in order to limit a finite thing that follows from it, an attribute would have to be finite, which is absurd. Now, what holds for an attribute holds also for an infinite mode: to limit a finite thing of the same kind, it would have to be finite. Equally, just as whatever follows from the absolute nature of something infinite cannot be finite, so whatever is finite cannot follow from the absolute nature of something infinite: it can only be caused by something finite, and that in turn by something finite, *ad infinitum* (E1p28,d).

Despite the intimate linkage of the proofs that, while infinite modes must follow, immediately or mediately, from attributes, and finite modes can only be caused by other finite modes, few commentators have been wholly undisturbed by Spinoza's apparent confession that finite modes cannot be immanently caused by God except with the help of other finite modes. If that is so, are they immanently caused by God, and conceived through God, or only through God and something else? Are they modes of God at all? And the same question can be asked, although for an opposite reason, about the infinite modes. Can what follows from what constitutes the divine essence, whether immediately or mediately, be immanently caused by something other than itself? Can there be more than a *distinctio rationis* between the absolutely infinite substance and its putative infinite modes?

The only statement from Spinoza we have about what the immediate and mediate infinite modes under any attributes are was elicited by von Tschirnhaus, who, with G.H. Schuller as intermediary, had asked him for 'examples of those things that are produced immediately by God, and of those that are produced by some infinite mediate modification' (Ep63—G IV, 276/1-2), adding that thought and extension seemed to him examples of the first kind, and intellect and motion of the second. In his reply, after tactfully intimating that thought and extension are attributes, not infinite modes, Spinoza offered the following:

> Finally, the examples which you ask for of the first kind are, in Thought, absolutely infinite intellect, but in Extension, motion and rest; of the second kind, however, the face of the whole universe (*facies totius universi*), which, although it may vary in infinite ways, remains always the same; on which see E2p13add L7s (Ep64—G II, 278/24-8).

Assuming that von Tschirnhaus was intended to interpret this in terms of Cartesian physics, and did, what would he have made of these examples?

I suggest the following. Motion and rest is the immediate infinite mode of nature as extended, first of all because, by her own immanent causation, nature is not a quiescent mass, but a plenum in which motions occur; and secondly because, by reference to those motions, finite extended things, or bodies, are distinguished as either in motion or at rest relative to one another. The attribute of extension, considered as constituting the essence of the extended substance that actually exists, constitutes an essence that involves those motions. Because of this, that substance immanently causes bodies within itself that move or are at rest relative to one another. Although the phrase 'motion and rest' would not, of itself, be taken to stand for an infinite plenum in which motions of a certain sort occur, in a correspondence between two adherents of Cartesian physics about 'things produced immediately by God', God being identified with nature, that is what it would stand for.

Spinoza's example of a thing produced by motion and rest as a mediate infinite modification is less difficult. According to Cartesian physics, it is a fundamental law of nature that the quantity of motion (that is, of momentum) in nature is constant; and this constancy underlies the specific laws by which the states of motion and rest resulting from any particular collision of bodies are determined. The 'face of the whole universe' therefore stands for the infinite Cartesian plenum in its double character: (1) as something in which internal motions unceasingly both bring new bodies into existence (by composition and division) and break them up, and vary their relative states of motion and rest; and (2) as something in which all changes are reducible to changes of relative motion and rest, and occur according to laws of nature, in particular, the conservation law. The infinite plenum in internal motion is always the same, like a face which remains the same although its expression constantly changes.[13]

We now have a definite description of each of the infinite modes under the attribute of extension that Spinoza has named; and since both describe the same thing—the absolutely infinite substance itself (see Figure I below)—the infinite modes they describe must, as existing individuals, be identical with that substance. How then, can they be its modes? A mode is not a substance, but an affection of substance: that is, something *other* than it that is immanently caused by it and conceived through it.

Kind of Mode	**Name**	**Definite Description**
Immediate Infinite Mode	Motion and Rest	The infinite three-dimensional plenum, in which are internal motions by which finite things can be distinguished as relatively in motion or rest.
Mediate Infinite Mode	*Facies Totius Universi*	The infinite three-dimensional plenum, the changes in the finite bodies in which all accord with laws of nature (e.g. conservation laws) that are always the same.

Figure 1

The simplest answer is that different ideas may be formed of the same actually existing thing: one fundamental, and the others derived from it by linkage. The fundamental idea of absolutely infinite substance is expressed in its definition—namely, 'a substance consisting of infinite attributes, each of which expresses an infinite and eternal essence' (E1d6). Such a substance, by virtue of an internal process expressed by each of its attributes, immanently causes modes ordered and connected in a certain way. It can be truly conceived without forming an idea of any of its attributes, or of the multiple nature of the process by which it immanently causes its modes. As we have seen in 5.4 and 6.1, from the absolute nature of each of its attributes, not as abstractly conceived, but as constituting a real thing, one of the kinds or natures of that internal process 'follows'.

Extension, as it constitutes the real absolutely infinite substance, is such that that substance has a constant quantity of internal motion by which finite things can be distinguished in it. This 'follows' from the real essence extension constitutes, not from the highest common factor of the essences our abstract conception of it allows us to imagine it might constitute. Our abstract conception of extension leaves it open whether an extended substance is internally in motion or not, and is therefore logically prior to our conception of the real extended substance as necessarily in motion. Again, the actual laws governing the constantly changing motions within the infinite extended plenum, bringing new finite beings into existence and destroying old ones, while they ultimately 'follow' from extension as it constitutes the real absolutely infinite substance, follow from it neither as conceived abstractly, nor as conceived merely as constituting a substance the conserved internal motions of which enable finite bodies to be distinguished in it.

The infinite modes of the absolutely infinite substance are therefore not modes in the sense of things immanently caused by another thing. Rather, they and the absolutely infinite substance are one and the same thing, of which a series of distinct concepts can be formed, those later in the series being 'conceived through' those earlier in it. That is, the immediate infinite mode of the absolutely infinite substance as constituted by any given attribute is conceived through that attribute as it exists in reality, and its mediate infinite modes (although Spinoza only mentions one, he does not exclude the possibility that there are more) are conceived through the immediate one, and any prior mediate ones.

The totality of the motions of finite bodies in the infinite plenum is the same thing as the internal motion of the plenum itself, looked at from the point of view of the finite bodies. If human beings could establish both (1) the laws of immanent causation according to which the internal motion in the plenum occurs, and (2) its state of motion and rest at any one time, then they could in principle calculate its state of motion and rest at any other time according to those laws, mentioning no finite bodies at all, but only regions of the plenum. Cartesian physicists thought chiefly in terms of the things and laws they could effectively study: human beings, finite physical bodies from stars to minute particles, and the laws of transient causation by which processes in those bodies are explained. Yet Descartes himself, in his cosmological speculations, sometimes thought about the physical system as a whole. Spinoza, in discerning the ultimate dependence of the transient causal system on the immanent one, did not break with Cartesian physics, but perceived one of its less obvious implications.

6.3. Motion, Eternity and Time

The infinite and eternal modes of God as extended both involve internal motion. And all motion, according to Cartesian physics, is local: it is the transference of parts of the infinite plenum that touch one another so that they touch other parts of it (cf. DPP II, d8).[14] Such transference presupposes a temporal order: at one time certain parts touch one another, and at a later time they do not. And if the relations of before in time and after in time are transitive, which Spinoza nowhere questions, this order must be linear. It appears to follow, therefore, that a mode can be eternal even though it involves processes the stages of which occur in linear temporal order.

At first sight, Spinoza's conception of eternity excludes the possibility that temporally ordered processes should occur in an eternal being. He defines eternity (*aeternitas*) as 'existence itself, insofar as it is conceived to follow solely from the definition of an eternal thing (*rei aeternae*)' (E1d8), adding as *explicatio* that, since eternal existence 'is conceived as an eternal truth', it 'cannot be explicated through duration or time, even if the duration is conceived to lack a beginning and an end' (E1d8exp). True, as Kline points out, he does not stick to this formal definition; for, in socio-political contexts, he uses 'eternal' in the sense of 'permanent', 'perpetual' or 'long-lasting', and 'eternity' as standing for 'a more-or-less property of certain individual and social practices and of certain socio-political institutions'. However, because in ontological discussions he does use 'eternity' according to his formal definition, Kline, with most commentators, concludes that in them 'eternal' must mean 'timeless', 'non-temporal', 'having no relation to duration'.[15]

If 'eternal' is so understood, what Spinoza says about the infinite modes he calls 'motion and rest' and *facies totius universi*' seems to be inconsistent: on the one hand, he describes those modes as 'eternal' even though motions are processes the stages of which are ordered by temporal relations; and on the other, he declares that whatever is eternal is timeless or non-temporal. Yet appearances, especially appearances about Spinoza's use of words, can deceive. What if, when he says such things as that eternity 'cannot be explicated through duration or time', he means something systematic and technical, which does not imply that there can be no temporal relations in anything eternal? Kline's demonstration that he uses 'eternity' and 'eternal' in both systematic and unsystematic senses should prepare readers for a similar double usage of related words; and those who look for it soon find it. Since he does not define 'time' (*'tempus'*) in the *Ethics*, it is best to begin with 'duration' (*'duratio'*), which he defines in Part II as 'an indefinite continuation of existing' (E2d5), adding 'I say "indefinite" because [such continuation] can by no means be determined by the nature itself of the existing thing, or even by its efficient cause, which indeed posits the existence of the thing, but does not take it away' (E2d5exp). Duration, in short, is the precarious continuation in existence of whatever is not self-caused: a continuation determined not by the cause that brought it into existence, but by the environment that sustains it.

That eternity cannot be explicated (that is, 'unfolded' or analysed) through duration, defined as the precarious continuation in existence of its finite modes, plainly does not imply that there can be no temporally ordered process in an

God as Cause and as Effect

eternal thing. Both eternity and duration are each defined as ways in which something exists (necessarily or not necessarily) and is caused (by itself or not by itself). If Spinoza can without embarrassment give the name 'motion and rest' to a mode he describes as eternal, presumably he saw no inconsistency in doing so. And the analyses in 4.1–2 of what he means by 'cause of itself' and 'necessarily exists' show that he was right: to be eternal in his sense is not incompatible with being internally in motion. Unfortunately, many able students of Spinoza, believing that he uses 'necessarily exists' as Maimonides or Descartes did, either misunderstand or disregard his related definitions of 'eternity' and 'duration'.

Bennett, for example, to whose work on Spinoza's concept of time I owe much, briskly dismisses the *explicatio* of the definition of duration, and declares that '"duration" is [Spinoza's] word for time considered as a perfectly uncut, undifferentiated continuum'.[16] Spinoza did not mean by 'indefinite continuation of existence' an uncut continuum: he recognized that the duration of most finite things is cut, in the sense of having a beginning and an end. The duration of a thing, as he conceived it, is indefinite with respect, not to how long it continues, but to its determination by the essence of the thing. The essence of a finite thing leaves how long it continues to exist undetermined, to be determined by external causes; whereas the essence of an eternal being determines that its existence has neither beginning nor end.

Although Spinoza does not formally define 'time' (*'tempus'*), his arguments that eternity cannot be explicated through time are parallel to his arguments that extended substance cannot be composed of parts capable of separate existence. Thus, in the authoritative *Letter on the Infinite* (Ep12), he argues that

> [as for] the existence and Duration of Modes, when we attend, as we often do, to their essence alone and not at all to the order of Nature, we can at will, and in no way thereby destroying the concept we have of them, determine [them], conceive [them] to be greater and lesser, and divide [them] into parts. Eternity, however, and Substance, since we cannot conceive [them] except as infinite, can undergo none of these, unless at the same time we destroy the concept of them. For this reason, they simply gabble, not to say run mad, who think that Extended Substance can be put together out of parts or bodies really distinct from one another. (Ep12—G IV, 55/4–13)

Here he plainly repeats his earlier strategy in showing that distinguishing finite bodies by means of motion and rest does not imply that nature is composed of really distinct finite bodies (cf. 6.1 above and E1p15s—G II, 58/19-60/4).

His argument here is that, although finite bodies enduring for finite times can be distinguished in an infinite and eternal extended substance, it does not follow that that substance can be broken up into really distinct parts, whether spatial or temporal. 'Measure, Time and Number' are 'Beings of reason', like the parts into which space is broken by the imagination. Such imagined separate parts are not to be confused with intellectually grasped modes of Substance, which cannot exist separately from it or from one another (G IV, 57/7-58/3). Duration is real, just as the finite modes of substance are real; but their reality cannot be upheld against objections like Zeno's except by recognizing that the spatial and temporal parts into which human beings imagine nature's eternal being as divided are not the same as nature's finite modes and their durations, but mere beings of reason (G IV, 58/4-15).

The passage quoted from the *Letter on the Infinite* shows that, in denying that eternity can be explicated through time, Spinoza thought of himself as using the word 'time' in a systematic sense, as meaning 'a time' or 'an interval of time'— 'measured time', as Bennett prefers to say.[17] It is confirmed by his observation in *Ethics* II that 'nobody doubts but that we also imagine time: namely, from this, that we imagine some bodies to be moved, with respect to others, more slowly, or more quickly, or equally quickly' (E2p44c1s—G II, 125/25-7). This echoes a fuller statement, in *Cogitata Metaphysica*, that

> to determine this duration, we compare it with the duration of other things that have a certain and determinate motion. *This comparison* is called *time*. Time, therefore, is not an affection of things, but only a mere mode of thinking, or, as we have said, a being of reason. For it is a mode of thinking that serves to explicate duration. (CM I, 4—G I, 244/24-6)

In saying that time, in this systematic sense, is a mere mode of thinking, Spinoza does not imply that whether two determinate motions which we compare have the same length or not is merely a matter of how we think. The time that Michelangelo took to paint the ceiling of the Sistine Chapel was four-and-a-half years, whether it is thought to be or not. It is the equality of two compared durations, that of Michelangelo's motions in painting the ceiling and the earth's motion in traversing four-and-a-half ellipses about the sun, not a real thing independent of that comparison. Yet although the comparsion is made by chroniclers, and does not exist in the world, it is otherwise with the durations whose continuations are compared, and with the motions whose durations they are. If there were not real motions for the chroniclers to compare, which really began and ended at the same time (non-systematic sense), there would be no 'times'.

Spinoza was therefore being perfectly consistent when he said both that motion and rest is an eternal mode of God as extended, and also that what is eternal is 'timeless', in his systematic sense of the word 'time'. Assertions that seem to contradict this do not when read in context. The often quoted remark 'in eternity there is neither *when, before,* nor *after*' (E1p33s2) is a case in point. Out of context, it would naturally be understood as 'in eternity nothing happens at one time rather than another, and so nothing happens before or after anything else'. But it occurs in the following passage:

> all God's decrees have been established by God himself from eternity. For otherwise he would be convicted of imperfection and inconstancy. But since, in eternity, there is neither *when, before,* nor *after*, it follows, from God's perfection alone, that he can never decree anything different, and never could have, or that God was not before his decrees, and cannot be without them. (G II, 75/10–15)

Spinoza is annotating a theorem that on its face is about the way and the temporal order in which God produces finite things. In his demonstration he expressly refers to the 'order of nature', and argues that if it could have been different then 'God's nature could also have been other than it is *now*' (G II, 73/26–7). In the course of his note, he argues that since God's production of things depends on his essence, there cannot be an interval of time when he decrees that they should be produced, because that would imply the existence of a time before, when he did not, and a time after, when he will not. It follows, not than an eternal being does not produce things in temporal order, but only that thinking of an eternal being as doing so by temporally ordered acts is not thinking of it from its own point of view, or '*sub specie aeternitatis*'.[18] From that point of view, an eternal being eternally decrees everything that ever has occurred, is occurring, or will occur in itself. None of the waves God immanently causes to break on a beach in a certain temporal order is more immediate to his necessarily existing essence than any other.

Many commentators now recognize that, since the motion and rest which Spinoza recognizes as an eternal mode are the motion and rest of physics, and hence presupposes a temporal continuum susceptible of division in thought, although not in reality, he therefore cannot have thought that a substance's eternity excludes the occurrence in it of processes that are temporally ordered.[19] Not long since, it was otherwise. That eternity excludes temporal order in the non-systematic sense was confidently taken to be 'what [Spinoza] said',[20] and what he wrote, not only about the infinite modes of extension but even about the finite ones, was construed, by main force, as anticipating Leibniz's doctrine that motion, rest, and the temporal relations they presuppose are no more than *phenomena bene fundata*.[21]

Students of Spinoza in the future may well be perplexed by the tenacity with which this interpretation was held, because no arguments for the view of post-Cartesian physics it ascribes to Spinoza can be found in the *Ethics*: they must be sought in Leibniz and the like-minded theorists. The explanation, I believe, is charity. When interpreters who were deeply influenced by absolute idealism, and who considered the object of physics to be merely an appearance of the object of metaphysics, found Spinoza to assert, on the one hand, that nature is infinite, eternal and indivisible, and on the other, that duration and time are found only in nature's finite modes, they were reminded of Parmenides, Leibniz, Hegel and F.H. Bradley, and had no doubt about what was before them. To demand proof that a philosopher agrees with an established truth he seems to be expressing is captious; and H.H. Joachim and H.F. Hallett believed it to have been established that time, in the unsystematic sense, is only an appearance. The authority their scholarship won them concealed from their successors how weak is the evidence for attributing to Spinoza the views of eternity and duration they did.

Times have changed. The days of an interpretation ill supported by Spinoza's texts are numbered when an acute commentator can write:

> Spinoza, ... on the view I advocate, must not only agree that motion-and-rest is timeless; he must deny the fundamental reality of all temporal passage. This is an heroic view, if also a mad one. ... Spinoza's error about Time and Eternity runs like a great, hidden fault-line through the whole extent of his system.[22]

What was charitable for Joachim and Hallett is so no longer.

6.4. The Non-Contingency of Finite Modes

The final seven propositions of *Ethics* I comprehensively assert the non-contingency of whatever is, whether absolutely infinite substance or mode—finite or infinite. Everything is declared to be necessary as immanently caused by the absolutely infinite being, not merely as transiently caused by it as modified by some finite modification (E1p29). Nor is that all. It is also declared that, in immanently causing what it does, the absolutely infinite being can do no other (E1p33), not because it is constrained by anything else, but because that is its nature (E1p32c2). There is no distinction in reality between what it is and what it can do (E1p34), or between what it can do and what it does (E1p35). Not only are its essence, its power, and its actions really identical, and necessarily so, but the possibility of its willing otherwise than it does is incomprehensible to it as to us, because it is unintelligible (E1p30).

It has already been shown that Spinoza did not confound causal necessity, even the necessity of immanent causation, with logical necessity (4.6). His position is not that the actual world is the only logically possible one, but that, given the actual world, it is contrary to the laws of nature that it has ever not existed or will ever not. The difficulty for necessitarians pointed out by Bennett, that 'it is hard to do good philosophy while staying faithful to the thesis that this is the only [logically] possible world', is not a difficulty for Spinoza.[23] The axioms of *Ethics* I are advanced as expressing true ideas about the structure of whatever is: ideas that, although they can neither be verified nor falsified by collecting empirical information, are accepted as truths about the essence of whatever is because, by comparison with others that are offered, they enable us to think more effectively and clearly than any rival.

Spinoza's radical denial of contingency (E1p29) is not inconsistent with his theorem that no finite mode can produce an effect unless it is determined to do so by another finite mode (E1p28). As has been shown in 6.2 with respect to the attribute of extension, both the existence of finite bodies and the effects they produce are 'distinguished' in the infinite extended plenum soley by virtue of the internal motions that plenum immanently causes in itself (E2p13addL1). When we think of the plenum as infinite substance, we think of internal motions as occurring in it according to laws of nature we can formulate only in part; when, distinguishing finite bodies in it, we determine their states of relative motion or rest and their effects, we think of it insofar as it constitutes those bodies. In each of these ways of thinking, we adopt a different point of view; but we do not think of two different substances or two different sets of modes. As Pierre Macherey has observed, 'Immanent causality and transient causality do not determine two independent orders of causality, at the intersection of which finite things are themselves produced: but it is one and the same order, that considered as a whole, acts absolutely in itself, and, considered as "*partes extra partes*", distributes its operations according to relations between individuals that have no autonomy because the reason for their being is not in themselves.'[24]

Bennett has suggested that Spinoza holds that, given a 'great proposition' *P*, stating 'the whole truth about the actual world, down to the finest detail, in respect of all times', the question 'Why is it the case that *P*?' is answerable.[25] That is not true if the whole truth about the actual world includes the truth about what the laws of nature are. True, Spinoza's denial of contingency commits him to determinism in the comprehensive sense, according to which the whole state of the universe at all times is determined, according to laws of transient causation, by its whole state at any time whatever; for he held that the laws of nature are such that, in principle, transient causes can be inferred from effects as well as effects from transient causes (E1a3). Yet that implies, not that the great proposition P is true, but only that, given the laws of transient causation, from any true comprehensive description, in terms of those laws, of the state of actual world at some given time, true descriptions of its states at all other times would follow. Spinoza does hold that the truth of determinism in this comprehensive sense follows from the set of the sets of laws of immanent causation for nature as constituted by some attribute; but he does not hold that there is anything from which the set of sets of laws of immanent causation follows: that set of sets of laws expresses what is ultimate—the divine essence. Spinoza is a necessitarian, but not an 'explanatory rationalist'.

He nevertheless distinguishes truths about individual finite bodies that follow from their essences or natures (e.g. that the body of Moses involves a certain proportion of motion and rest) from those that depend on the common order of nature (e.g. that Moses lived to be a hundred and twenty). Bennett has complained that 'philosophical moves' such as this 'are invalid if there is no contingency'; for such a use of the concept of a thing's essence, meaning 'those of its properties it could not possibly lack', would be 'flattened into either falsehood or vacuous truth if there are no contingent truths'.[26] In 4.1, I have argued that a thing's essence is not a set of properties; and Diane Steinberg and Don Garrett have independently shown that Spinoza's necessitarianism does not flatten into falsehood or vacuity the distinction, in a finite thing's history, between what depends on its essence and what depends on external causes. That necessitarianism implies neither that all a finite body's properties are essential to it, nor that none of its properties can change, but only that the series of its actual changes constitutes its only possible biography.[27]

In repudiating contingency Spinoza also repudiated teleology. The laws governing the immanent causation of motion in the infinite extended plenum exhibit the order and connection of modes under all attributes; and that order is not teleological. Nature's laws, whether of immanent or of transient causation, lay down, not what ends nature strives to bring about, but rather what follows from nature's infinite essence, as expressed in her attributes (cf. E1p16, p32c1,2). 'Nature,' therefore, 'has no end set before her, and ... all final causes are nothing but human fictions' (E1p36ap—G II, 80/3-4). Indeed, Spinoza argues,

> this doctrine concerning the end turns nature completely upside down. For what is really a cause, it considers as an effect, and conversely. What is by nature prior, it makes posterior. And finally, what is supreme and most perfect, it makes imperfect. (G II, 80/9-14)

It is not because she satisfies some standard human beings have foolishly set up that nature is perfect, but because she is absolutely infinite, and because, according to the laws that express her essence, what she does, her 'course', cannot be other than it is. Since in practice there is no human end that the course of nature—that is, of God—consistently subserves, all claims to knowledge of God's ends must eventually be exposed as deceits.

6.5 Spinoza's Dualism: Pairing Within the Divine Attributes

In *Ethics* I, Spinoza mentions no specific divine attribute in either his axioms or his theorems. It is true that, in the examples he gives in scholia, and occasionally in his proofs, he assumes that extension and thought are divine attributes; but the validity of his proofs does not depend on that assumption. The only properties of God he professes to establish are trans-attribute, such as that he is indivisible and the cause of all things. In *Ethics* II, however, he proceeds differently. He lays down two existential axioms: that 'Man thinks' (E2a2), and that 'We feel (*sentimus*) a certain body to be affected in many ways' (E2a4). Besides implying that the universe is not empty, for it contains us—human beings who think of themselves as embodied—they incidentally identify two attributes we cognize. A third axiom then restricts the attributes we cognize to these two: 'We neither feel nor perceive any singular things except bodies and modes of thinking', or, as the *Nagelate Schriften* puts it, 'We neither feel nor perceive anything of

Natura Naturata except bodies and modes of thinking' (E2a5—G II, 86/6-8).

The first existential axiom is self-evident: no finite intellect constructing as best it can an idea of how things are can do other than begin with the ideas it has; and no reflective human being that ventures such a construction can fail to perceive that his idea of himself as thinking cannot be false (cf. 3.2). Given this axiom, together with what has been shown in Part I, that 'particular things are nothing but affections of God's attributes' (E1p25c), unless thinking can be shown to be a mode of some more fundamental essence it follows that 'Thought is an attribute of God, or God is a thinking thing' (E2p1). Proving that 'Extension is an attribute of God, or God is extended' (E2p2), is more difficult. Despite Spinoza's statement to the contrary, it plainly cannot be proved 'in the same way as ... the preceding Proposition' (E2p2d); for there is no axiom parallel to 'Man thinks', asserting the existence of any mode of extension. That 'We feel a certain body to be affected in many ways', as all readers of Descartes are aware, does not by itself entail that there is a particular extended thing that (by E1p25c) is an affection of one of God's attributes. However, it does entail that that extension is conceived. If that is so, since extension as conceived expresses an infinite essence (see 6.2), it follows, by the principle of substance plenitude, that extension is an attribute of the absolutely infinite being.

With the proof that actually existing beings, human thinkers, are modes of God, Spinoza has passed from proving that whatever is includes an absolutely infinite being to proving that an absolutely infinite being actually exists. Did Spinoza distinguish proving the one from proving the other? That he added a scholium to his proof that thought is an attribute of God, in which he pointed out that it can be proved simply from the fact that we can conceive an infinite Being by attending to thought alone (E2p1s—G II, 86/25-8), suggests that he did not. Yet would he have furnished a proof that assumes the existence of a particular thinking thing (E2p1d), and enunciated an axiom of the sort it assumes, if he had not had some inkling of the distinction?

Spinoza's restrictive axiom, that we neither feel nor perceive anything but bodies and thoughts, is presumably offered as a truth every reflective scientifically-minded reader will endorse. However, if the doctrine of *Ethics* I is true, that God has infinite attributes, and every mode is constituted by every attribute, why do human beings, as modes of God, not perceive all the other attributes that constitute God's essence? This question was put to Spinoza by von Tschirnhaus, with a supplementary question that shows he divined Spinoza's answer:

> will it please you, Sir, to convince us by some constructive (*ostensiva*) proof, and not by a reduction to impossibility, that we cannot cognize more attributes of God than thought and extension: [and] besides, whether it follows from this that creatures consisting of other attributes can on the other hand conceive no extension, and that thus it would seem that as many worlds are constituted as there are attributes of God? (Ep63—G IV, 274/19-20, 275/1-10)

If a certain finite mode of God as extended is a human body, and as thinking is a mind thinking primarily of that body, then corresponding to each other attribute constituting it, it is presumably also a mind thinking primarily of itself under that attribute. If so, each attribute other than thought will be the object of a distinct mind in the divine intellect; and, for thought at least, there will be as many distinct worlds as there are attributes, although their order and connection will be identical.

Spinoza's answers confirmed von Tschirnhaus's idea. Since a human mind, he wrote, is primarily constituted by the idea of a human body, and nothing else (E2p13), it 'neither involves nor expresses any other attributes of God than Extension and Thought' (Ep64—G IV, 277/18-9). And then, prompted by a further letter, he added this:

> although each thing is expressed in infinite ways in the infinite intellect of God, nevertheless those infinite ideas by which it is expressed cannot constitute one and the same mind of a singular thing, but an infinity: since each one of these infinite ideas has no connection with any other.[28] (Ep66—G IV, 280/8-12)

The infinite intellect of God consists of an infinity of infinite ideas of himself, one for each attribute besides thought; and each idea in that infinity is accompanied by an idea of that idea, and a further idea of that idea, to infinity (see 3.1). Since the objects of each of this infinity of ideas are conceived through really distinct attributes, they have nothing in common. They may therefore be considered an infinity of really distinct infinite minds.

It follows from this, not merely that the attribute of thought is more comprehensive than all the others, but that the infinity of infinite minds of which it consists are each of them paired with one of the infinity of God's attributes besides thought. There is an infinite mind whose object is God as extended, and then, for each of God's attributes other than thought and extension, $A_1, A_2, \ldots A_n$, there is an infinite mind whose object is God as A_1, an infinite mind whose object is God as $A_2, \ldots$ and an infinite mind whose object is God as A_n.

Spinoza is a substance monist: his God or Nature is a substance constituted by every attribute expressing an infinite essence, not a union of distinct substances, like a Cartesian human being. And although he is an attribute pluralist, he is not an attribute dualist; for he does not restrict the attributes constituting the essence of his God to two, although he holds that only two can be cognized by human beings. However, since within his God's unitary substance each infinite attribute is paired with an infinite mind, just as each Cartesian human body is paired with a human mind, he can be accurately described as an attribute-mind dualist. His dualism is an exclusive pairing of each attribute besides thought with a distinct mind of which it is the sole object, the attribute of thought being the totality of those distinct minds. Since each attribute is really distinct and is conceived through itself (E1p10), the attribute of thought can be reduced neither to any attribute besides thought, nor to their totality: it is on exactly the same footing as the others and equally immediate to God. Spinoza allows no possibility of reducing even human thought to processes in human bodies, which used to be the programme of materialism when philosophers were serious about it. From no point of view is he a materialist.

Notes

[1] Cf. Gueroult (1968), chs. 8–12, according to which God is treated as

cause in *Ethics* I, 16–20, and as effect in *Ethics* I, 21–9.
2. Cf. Maimonides, I, 35 (42a–43a/79–81); Descartes, *Princ. Phil.* I, 23 (AT VIII-1, 13/24–30).
3. Cf. Descartes, *Princ. Phil.*: (i) I, 30–5, 42–5, 70–5 (on distinguishing what is grasped by the intellect from what is not); (ii) II, 4, 22–3 ('all the matter in the whole universe is of one and the same kind'); and (iii) II, 23–33 (how finite bodies in an infinite plenum are distinguished from one another by their movement relative to one another). Cf. DPP, I p13–15; II d8–9, p65 (G I, 191/24–192/14).
4. My account of the fundamentals of Descartes's physics is derived from *Princ. Phil.* II and from Spinoza's DPP II. It is not, I believe, controversial.
5. Bennett (1984), pp. 88–110; esp. 92–3, 97, 100.
6. Descartes, *Princ. Phil.* II, 33.
7. Bennett (1984), p. 101.
8. Grene and Nails (eds) (1986). The two fundamental historical studies in this collection, André Lecrivain, 'Spinoza and Cartesian Mechanics', and Heine Siebrand, 'Spinoza and the Rise of Modern Science in the Netherlands', confirm A. Rupert Hall's observation that 'it is impossible to open any book on physical science written between 1650 and 1720 ... without recognising [Descartes's] shadow' (*From Galileo to Newton: 1630–1720*—London: Fontana, 1970, p. 120). In a useful article, David Lachterman describes Descartes's physics as 'confront[ing] its partisans and opponents alike as a body of principles rent by tensions, incompatibilities and discrepancies' (Lachterman (1978), p. 81), but it would be equally true so to describe quantum mechanics in 1950, and would convey an equally false impression.
9. Savan (1986), p. 97.
10. Nancy Maull, 'Spinoza in the Century of Science', in Grene and Nails (eds) (1986), p. 12.
11. Savan (1986), p. 99.
12. According to Wolf, there is an 'enormous difference' between Descartes's conception of matter and Spinoza's. 'For Spinoza Extension or Matter is essentially Physical Energy' (W1, 62). If so, Spinoza anticipated ideas of the nineteenth century—without betraying it in his correspondence.
13. Hallett rightly objects to taking '*facies totius universi*' as standing for what Spinoza calls 'the common order of nature', but his recommendation that '*facies*' be translated as 'fashion' or 'make' (Hallett (1957), p. 32 n.2) is as gratuitous as his objection to the phrase '*res extensa*'.
14. Although motion is not defined in the *Ethics*, the Cartesian conception of it is presupposed in what Spinoza says about finite bodies in *Ethics* II, in particular that 'Bodies are distinguished from one another by reason of motion and rest, speed and slowness, and not by reason of substance' (E2p13addL1).
15. Kline (1982), p. 263.
16. Bennett (1984), p. 203.
17. Bennett (1984), p. 202.

18 The Latin phrase '*sub specie aeternitatis*' or '*sub aeternitatis specie*' (the order of the nouns makes no difference) occurs eighteen times in the *Ethics*: thrice in Part II and fifteen times in Part V (Gueret, Robinet and Tombeur (1977), p. 309). Curley distinguishes two senses in which Spinoza uses '*species*': (i) as equivalent to 'specific kind' (or to the Dutch '*gedaante*' or '*soort*'); and (ii) as equivalent to 'appearance' (or to the Dutch '*schijn*'). Curley holds that in '*sub specie aeternitatis*' it is used in sense (i); but I accept Gueroult's argument (against Appuhn, Baensch, Hallett, Lewis Robinson and others) that it is sense (ii), 'from the point of view of eternity' (Gueroult (1974), Ap. 17, pp. 609–15; cf. C, 662, 698).

19 Wolfson's freedom from Platonic and Hegelian preconceptions was liberating (cf. Wolfson (1934), I, pp. 358–69); but Martha Kneale first worked out the non-idealist interpretation I adopt (Kneale (1968), pp. 236–40). Cf. Bennett (1984), pp. 196–11.

20 Hardin (1977), p. 137.

21 Cf. Mates (1986), pp. 198–203, 228–32. For a recent example of the attribution of Leibniz's position, see Hardin (1977), pp. 130–1.

22 Delahunty (1985), pp. 294–5.

23 Bennett (1984), p. 114.

24 Translated from a forthcoming paper presented by Pierre Macherey to a conference in Jerusalem in March 1987.

25 Bennett (1984), p. 115.

26 Bennett (1984, p. 114.

27 This section has been influenced throughout by forthcoming papers by Don Garrett, Pierre Macherey, and Diane Steinberg; and by conversation or correspondence with their authors.

28 Confirming that this is Spinoza's considered view, 'although [he] is not very explicit on this point in the *Ethics*', Curley notes the following comments on it: Pollock (1880), pp. 159–63; Joachim (1903), pp. 134–8; Curley (1969), pp. 147–51; Gueroult (1974), pp. 45–6, 78–84, 91–2 (C, 450 *n*.9).

7 Human Beings (I): Cognition

7.1. Human Individuals: Body and Mind

In his prefatory note to Part II, Spinoza announces that the remainder of the *Ethics* will be confined to those things following from God's essence that 'can lead us, by the hand as it were, to cognition of the human Mind and its highest blessedness' (E2pref—G II, 84/10–12). Since human minds are finite modes of the infinite mind whose object is God as extended (see 6.5), and since every mode of thinking involves an idea of an object (E2a3), each human mind must involve an idea, and the object of that idea must be something extended. But what? Since each human mind feels a certain enduring individual body, as distinct from others, to be affected in many ways (cf. E2a4), it must be that individual body, and not extended substance as a whole (E2p13d—G II, 96/6–10). And that body must actually exist (E2p11); for 'when singular things are said to exist, not only in so far as they are comprehended in God's attributes, but in so far also as they are said to endure, their ideas also involve the existence through which they are said to endure' (E2p8c—G II, 91/8–11). 'The primary constituent[1] of the actual being of a human Mind', Spinoza therefore concludes, 'is nothing other than the idea of a certain actually existing singular thing' (E2p11), namely, 'a Body, or a certain mode of Extension actually existing, and nothing else' (E2p13).

Even before he divulged that the actually existing individual that is the object of the human mind is a human body, Spinoza confessed that his readers would 'think of many things that will give them pause' in this argument, and begged them 'to continue with [him] slowly, step by step' (E2p11s—G II, 95/8–10). And his next step, before directly considering the things that would given them pause, was to determine the nature of the human mind's object: the actually existing individual human body. It is uncontroversial that each human body is 'composed of a great many individuals of different natures, each of which is highly composite' (E2p13add—G II, 102/20-1); and it is commonly inferred that it is therefore the aggregate of the individual parts that compose it. This inference Spinoza rejected. In its place, he proposed a functional view of what all composite finite bodies are, human bodies among them. It is largely Cartesian (E2p13add—G II, 97/16-103/5).

Although he rejects atomism—the doctrine that Nature as extended consists of finite bodies that cannot, by the laws of nature, be cut into others—he does not deny that in nature at any time certain bodies are *simplicissima*, that is, distinguished from one another only by differences of external motion and rest in relation to one another (cf. G II, 99/23-5; 101/28-102/1). It does not follow that they are of the same magnitude, as Joachim thought:[2] the quantity of motion of one *corpus simplicissimum* could differ from that of another solely because of its different size. In turn, non-simple bodies are composed of *corpora simplicissima* in the following way:

> When a number of bodies, whether of the same or of different size, are so constrained by other bodies that they lie upon one another, or if they so move, whether with the same degree or different degrees of speed, that they communicate their motions to each other in a certain fixed (*certa*) manner, we shall say that those bodies are united with one another and that they all together compose one body or Individual (*corpus, sive Individuum*) which is distinguished from the others through this union of bodies. (G II, 99/27-100/5)

This, as Joachim points out, is implicitly recursive: it lays down how a body can be composed of other bodies, whether they are themselves simple or composite.[3] Composite bodies, in short, are distinguished neither by the identity nor the physical properties of the bodies that compose them, but solely by the manner in which those bodies communicate motions to one another.

Spinoza neither endorses nor repudiates Descartes's fundamental law governing collisions of bodies: that 'if a body collides with another body that is stronger (*fortiori*) than itself, it loses none of its motion; but if it collides with a weaker body, it loses a quantity of motion equal to that which it imparts to the other body.'[4] He confines himself to the specific law that 'when a body in motion strikes against another which is at rest and cannot give way', then it is 'reflected' in such a way that the angle of incidence is equal to the angle of reflection (E1p13adda2—G II, 99/16-22). As Gueroult points out, this rule 'is especially important for Hobbes and Spinoza, who ... base on it the mechanism of the cerebral conditions of perception, that mechanism being conceived as linked to the rebounding of the animal spirits from the cerebral surfaces which they strike'.[5]

The composites of which human bodies are composed are of three kinds: hard (those 'whose parts lie upon one another over a large surface'), soft (those 'whose parts lie on one another over a small surface'), and fluid (those 'whose parts are in motion') (G II, 100/12-15). From infancy to death, the parts of each human body, like those of a compound pendulum,[6] preserve a constant pattern of internal motion and rest. They are 'as it were, continually regenerated', being replaced during growth by larger parts: for example, the heart becomes larger, the arteries and veins longer, the blood more copious (G II, 102/29-30); but that does not alter the fixed manner in which they communicate motion to one another (for example, that in which the heart's motion communicates motion to the blood). The body dies when its external environment either ceases to enable it to replace worn-out parts, or prevents healthy ones from continuing to function, whether by accelerating or slowing its heartbeat beyond a fixed range or by causing it to lose too much blood.

An individual human mind is primarily constituted by that part of God's infinite intellect that has God as extended for its object, but only in so far as it is an idea of a certain actually existing human body, and nothing else (E2p13). The same composite finite mode which, as extended, is a human body is also, under the attribute of thought, a human mind. Yet although a given human individual's mind and body are in this sense the same thing, constituted respectively by the really distinct attributes of thought and extension, they cannot be causally related to one another, because those attributes are really distinct. Except through one attribute or another, trans-attribute relations between substance and mode, or between mode and mode, cannot be conceived at all. The finite mode that is a human mind can be trans-attributively related to other finite modes; but to conceive that relation, either those other finite modes must be conceived through the attribute of thought, or both that mind and those of other modes must be conceived under some common attribute other than thought. What is conceived through one attribute cannot be conceived as trans-attributively related to what is conceived through another.

7.2. Representation Without Adequate Cognition

Nobody has presented more effectively than Margaret Wilson what in Spinoza's theory of the human mind gives his readers pause.[7] A true idea of the human mind must account for common beliefs about specific contents of human minds, just as a true idea of motion must account for common beliefs about specific motions, perhaps correcting the, but not by resorting to ideas themselves suspect. But, Wilson objects, in holding that the mind of an arbitrary human being, say Peter, is the idea in the divine mind of that human being's body, Spinoza contradicts four common beliefs about the human mind that are undeniably true. They are these (1) Ideas in human minds are possessed by finite human beings: Peter's ideas are his, not God's—more technically, Peter is their 'subject', not God. (2) Peter's idea of his own body is neither complete nor wholly true; and yet, as Wilson reminds us, Spinoza implies that 'whatever happens in the individual (*singulari*) object of any idea, there is cognition of it in God' (E2p9c), and she points out that 'this carries down to changes of the relation of the simplest parts'.[8] (3) Most of the ideas in any actual human mind are of things other than the corresponding body—of other minds, human and divine, of animals, of the innumerable things in the material world. For if 'the idea that constitutes the human mind' is 'just the idea of the human body', then it appears that there can be no ideas in the human mind that are not 'of parts, processes, or aspects of the human body'.[9] And finally, (4) finite minds are much fewer than finite bodies. If, as Spinoza maintains, there is an idea in God's mind of every finite body whatever, it appears that there must be a mind corresponding to each finite body.

Anticipating objections like these, Pollock took the desperate course of denying the plain sense of Spinoza's text (e.g. E2p11s), and reading his declaration that 'a mode of extension and the idea of that mode are one and the same thing' (E2p7s—G II, 90/8-9) as saying no more than that the 'parallelism and mutual dependence' of extension (or body) and thought (or mind) are 'not a mystery but an elementary fact', so that asking 'why mind should correspond with matter' is like asking 'why the convexity of a curve should answer to the concavity'.[10] Thus, when Spinoza refers to the 'object (*objectum*) of the idea constituting the human mind' (E2p12), Pollock takes him to mean, not what that idea represents, but what in God as extended is causally parallel to it. He could be right only if, in technical epistemic contexts and without a word of explanation, Spinoza had used both the noun '*objectum*' and the Latin expression rendered into English by 'idea of' followed by a noun[11] with deliberate ambiguity: to stand for what an idea represents and for an idea as representing it, and also for what under an attribute other than thought is causally correlated with an idea, and for an idea as correlated with it. '[I]t is important to observe', Pollock adds,

> that in this [second] sense, *idea* has a far wider application than in the first and more familiar sense. The material correlate which is called the object of idea may be living organism, but also it may not. The idea may coincide with a concept in a conscious mind, or with a conscious mind forming concepts, but also it may not.[12]

In other words, when Spinoza speaks of the idea in God that is 'of' a given actually existing human body, he means, not an idea that represents that body, but merely one that is causally parallel with it.

Although some have refused, many commentators have followed Pollock in this violent reading of Spinoza's text.[13] Yet is has a worse defect than violence: it is suicidal. It meets an objection by jettisoning an essential part of what is objected to. That God as extended is causally parallel to God as thinking is only half of Spinoza's doctrine of God as constituted by those attributes. Its other half is 'gnoseological' (to use Gueroult's term): namely, that God as extended is truly represented by the infinite idea that is God as thinking (E2p7c). Its gnoseological half, together with the axiom that (true) cognition of a thing involves cognition of its cause (E1a4), implies that God's true cognition of himself as extended must truly represent his causal order and connection as extended. But since (by E2p7) God's causal order and connection as thinking is the same as his causal order and connection as extended, his causal order and connection as thinking of himself as extended must be the same as his causal order and connection as extended. Hence the *modi cogitandi* in God that constitute the idea representing Peter's body must have the same causal order and connection as the modes of extension they represent. Admittedly, they appear not to have: the ideas composing Peter's mind seem for the most part not to represent causal order and connection of the modes composing his body. But unless that appearance is deceptive, an essential part of Spinoza's theory of the relation of God as thinking to God as extended must be rejected as false.

Can the objections listed by Wilson be met without resorting to Pollock's suicidal defence? The first of them may be brushed aside. Admittedly, it outrages common opinion that human beings are not the substantial subjects of their ideas, but that God is. Yet nothing in human experience contradicts Spinoza's doctrine that all human ideas are modes of God's infinite intellect. When reasoned argument is consistent with experience, common opinion cannot withstand it.

The second objection in Wilson's inventory is more serious. If the mind of each human being is God's idea of that human being's body, then Spinoza's conclusion seems to follow that nothing can happen in that body which is not perceived by the Mind' (E2p12). Yet that seems plainly false. Human beings perceive relatively little that happens in their bodies: they do not, for example, perceive what the corpuscles of their blood are doing. If Spinoza is right about the relation of human minds to God, therefore, it appears that their minds cannot be ideas of their bodies.

Spinoza meets this objection by denying that an idea of all

that happens in a human body and nothing else involves cognition of that body's parts, or of its structure and functioning. Nobody has bettered Matheron's exposition of why he denies it, which in English would run:

> The [human] mind *is* the idea of the [human] body actually existing. But it *does not have* the idea of the body actually existing: it is God who has that idea; and he has it only in measure as he also has ideas of the external causes that make our body exist, then the causes of those causes, and so *ad infinitum*. The mind, therefore, does not as such cognize the body (E2p19d). However, it does cognize it from another direction: thanks to events which happen to it. Since it *has* ideas of affections of the body, and since those ideas entail the nature of the body, it perceives the body in perceiving its affections (E2p19d): such is the only way vouchsafed it of being conscious of its object.[14]

As Matheron reminds us, cognition of a finite thing is through its cause. Hence, since the ideas human beings have of the laws of immanent causation are inadequate, and go little further than that they involve conservation, adequate human cognition of a finite mode involves not merely an idea of that mode, but also, linked with it, an idea of its transient cause, an idea of the transient cause of that transient cause, and so on (see 3.4–5).

Accordingly, if your mind is that 'part of the infinite intellect of God' (E2p11c—G II, 94/31-2) which constitutes the idea of a human body actually existing *and of nothing else*, everything is excluded from your mind, as idea of your body and nothing else, that you can cognize only through independent ideas of external causes. Your mind is confined, for its primary material, to ideas of what is actually happening in your body, and of the effects of those happenings, so far as ideas of those effects follow from ideas of those happenings alone. Spinoza's catalogue of what this excludes is formidable. Most of it follows from the theorem that 'The human Mind does not cognize the human Body itself, nor does it cognize that it exists, except through ideas of affections by which the Body is affected' (E2p19). A given human body is brought into existence, and is 'as it were, continually regenerated' by the effect on its various parts of many other bodies. Hence God's infinite intellect, in so far as it constitutes the idea of that human body and nothing else, has only an inadequate idea of it, because it does not have ideas of the other bodies that are its causes (E2p19d—G II, 108/9-14).

A human body, we must remember, is an individual consisting of parts that 'communicate their motions to one another in a certain fixed manner' (E2p13add—G II, 99/27-100/5). Nothing about its parts belongs to its essence except the manner in which their internal motions are communicated: neither their size relative to external bodies, nor their internal composition. Hence Spinoza infers that ideas of those parts, and of their parts, will not be in the divine intellect in so far as he has the idea of the human body, but only in so far as he has other ideas (E2p24d—G II, 110/30-111/12). Your perception of all the affections of your body, therefore, does not involve cognizing even its affected parts, much less their microstructure. Nor is that all. As derived from ideas of its affections, your idea of your body furnishes no adequate cognition of its nature or essence—of the fixed manner in which its parts communicate their motions to one another (E2p27). For, while your body was caused to exist and is preserved in existence by bodies outside itself, God's idea of it, taken by itself, does not include ideas of those external bodies, and hence is not an idea of it through its cause (E2p28s). Not only does God's idea of your body, and nothing else, not yield adequate cognition of your body's essence, but neither does it yield adequate cognition of its affections (E2p28) or duration (E2p30).

In saying that your mind 'perceives' every happening in your body, Spinoza therefore implies no more than that you must have some idea of all that is happening in it, not that your idea must be clear or adequate. This throws light on a related doctrine to which he is committed, although Parkinson describes it as 'little more than a curiosity'.[15] Since his reasons for identifying the mind of each human being with the idea in the divine intellect of that human being's body are 'completely general', and 'do not pertain to man more than to other Individuals' (E2p13s—G II, 96/26-7), he cannot escape concluding that for every finite individual body, as for every human body, there is a mind. That being so, all finite bodies 'thought in different degrees, are nevertheless animate' (G II,

96/27-8). But God's idea of a grain of sand, taken by itself, being cut off from any idea of its cause, will not be cognition, and will be barely distinguishable from inanimateness.

By thus blunting the objection that according to his theory, every *corpus simplicissimum* is equipped with intelligence or even sensation, Spinoza has sharpened another: that the ideas in the divine intellect of individual human bodies seem much the same as those of any finite body whatever. That takes us to Wilson's third objection: that human beings, whose minds Spinoza holds to be primarily constituted by ideas of their own bodies, in fact cognize little about their bodies, but a great deal about their neighbours and their immediate material environment. Spinoza's explanation of why they are largely ignorant of their bodies makes it even more difficult to understand how they can be less ignorant of other things. Can he explain that?

7.3. Extra-Cogitative Parallelism (I): Imagination

If human minds surpass the minds or souls that correspond to meaner finite bodies, then the human body must surpass those other finite bodies. For everything Spinoza finds in the human mind, this 'extra-cogitative' parallelism (the phrase is Gueroult's)[16] compels him to find an analogue in the body that is that mind's primary object, and at the same time strictly to observe the real distinction between extension and thought. As he begins his search, he gives notice that he will work on the following hypotheses:

> [I]n proportion as a Body is more capable than others of doing many things at once, or being acted on in many ways at once, so its Mind is more capable than others of perceiving many things at once. And in proportion as the actions of a body depend more on itself alone, and as other bodies concur less with it in acting, so its mind is more capable of understanding distinctly. And from these [truths], we can cognize the excellence of mind over others, and also see the cause why we have only a completely confused cognition of our Body.... (E2p13s—G II, 97/8-15)

Assuming these hypotheses, he proceeds to show that an idea of any affection of your body that excludes its being caused by another must represent that affection as caused by something outside your body.

He begins by trying to prove that 'The idea of any mode in which the human Body is affected by external bodies must involve the nature of the human Body and at the same time the nature of the external body' (E2p16). Stipulating that an idea 'involves' the nature of an external body if it 'does not exclude the existence or presence of the nature of [that] body, but posits it' (E2p17d—G II, 104/27-9), he argues that, since all the modes in which a body is affected follow from the nature both of the affected and of the affecting body, the idea of them (by E1a4) will necessarily involve the nature of each (E2p16d—G II, 104/2-5). This argument fails; for it holds only of true ideas of such modes: ideas that do not represent them as internally caused or uncaused. An idea of a mode of your body which represents it as uncaused, or as caused by another of its modes, will not represent it as caused by something outside your body even if it is so caused.

Fortunately, both proposition and proof can be acceptably revised. Suppose that somebody pulls your ear, and that your complex idea of your body contains the following elements: (i) an idea of the region relative to the side of your head that the lobe of your ear now occupies; (ii) an idea of the region relative to the side of your head that it occupied a moment ago; (iii) an idea of bodies generally that excludes the uncaused transference of the lobe of your ear from the latter region to the former; (iv) an idea of the motions of the rest of your body, which excludes them as causes of that transference. Although a body external to your own is not the ideatum of any of these ideas, attention to what they exclude shows them to be linked to a further idea, namely (v), an idea of an external body as cause of the transference of the lobe of your ear from the latter region to the former. This idea 'posits' the existence of that external body; of the character of which you can form a more or less definite idea, perhaps a false one, in measure as you have ideas of affections of your body that could produce such transferences (for example, pulling your own ear). Furthermore, you will not only regard the transference of the lobe of your ear as caused by the external body you thus conceive, you will regard that external body 'as actually existing, or as present' to you, until your body 'is affected with a mode[17] that excludes the existence or presence of that body' (E2p17).

Corresponding to this revision of its proof, the proposition proved may be restated as: If a human body is affected by a mode caused by external bodies, and if the human mind primarily constituted by an idea of that body cognizes that all its affections are caused by bodies internal or external to it, then if its idea of that mode is such as to exclude the idea of its being caused by bodies internal to it, its idea of it must involve the nature of the external bodies that cause it. With this proposition as point of departure, Spinoza can proceed to construct a theory of human cognition of the external world.

The next step is to show that such cognition is not confined to external bodies now acting on the body of whoever cognizes them. According to Spinoza's physiology, the bodily counterpart of an idea of an external body is a mode of the brain, one of the body's softer parts, produced by the effects of the external body on the sensory surfaces of the body in question. Such modes can endure after they are produced; and as long as they do, the mind primarily constituted by the idea of that body will have an idea of them. In order not to introduce unfamiliar (*inusitata*) words, Spinoza calls more or less lasting modes of this kind 'images' of the things that cause them (E2p17s—G II, 106/6–9). An image is therefore physical, a certain configuration of some of the softer parts of the brain. It is not a representation of the external body that caused it, although its character will be a physical projection of some of that body's properties.

No mode of a human body can properly be called an image of the body that causes it unless it has a part in that body's life analogous to that which the idea of that external body has in the corresponding mind's life. Ideas of external bodies are not merely effects of causes external to the mind, but are themselves causes of both mental actions and mental 'passions'. What Spinoza says of images in *Ethics* II is less than satisfactory, because he does not introduce the concepts of action and passion until *Ethics* III. However, in view of his treatment of human action in *Ethics* III and IV, it is reasonable to ascribe to him the conception of a bodily image as a mode of the body that is both caused by an external body, and, given the bodily states that correspond to what he calls mental 'affects', causes bodily reactions to that external body, or to other external bodies in causal relations with it. A mode of your brain caused by the ringing of your alarm clock, which, together with a tendency of your body not to linger in bed after a mode of that kind occurs in it, can reasonably be considered to play in the life of your body a part analogous to that played in the life of your mind by the idea of the clock's ringing, together with your desire not to linger in bed after you hear it ring.

Any body capable of many things, according to Spinoza, must be able to form highly complex images of its environment that will be part of the cause of the various adjustments it makes to changes, present and future, in that environment. The corresponding mind will form two kinds of ideas of those images: (1) ideas of them simply as modes of that body; and (2) ideas of them as modes with external causes of certain kinds (cf. E2p14d—G II, 103/12-14). A supermarket supervisor's ideas of the display on his television screen is likewise of two kinds: (1) ideas of it as a pattern of light; and (2) ideas of that pattern as caused by the external bodies affecting a television camera. Far from being a paradox, Spinoza's view was already scientific common-sense in his own day, as its descendants are in ours.

Given the human mind's capacity to form ideas of external bodies from ideas of their images, the set of those ideas is enlarged by virtue of a proposition that has been labelled Spinoza's 'Association Law'. It runs, 'If the human Body has once been affected by two or more bodies at the same time, then when the Mind subsequently imagines one of them, it will immediately recollect the others also' (E2p18). The nature of Spinoza's proof of this is best brought out by restating the cardinal point proved in it: that if your environment produces in you an image of a body that is part of a complex image of several bodies, you cannot imagine that body without imagining the others (E2p18d). If your environment later produces in you an image of that same body without its former companions, the association will be excluded, at least for a time; but it will be strengthened if, instead, your environment repeatedly produces in you the same complex image. That is why, when they see a hoof-print, soldiers associate it with cavalry and wars, while farmers associate it with ploughing and harvests (E2p18s—G II, 107/21-9). Another of Spinoza's examples, that of the association of the Latin word *'pomum'* with apples, suggests a mechanism of image formation more akin to what B. F. Skinner has called 'operant conditioning'. Children learning Latin as their mother tongue may first learn to utter *'pomum'* in the presence of an apple, but they soon learn to convey thoughts about absent apples by uttering it. What reinforces the association is less the repeated causing of complex images of apples and utterances of *'pomum'* than repeated sequences of utterances of *'pomum'* and subsequent expected transactions with apples.

All developed human beings come, in these ways, to have ideas of numerous external bodies actually existing, among them ideas of human bodies other than their own, whether present or absent, living or dead (E2p17s—G II, 105/30-106/6). For example, Peter can have an idea of Paul's body, whether Paul is alive or dead; and Paul an idea of Peter's, whether Peter is alive or dead. In addition, as Hallett has pointed out, Peter will also come to have ideas of his own body of the same kind as his idea of Paul's. Since his brain can receive images of parts of the body of which it is a part, he can derive ideas of those parts from his ideas of those images. Yet those ideas will not be part of the idea that primarily constitutes his mind.[18] If he inspects the back of his head in a double mirror, he forms an idea of the same kind as his idea of the back of Paul's.

Suppose now that Peter and Paul are inseparable identical twins, and that for everything of which Peter has an idea, Paul has an idea too. Peter's mind contains ideas both of Peter's actually existing body, its parts and their states, and also of Paul's, and Paul's also contains idea of those very same objects. How, on Spinoza's view, can their minds be two and not one? Spinoza's answer is that the infinitely many ideas in the divine intellect include (i) a composite idea of which the primary constituent is an idea of Peter's body that represents all its modes or affections, and nothing else, among these affections being images of Paul's body; and (ii) a similar composite idea of Paul's body, among the components of which is an idea of an image of Peter's body. The components of each of these composite ideas will be either primary (that is, not caused by other components) or derivative (not primary); and even though (as will almost never happen) both have ideas of the same objects, the ideas that are primary in the mind of one will be derivative in the mind of the other, and vice versa.

Let ideas be represented by '$I(\ )$', each with a name of its object in the parentheses, and with one of the subscripts 'p' or 'd' after 'I' to indicate whether the idea it stands for is primary or derivative. And let the various objects of ideas be represented as follows: (i) modes of a body that are not images by 'M_1' ... 'M_n'; (ii) modes that are images by '$E[\ ]$' (each with the name of what causes it in the brackets), and (iii) all other objects by 'O_1' ... 'O_n'. Then, indicating modes of Peter's body by the subscript 't', and those of Paul's by the subscript 'u', the composite idea of which the primary constituent is an idea of Peter's body may be represented as:

$I_p(M_{t1} ... M_{tn}, E_t[M_1] ... E_t[M_n], E_t[O_1] ... E_t[O_n])$ & $I_d(M_1 ... M_n), O_1 ... O_n$.

Conformably, the composite idea of which the primary constituent is an idea of Paul's body may in turn be represented as:

$I_p(M_{u1} ... M_{un}, E_u[M_1] ... E_u[M_n], E_u[O_1] ... E_u[O_n])$ & $I_d (M_1 ... M_n, O_1 ... O_n)$.

In Peter's mind, only modes of Peter's body are objects of its primary components, while those of Paul's are among either the causes of images of which Peter has primary ideas, or the objects of his derivative ideas. In Paul's mind, on the other hand, only modes of Paul's body are objects of its primary components, and those of Peter's are among either the causes of images of which Paul has primary ideas, or the objects of his derivative ideas.

7.4. Extra-Cogitative Parallelism (II): Reason

How our ideas of external things are connected depends on how those things affect our bodies, and not on their nature or causes. Yet human beings connect their ideas not only 'according to the order and connection of the affections of the human Body', but also 'according to the order and connection of the intellect, by which the Mind perceives things through their first causes, and which is the same for all men' (E2p18s—G II, 107/9–13). How can any human mind, yours for example, form and connect ideas of things through their first causes, which must be the same for all?

In approaching this question, Spinoza's first step is as profound as it is simple. Since God cognizes everything as it is, and hence adequately, an idea in your mind is adequate if it is identical with God's idea of its object: that is, if God's idea of that thing is identical with the idea he has of it so far as he constitutes the idea of your body, and nothing else. Now ideas of 'things that are common to all, and are equally in the part and in the whole' are necessarily in God so far as he constitutes the idea of your body, and nothing else (E2p38). All such things are essences; for while individual essences can be common to many existents, individual existents cannot. Essences that are common to all are either trans-attribute, or follow solely from the nature of some attribute constituting God's essence. The undefined terms of *Ethics* I stand for things that are common to all in this sense, except for those whose sense is elucidated by referring to the structure of ideas (such as 'being' and 'essence'), or to their linkage (such as 'necessary' and 'possible'). Trans-attribute essences that are common to all are: those of a cause and of an effect, or a concept (or idea) and of an object of a concept (or ideatum). The attributes, since they each constitute God's essence, are also common to all. And since from the absolute nature of each attribute, as constituting an actual essence, there follows an eternal process in the divine substance by which finite modes come into being and cease to be in temporal order, the essence signified by the phrase 'a temporally ordered thing' is also implicitly recognized as common to all.

Spinoza proceeds to show that there are also external things affecting their bodies that human beings can adequately cognize without conceiving them through common notions. Suppose that an affection or mode M of a given human body B is caused by another body by virtue or some property which both share, say F. Then God will conceive M, through its cause, that is, through another body in so far as it is F. Now God has the idea of F, not only in so far as he has ideas of bodies external to B, but also in so far as he has an idea of B and nothing else, that is, in so far as he constitutes the human mind whose object is B. Since that human mind must have an adequate idea of F, human beings have the materials for forming adequate ideas of external bodies by which their bodies are affected, provided that one affects the other by virtue of essences commmon to both (E2p39). 'Because of this', Spinoza observes, 'the [human] mind is more capable of perceiving many things adequately, the more its Body has in common with other bodies' (E2p39c). This theorem is cardinal to much he will say about what human beings can cognize about one another.

Apart from ideas of these two kinds, and those that can be derived from them, all the ideas in your mind, or in anybody else's, are inadequate and confused. In the *Ethics*, Spinoza divides such inadequate and confused ideas into: (i) ideas of 'singular things that have been represented to us through the senses in a way that is mutilated, confused, and without order for the intellect' (E2p40s2—G II, 122/3–5); and (ii) ideas derived 'from signs, e.g. from the fact that, having heard or read certain words, we recollect things, and form certain ideas of them, which are like them, and through which we imagine the things' (G II, 122/7–9). Each of these two ways of regarding (*contemplandi*) things Spinoza calls 'cognition of the first kind, opinion, or imagination' (G II, 122/9–11). Most of the ideas we live by belong to this way of regarding things, and are therefore confused and inadequate.

We must therefore use our common notions and adequate ideas of the properties of things, which Spinoza calls 'cognition of the second kind', to construct 'an adequate idea of the formal essence of certain attributes of God', and, having done so, to proceed to 'the adequate cognition of the essence of things', which he calls 'cognition of the third kind, or intuitive knowledge (*scientia intuitiva*)' (G II, 122/14–19). Spinoza illustrates how the two kinds of adequate cognition differ, and how both of them differ from imagination, by the following analogy with the three ways in which the proportions of numbers to one another can be cognized:

Suppose that there are three numbers, and the problem is to find a fourth which is to the second as the third is to the first. Merchants do not hesitate to multiply the second by the third, and divide the product by the first, because they have not yet forgotten what they heard from their teacher without any demonstration, or because they have often found this in the simplest numbers, or from the force of demonstration in Euclid VII, 19, viz. from the common property of proportionals. But in the simplest numbers none of this is necessary. Given the numbers 1, 2, and 3, nobody fails to see that the fourth proportional number is 6, and we see this much more clearly because we infer the fourth number from the ratio which, in one intuition,[19] we see the first number to have to the second. (G II, 122/19-30)

Alexandre Matheron has elucidated the idea underlying this analogy;[20] and in what follows, I try to convey the gist of his conclusions.

A merchant may find the number that is to 9,913 as 931 is to 161 by applying 'the rule of three' he has been taught: to wit, whenever he has three numbers, a, b, and c, and wants to discover a fourth x, that is to b as c is to a, then $x=(b \times c) \div a$. So he multiplies 9,913 by 931, obtaining the product 9,229,003, and divides that product by 161, arriving at the desired number 57,323. That merchant may well not understand why the rule he applies yields the number he seeks; and if so, his cognition of it is imaginative rather than rational, and hence inadequate. Now consider a second merchant, who, like many among Spinoza's Dutch contemporaries, understands Euclid's proof from the nature of multiplication and division that, given any set of four numbers, a, b, c, and d, if $a \div c = b \div d$, then $d \times a = c \times b$. Applying what he understands to the problem of finding, for the set 161, 9,913 and 931, what fourth number x is to 9,913 as 931 is to 161, he can perceive that, since $x \times 161 = 931 \times 9,913$, then $x=(931 \times 9,913) \div 161$, and compute that x is 57,323. Since he grasps Euclid's demonstration that any number x that is proportional to b as a is to c must be equal to $(b \times c) \div a$, he cognizes the result 'from the force of' that demonstration, and hence adequately and rationally. For the smaller numbers, however, like 1, 2, and 3, such a merchant does not need Euclid. When asked what number is to 2 as 1 is to 3, he will perceive both that 3 must be in the same ratio to it as 1 is to 2, and also, *uno intuitu,* what the ratio of 1 to 2 is, namely half. Moreover, he will understand that 3 is to 6 as 1 is to 2 better than he understands that 9,913 is to 57,323 as 161 is to 931, because there he does not 'see' what the common ratio is.

At first sight it is perplexing that Spinoza illustrates the highest kind of cognition, *scientia intuitiva*, by an elementary perception we can all share, while degrading to the second and lesser kind the practically more powerful cognition reserved for those who understand a fairly deep Euclidean proof. Perplexity vanishes, however, when it is remembered that he is grading kinds of cognition as evident, and not as useful or deep. We resort to cognition of the second kind only when we cannot see clearly. Spinoza should not be presumed to have foreseen that the sciences of actually existing entities would themselves be mathematicized, or that they would ever have the complexity of mathematics, which treats of entities of reason generated by our mental operations. There is no evidence that he expected physics to advance beyond the correction of the fairly simple Cartesian system.[21]

He thought of the study of human affairs much as he did of physics. The fundamental truths of the *Ethics* are not complicated, and you need not be mathematically sophisticated to grasp them. Yet once grasped, those truths enable you, beginning with adequate ideas of extension and thought as attributes of God, to proceed to adequate cognition of the essence of things. As Matheron has put it, 'Spinoza ... simply wants to say to his readers, "Follow me all the way to the end and you will come to know your nature, starting from the nature of God, *in the same way* and *just as well* as you understand the equality $1/2 = 3/6$".'[22]

A number of students of Spinoza have perplexed themselves with the ill-conceived question 'What kind of cognition is expressed in the text of the *Ethics* itself?'[23] Cognition is a matter of ideas, not of words. Spinoza implies not only that his own cognition of what he writes in the *Ethics* is of the third kind, except when he makes plain that it is imaginative, but also that the *Ethics* will lead anybody fit to study it to cognition of the same kind (cf. E2pref—G II, 84/10–12). Nobody can learn from the *Ethics* who does not distinguish a fair number of the adequate ideas expressed in it from the imaginative ones with which they are usually confounded; but for anybody who does, studying it will be a progress from

7.5 Intra-Cogitative Parallelism: Ideas of Ideas

As we have seen in 7.1, there is necessarily in God an idea of everything that follows from any of his attributes (E2p3). Hence, since ideas themselves are among the things that so follow, there is necessarily in God an idea of every idea there is in him. This has consequences that are awkward. Consider three finite modes of God as extended, the bodies a, b, and c, of which a is the transient cause of b, and b of c. Those same three modes of God as thinking will be three ideas or representations $I(a)$, $I(b)$, and $I(c)$. And since the order and connection of things must be the same in thought as all other attributes, it is a general recursive principle that if x, y, and z are objects of ideas, and $I(x)$, $I(y)$, and $I(z)$ God's ideas of those objects, then if x causes y, and y causes z, $I(x)$ causes $I(y)$, and $I(y)$ causes $I(z)$. According to this principle, it follows that $I(a)$ is the cause of $I(b)$, and $I(b)$ of $I(c)$. The parallelism of a, b, and c, with $I(a)$, $I(b)$, and $I(c)$ is extra-cogitative. Now, since the ideas in that parallelism are modes in God following from the attribute of thought, God must have, not only ideas of them —$I(I(a))$ causing $I(I(b))$, and $I(I(b))$ causing $I(I(c))$—identically ordered and connected, but also further ideas of those ideas, *ad infinitum*. These parallelisms are intra-cogitative.

The awkwardness of countenancing such infinite series is succinctly brought out by Bennett.[24] According to the principle of extra-cogitative parallelism, ideas and bodies are the same modes, constituted by two different attributes, and there is only one causal network that connects them. A related principle must also hold for intra-cogitative parallelism: ideas (of any level) and ideas of those ideas must also be the same modes, although constituted not by two different attributes, but by two different levels within the same attribute. Yet on the face of it, the differences between ideas of bodies, ideas of ideas of bodies, and so on, vanish above the first few levels; and if they do, is not the infinity of levels a sheer illusion, generated by permitting repeated 'useless redescriptions' of the lower levels?[25]

Bennett, of course, sees what Spinoza's answer is: that the levels are distinct from one another because what they represent is different. With respect to their formal being, ideas are all on a level. They are all representations. Individual ideas are distinguished from one another both by what they represent, that is, by their objects, and by their place in the causal network. Yet ideas of different levels always differ in what they represent. Just as an idea of a body represents a body while an idea of that idea does not, so an idea of an idea of a body represents an idea of a body, while an idea of that idea does not. With an acknowledgement to Gueroult, Bennett gilds Spinoza's lily:

> I take Spinoza to be saying here that $I(I(x))$ picks out the intrinsic properties of $I(x)$ but not its representative ones; it sees down into $I(x)$ as a psychological particular, but does not take in what it represents or is about, i.e. does not see through it to x.[26]

This seems to me a mistake which Gueroult does not make. When you form a representation of a representation of a horse, you are forming a representation of a representation, and not of a horse. Yet a representation of a representation of a horse is not the same as a representation of a representation of a giraffe; they cannot be good representations unless each 'reaches through' to what the representation it represents is a representation of. A good painting of a good painting of a horse is not a painting of horse; but you ought to be able to tell that it is not a painting of a giraffe.

While conceding its intelligibility, Bennet condemns Spinoza's theory of intra-cogitative parallelism as 'profligate':[27] an infinite hierarchy of ideas of ideas is to much. At the same time, he perceives why Spinoza held it. If God cognizes everything that follows from his essence, immediately or mediately, then for every idea there is in God there must also be an idea of that idea. In addition, like many of his contemporaries and ours, Spinoza agreed with Descartes that human beings cannot cognize anything without cognizing that they cognize it; and so concluded that, like God, they cannot cognize anything unless they have an infinite hierarchy of ideas: an idea of the thing cognized, an idea of that idea, and so on *ad infinitum*.

> [T]he idea of the Mind, [he writes], that is, the idea of the idea, is nothing but the form of the idea insofar as this is considered as a mode of thinking without relation to the object; for as soon as anybody knows (*scit*) something, he thereby knows that he knows it, and at the same time knows that he knows that he knows, and so *in infinitum* (E2p21s—G II, 100/19–23).[28]

Spinoza is not asserting that any human being's mind has an infinite number of distinguishable objects before it, but only that since, like God, he is necessarily conscious of all his ideas, an infinite hierarchy of ideas must accompany his every idea. Given Spinoza's conception of God, it cannot be denied that God as infinite intellect has an idea of each of his ideas, but there is no need to infer that, as constituting the essences of individual human minds, God has such ideas of ideas.

7.6 Human Error

Since all propositions can be expressed as answers to questions, if cognition is propositional, ignorance is not believing the true answer to a question, and error is believing a false answer to one. Spinoza asserts that human beings are ignorant of much, and it has been shown in 7.2 that his theory of cognition can account for it. He also asserts that human beings believe much that is false, and hence err about much. Yet, although he acknowledges that 'to be ignorant and to err are different' (E2p35d—GII, 117/6–7), he professes to show 'how error consists in the privation of cognition' (E2p35s—G II, 117/10–11). Bennett therefore charges him with inconsistently trying to reduce error to a form of ignorance.[29]

Spinoza would demur, on the ground that the charge falsely assumes that the difference between ignorance and error can be adequately elucidated in terms of assent to propositions. Propositions, on his view, are true or false only because they are associated with ideas. Every idea is a regarding of a presented individual as somthing (cf. 3.2–3); and it is false if it is the regarding of a presented non-being as something. To err is to have a false idea; and the problem of error is how human beings come to have false ideas. According to Spinoza's theory of cognition as expounded in 7.1–5, this problem is serious but not intractable. All ideas, as they occur in God, are true (E2p32) by virtue of the fundamental extra-cogitative parallelism. The part of God's infinite intellect that has God as extended for its object is an infinite causal network of ideas, in exact correspondence with the infinite causal network of nature as extended, each item in the former, by virtue of its linkages with its fellows, truly representing the corresponding item in the latter. Even when an idea of some finite body is considered in itself, apart from any presentation of its external cause, there is 'nothing positive in [it], on account of which [it is] false' (E2p33). (By something 'positive' Spinoza simply means something presented, which can be regarded as formally real). Furthermore, anything presentable in an idea must be presented in the infinite network of ideas in God, and, so presented, must be part of God's infinite true self-representation (E2p33d). The problem of error confronting Spinoza is therefore this: since what is presented is positive, negative presentations are impossible; but unless negative presentations are possible, no idea can be the regarding of a presented nonthing as a thing.

Spinoza's solution depends on his doctrine of the linkage of ideas (see 3.4–5). No idea can present anything negative; but ideas can be linked with others both as excluding them, and as excluding their exclusion. As we have seen in 3.4, Spinoza recognizes that human beings can combine simpler ideas into complex ones. This is a common source of error. For example, the idea of a figure inscribed in a circle and the idea of a rhombus (an equilateral quadrilateral, none of whose interior angles is a right angle) are true ideas of essences; but when combined into the idea of a rhombus inscribed in a circle, the complex idea thus formed is false: a representation of a nonthing as a thing. The reason for this is that the idea of the rhombus excludes that of a circle circumscribing it, and that of the circle excludes that of a rhombus inscribed in it. True, beginners at geometry may form the idea of a rhombus inscribed in a circle, and try to construct one: their error is not cognizing what is excluded by the positive content of the ideas of its components (cf. E1p11d—G II, 53/3–5).

More complicated examples appear when one turns from what is excluded by pure essences to the essences of actual existents—from geometry to physics. Aristotle's idea of motion represents it, not as a state that needs an external cause to change it, but as a change of state (from being in one position to being in another) that needs an external cause to sustain it; and this complex idea is shown to be false, although composed of elementary ideas that are in themselves materially true, because when it is combined with other ideas that are true, it excludes the truth of elementary ideas of projectile motion.

These examples of errors of reason do not violate Spinoza's theory of mind, but illustrate it. He provides others in his denunciations of superstition in philosophical theology (E1ap), and of Cartesian interactionism (E5 pref.). Errors of imagination also involve exclusions, but of a different sort. (One of his examples (in E2p35s) has been examined in 3.2.) The complex idea of your body that is the primary constituent of your mind represents your body, and derivatively its environment, but only as they are disclosed by your ideas of its affections. This idea is 'mutilated' in the strict sense: it is a part of the complete and true representation in God of your body and its environment, but only a part: it is cut off from most of the ideas that are linked with it in God—ideas of the external causes that sustain your body.

Notes

[1] Spinoza's words '*primum, quod actuale Mentis humanae esse constituit*', are usually rendered 'the first thing that constitutes the actual being of the human Mind' (e.g. C, 456). Although '*primum*' can mean 'the first thing', in this context its sense is 'primary' or 'basic', and the relative clause '*quod ... constituit*' shows Spinoza to be picking out a constituent of the human mind's actual being as primary or basic.

[2] As Gueroult points out, Joachim (Joachim (1903), p. 83 n.1) inferred that 'since *corpora simplicissima* are distinguished one from another solely by motion and rest, they cannot differ in size', although that is 'an implication which cannot be found in Spinoza' (Gueroult (1974), p. 163; and cf. pp. 160–5, esp. 160–1).

[3] Joachim (1903), p. 83 n.1.

[4] Descartes, *Princ. Phil.* II, 400 (AT VIII-1, 65).

[5] Gueroult (1974), p. 155 *n*.45

[6] I owe this comparison to Gueroult (1974), pp. 158–60, 171–6, 555–8.

[7] Wilson (1980), pp. 104–10.

Human Beings (I): Cognition

8. Wilson (1980), p. 108.
9. Wilson (1980), p. 109.
10. Pollock (1880), p. 193.
11. Namely, the word *'idea'*, followed by a noun or noun phrase in the objective genitive.
12. Pollock (1880). p. 133.
13. E.g. for Pollock are Barker (1938), pp. 136–44, and Bennett (1984), pp. 154–9. Hallett (1949) indignantly complains that Pollock and Barker attribute a 'callow confusion' to Spinoza (p. 169): his criticism of Pollock seems to me just, of Barker less so—cf. Bennett (1984), p. 156 n.3. The case for a straightforward reading of Spinoza is more soberly put by Parkinson (1953), pp. 105–7 (note his reference to Ep64 (G IV, 277/19–20), Matheron (1969), pp. 33, 68, and Gueroult (1974), 115–42.
14. Matheron (1969), p. 68.
15. Parkinson (1953), p. 106.
16. Both the expressions 'extra-cogitative' and 'intra-cogitative', and the reasons for introducing them are elucidated in Gueroult (1974), pp. 15–16, 66–70.
17. Following Curley's advice, but not his text. The *Nagelate Schriften* reads 'mode' (*wijze*); and the *Opera Posthuma* reading, '*affectus*', if Spinoza wrote it, was a slip for '*affectio*' (C, 464 n.42).
18. Cf. Hallett (1949), p. 171.
19. Curley renders '*uno intuitu*' as 'in one glance', which suggests something shorter than an *intuitus* need be. Since Curely translates '*intuitiva*' as 'intuitive' fourteen lines above, a parallel translation of '*intuitus*' seems least misleading. Cf. Matheron (1986), p. 136.
20. Matheron (1986). In this paper Matheron 'concentrate[s] principally on' TdIE, 18–29—G II, 10–13; because those texts not only 'are most in need of elucidation' but 'best elucidate the example' he 'sav[es] the *Ethics* for the end' (ibid. p. 125).
21. Cf. Hall and Hall (1964), esp. pp. 345–8, 252–6. Curley's defensive note (C, 178–9 *n*.3) does not meet the Halls' point that Spinoza makes his hypotheses untestable.
22. Matheron (1986), p. 149
23. E.g. Parkinson (1969), p. 94–100; Floistad (1969), pp. 101–2, 123–7; Hubbeling (1987), pp. 228–9.
24. Bennett (1984), pp. 184–91. This is in part a commentary on Gueroult (1974), pp. 244–56.
25. Bennett (1984), p. 186.
26. Bennett (1984), p. 187; but cf. Gueroult (1974), pp. 255–6.
27. Bennett (1984), p. 187.
28. Cf. Gueroult (1974), p. 249 with Bennett (1984), p. 187.
29. Bennett (1984), pp. 167–84. This is elaborated in Bennett (1986). I do not go into Bennett's treatment in detail, brilliant though some of it is, because it seems to me to be undermined by its neglect of the elementary points I shall make.

8 Human Beings (II): Action and Passion

8.1 Human Individuals as Functional Entities

In *Ethics* III Spinoza turns from what human beings think to what they do. While not denying that what they do is in large measure caused by what they will to do, he has already given notice, in the long scholium with which *Ethics* II concludes, that he rejects the traditional doctrine, reasserted in a post-Aristotelian form by Descartes, that will is a human power or faculty distinct from intellect (E2p49s—G II, 132/23–135/31).

That doctrine is cardinal to Descartes's last major work *Les Passions de l'âme*, published in 1649, which Spinoza himself read in Samuel Desmarets' Latin translation of it, *Passiones Animae*.[1] It underlies Descartes's distinction, in that work, between two functions of the human mind: actions, or acts of will (*volontés*); and passions, or perceptions. Perceptions are caused either by the mind itself (perceptions of its acts of will), or by the body. Of the latter, some (feelings of joy, anger and the like), while depending on the nerves, are referred to the soul. Although their proximate cause is unknown, these 'passions of the soul' are 'caused, maintained and strengthened by some movement of the [animal] spirits'; and therefore cannot be directly controlled by the will. They can, however, be indirectly controlled by it, 'through the representation of things which are usually joined with the passions we wish to have and opposed to the passions we wish to reject'.[2]

Rejecting Descartes's distinction between will and intellect, Spinoza dismissed this theory as 'show[ing] nothing but the cleverness of [Descartes's] understanding' (E3pref—G II, 137/25–138/5). In doing so, however, he was anticipated by Thomas Hobbes in a series of books, of which the most important are *Leviathan* (1651), *De Cive* (1951), and *De*

Corpore (1655).³ According to Hobbes, human beings are complex bodies, each with a distinctive vital motion 'begun in generation, and continued without interruption through their whole life; such are the *course* of the *Bloud,* the *Pulse,* the *Breathing,* the *Concoction, Nutrition, Excretion,* &c'. This motion can continue only if their bodies can obtain from their environment what they need to preserve it: air, food, clothing and shelter, and immunity from predation. Like all animals, human beings obtain these things by '*Animall motion,* otherwise called *Voluntary motion*; as to *go,* to *speak,* to *move* any of our limbes, in such manner as is first fancied in our minds'.⁴ The higher the animal, the better able it is to obtain what it needs by adapting its animal motions to its environment.

Human beings are the highest animals. Like all animals, as infants they 'endeavour' in certain bodily states to suckle and excrete, do so, and find doing so such that, when those states recur, they endeavour to do it again. Hobbes therefore held them to be so constituted that, experience teaches them both how to do more and more things, and which of those things are pleasant, that is, such that it is natural to endeavour to repeat them, and which are not.⁵ Thus what is pleasant is what is desired; and desire is endeavour or appetite to do. Human beings are physically so constituted that their animal or voluntary motions are always such as they imagine will enable them to do what they desire. They seldom desire what will endanger the continuation of their vital motions, but sometimes they do. In general, 'whatsoever is the object of any man's Appetite or Desire; that is it, which he for his part calleth *Good* .... There being nothing simply and absolutely so; nor any common Rule or Good and Evil, to be taken from the objects themselves ....'⁶

In *Ethics* III and IV, taking much from Hobbes, Spinoza radically reworks the theory of human behaviour advanced by Descartes in *Les Passions de l'ame.* By adopting most of the Latin terminology of Descartes's translator, not always happily,⁷ he made it plain that he thought it unprofitable either to devise a terminology of his own or to analyse the beliefs implicit in what his fellows familiarly said and presumably thought about one another's doings.⁸

He begins by introducing new senses of Descartes's 'action' (*'actio'*) and 'passion' (*'passio'*). Stipulating that a cause is 'adequate' if an only if 'its effect can be clearly and distinctly perceived through it' without reference to anything else, and 'partial' or 'inadequate' if its effect can only be so conceived through something else as well (E3d1), he defines a human being as 'acting' (*'agere'*) if and only if he is the adequate cause of something that happens, and as 'suffering' or acted on (*'pati'*) when something happens within him, of which he is only a partial cause (E3d2). The happenings or 'affections' thus caused can increase his power of acting (*potentia agendi*), or decrease it, or leave it unchanged (E3p1). Individual human beings thus remain the same through increases and decreases of their power of acting. However, contrary to Descartes, their bodies and minds do not interact: their actions as extended (as bodies) are explained wholly through the attribute of extension, and as minds wholly through that of thought (E3p2). Hence the actions of a human mind are caused solely by its adequate ideas, and its passions solely but its inadequate ones (E3pl,3); and neither are caused by affections of the body.

The first controversial proposition in *Ethics* III is that 'No thing can be destroyed except through an external cause' (E3p4). The chief problem it poses is what it means.

As applied to bodies, understood in the Cartesian sense as extended solids, each an aggregate of parts (in the simplest case, of one part) with one proper motion relative to the bodies that surround it,[8] it would mean that no body can be destroyed —that is, broken up—by anthing it does as a whole, or by anything its parts do. That would be a paradox in the Zenonian manner, philosophically interesting only if the flaw in its proof were hard to detect. Examples abound of Cartesian bodies being destroyed by causes that are not external: most obviously, by natural death. All animal bodies, if they survive external perils, in the end die and decay into their elements because, owing to their normal functioning, their internal parts gradually wear out.

Although Spinoza's proposition, understood as applying to extended solids, is obviously false, his proof of it has been saluted by Bennett, the profoundest of its critics, as 'a real achievement'.[9] It runs:

This proposition is evident through itself. For the definition of anything affirms, and does not deny, the thing's essence, or it posits the thing's essence, and does not take it away. So while we attend only to the thing itself, and not to external causes, we shall not be able to find anything in it which can destroy it. (E3p4d—G II, 145/24-8)

Four steps can be distinguished in this compact statement. (1) A non-external cause is one that follows, according to laws of nature, from the thing's essence, and hence one that is expressed in its definition. (2) A thing's definition, given (1), expresses what causes it to be, not what causes it not to be. (This step tacitly relies on the principle that things are conceived through their causes.) (3) If its essence entailed its destruction, it would be correctly defined as being such as to cause itself not to be. (4) Therefore, given (2) and (3), the definition of a self-destructive thing must be self-contradictory: combining lawfully sufficient conditions both of its existence and of its non-existence. A thing so defined could no more exist than a square circle.

Bennett not only accepts the first three of these steps,[10] but also concedes that, if transient causation were a timeless geometrical realation, the fourth would follow. However, he rejects it on the ground that the transient causation by which things are destroyed is temporal. A definition can lay down causal conditions that are lawfully sufficient both for the existence of a pendulum clock for a certain period of time (the time it takes for its weakest moving part to wear out), and also for its non-existence after that period. Spinoza's proof fails, therefore, because it 'neglect[s] ... the fact that causal laws cover stretches of time'.[11]

The admitted power of Spinoza's proof invites another approach: instead of assuming that the proposition it purports to prove is evidently false, and investigating why its proof fails, why not assume that the proof is sound, and inquire what it proves? We have already seen how Spinoza, retaining old names, introduces new ideas by innovations in his axioms and proofs. The theory of affects in *Ethics* III and IV, I shall now try to show, is the most sustained example in his writings of that technique.

As we have seen in 7.1, Spinoza in *Ethics* II defines a complex body not physically, as an aggregate of component bodies brought into being by certain causes, but functionally, as a 'union' of whatever component bodies continue to communicate motion to one another in a certain fixed manner (E2p13addD—G II, 99/27-100/5; L4—G II, 100/17-20). His definition presumably owes something to Hobbes's identification of an animal body as one that conserves a single 'vital motion'. Given that definition, steps (2) and (3) of his proof of *Ethics* III, 4 are:

(2) a thing's definition lays down what conditions its parts and their arrangement must satisfy if it is to exist, not what conditions would ensure that it ceases to exist;

and

(3) if its destruction followed from its essence, its definition would have to lay down conditions that would ensure that it ceases to exist.

That an animal body dies of old age, because its functioning parts have ceased to be able to renew themselves from their environment, is no more a function of it as a body than that it is a function of a mechanical clock that its parts wear out from friction. The friction of a clock's parts on one another is external to them as functional, just as the physiological interactions of the parts of animals that cause them to cease to be able to renew themselves are external to them as functional.

Bennett recognizes this possibility, but he does not go far enough into it.[12] Read in the light of his definition of a complex body, Spinoza's proof proves that self-destruction can neither be among the functions by reference to which a complex body's essence is defined, nor can follow from those functions. Why not interpret the proposition that 'No thing can be destroyed except through an external cause (E3p4) as saying that? The only answer can be: because Spinoza uses it in proofs that are invalid if it means that. Does he? I contend that he does not. On the contrary, as we shall see when he discusses Seneca's suicide, he uses it to show that, when a functioning human being does something that destroys its body, its self-destructiveness is not functional, but arises from some external circumstance. There is a deep reason why Spinoza insists on thinking of human beings in this way. The common notions of science enable us to form adequate ideas of human bodies as functional entities; and by forming such adequate ideas we can 'consider human actions and appetites just as if it were a question of lines, planes, and solids' (E3pref—G II, 138/26-7).[13]

8.2. Persevering in One's Own Being

Those who misunderstand Spinoza's proposition that no thing can be destroyed except through an external cause can hardly avoid misunderstanding that to which he now proceeds: that 'Each thing, so far as it can by its own power, strives (*conatur*) to persevere in its own being' (E3p6). Refining the interpretations of a number of predecessors, Bennett reads it as an ambiguous 'self-preservation doctrine', which Spinoza proves in the fairly harmless non-teleological sense that if a thing does something, it will be self-preserving, but which he goes on to use in the harmful teleological sense that if a thing would be preserved by doing something, then (if it is in its power) it does it.[14] Bennett's reasons for this interpretation, and mine for rejecting it, will appear as we follow Spinoza's own argument.

The cardinal point in any interpretation is what it takes 'persevering in its own being' to mean. By the being (*esse*) of a thing, Spinoza means what he will later call its 'actual essence': its essence as existing, and not as a mere possibility. It is to be conceived functionally. Since singular things are modes expressing, in a determinate way, Nature's power of acting, Spinoza argues,

> no thing has anything in itself by which it can be destroyed, or which takes its existence away (by E3p4). On the contrary, it is opposed to everything which can take its existence away (by E3p5). Therefore, as far as it can, and it lies in it, it strives (*conatur*) to persevere in its being. (E3p6d—G II, 146/13-17)

Mention of p4 is not 'otiose', as Bennett complains, because the functional way of conceiving a thing's essence is introduced by that proposition; and by mentioning it Spinoza prepares his readers for the introduction of a parallel functional sense of persevering in one's being. Just as to be is to function, to persevere in one's being is to continue to function.

Not content with these innovations, Spinoza also transforms the customary sense of the verb '*conari*' ('to strive'). As a rule, it means to try; and it suggests effort, especially persistent and even intelligent effort. As Bennett says, '[I]ts ordinary meaning is teleological: to try to climb a mountain is to do things because you think that they will get you up the mountain.'[15] However, as his proof shows, Spinoza uses '*conari*' as applying to all bodies, animal or mineral. A sand-castle strives, in his sense, not to be washed away; yet it does not do things because it thinks that they will prevent its being washed away. Proposition and proof together are designed to teach readers to think of all persevering in one's own being, or continuing to discharge the function that defines one's being, as a *conatus* or striving. If the function that defines your being is doing things you think will get you up a mountain, then doing these things is striving to persevere in your being; but if continuing at rest as a sand-castle until something washes you away or otherwise destroys you is the function that defines you, then continuing to be at rest is striving to persevere in your being.

Far from inviting us to conceive sand-castles as dedicated self-preservers, Spinoza is inviting us to conceive dedicated self-preservers as like sand-castles. In both, striving to persevere in being is a kind of inertia:[16] provided that they satisfy their functional definitions, and are appropriately arranged, their component parts will communicate motion to one another in the fixed manners by which their different essences are defined, unless something (by definition of contrary nature) causes them to stop (cf. E3p6d—G II, 146/13-17). That is why 'the *conatus* by which each thing strives (*conatur*) to persevere in its being' involves 'no finite time, but an indefinite time' (E3p8). Nothing in a complex body's essence, so conceived, limits its continuation in existence. That this *conatus* is inertial also appears in Spinoza's proof that it is a thing's 'actual essence' (E3p7). The proof amounts to this: a thing's power and its essence are the same; but its power is nothing but the *conatus* by which it produces whatever effects follow from its determinate nature, that is, by which it perseveres in its being; hence a thing's essence is the *conatus* by which it perseveres in its being

Human Beings (II): Action and Passion   153

(E3p7d). These identifications—*conatus* = power = actual essence—do not imply that what was thought to be inert in fact brims with activity, but rather that the activity of even the most active things is a kind of inertia, a continuing to be as usual.

If Spinoza is to retain the fundamental psychological terms 'appetite' ('*appetitus*'), 'will' ('*voluntas*'), and 'desire' ('*cupiditas*'), he must redefine them in terms of *conatus* in this inertial sense. He therefore stipulates that 'appetite' is to stand for the *conatus* of a human being so far as reference is being made to his mind and body together, 'will' for that same *conatus* so far as reference is being made only to his mind, and 'desire' for that *conatus* or appetite so far as those who have it are conscious of it. All three stand for the tendency of human beings to continue to function each as they are, and not for tendencies on their part to try to makes themselves what they are not. So defined, there are only *distinctiones rationis* between them. Thus the words 'appetite' and 'desire' both stand for the same thing, although 'desire' is used when the speaker wishes to indicate that human appetite is necessarily in some measure conscious (E3p9s).

As Matheron has pointed out, by identifying the actual essences of human beings with their *conatus* or appetites, Spinoza implicitly both refines his conception of the human body, and parts company with Hobbes's view of what it is for an animal to persevere in its being. As we have seen, he identifies the essence of a finite body with a possible union of component bodies that communicate their motions to each other in a certain fixed manner; and by equating essence with power of acting he elaborates the concept of what such a 'fixed manner' may involve. In Matheron's words:

> What is preserved here is not the vital motion abstractly separated from the whole in which it is integrated: it is, in its totality, the system of motion and rest the formula of which defines our individuality. We will to live, it is true, and in a sense only to live; but life is not reduced to the simple circulation of the blood or to other elementary biological functions. To live is to live *according to my individual essence*; for, when I lose that, I die, even if my blood continues to circulate (E4p39s).[17]

Persevering in one's being is not the same thing as continuing to live in the biological sense. This appears in what Spinoza says about Seneca in his brief discussion of suicide. Suicide can either be a symptom that the parts of a human body have already ceased to be a functional unity, as in the case of suicidal madness, or it can be a perseverance in one's own being in external circumstances in which so persevering will *per accidens* cause one's death.

> Somebody may kill himself [Spinoza writes] because he is compelled by another, who twists his right hand (which happened to hold a sword) and forces him to direct the sword against his heart; or because he is forced by the command of a tyrant (as Seneca was) to open his veins, i.e. the desire to avoid a greater evil by [submitting to] a lesser. (E4p20s—G II, 224/24–8)

To this, Bennett objects that the cases are dissimilar: in the former, the 'movements of the victim's hand are *at that very moment* being caused by the other person's hand', but in the latter, 'Seneca's body was not transmitting forces from the outside, [t]he causally sufficient conditions for his act were stored within him'.[18] The objection fails because that dissimilarity is beside the point. In the first case, the victim's persevering in being was simple physical perseverance—his hand did not dissolve so that he ceased to hold the sword. In the second, Seneca persevered in being a human being who in adverse external circumstances rejected the greater evil. Nero wickedly created an external situation in which, by so persevering, Seneca would kill himself. The proposition 'No thing can be destroyed except through an external cause' (E3p4) teaches us to regard Seneca's behaviour, while self-destructive in fact, as not functionally so.

Bennett's ultimate reason for rejecting such interpretations (he discusses Matheron's, of which mine is a variant) is that, even if propositions 4–8 can be interpreted functionally in accordance with their proofs, 'there are eleven propositions in [*Ethics* III], starting with proposition 12' which 'are teleological not because they contain "try" [i.e. "*conari*"] but because they infer facts about conduct from facts about the results of the conduct, i.e. they have the form, "If it would lead to P, he will do it"'.[19] That, however, is a mistake: all those propositions contain a further conditional phrase, 'so far as it can', or some equivalent. Consider proposition 12: 'The Mind, so far as it can, strives to imagine those things that increase or aid the Body's power of acting.' Its proof follows the same 'inertial' lines as the proof that everything, as far as it can by its own power, strives to persevere in being: that is, it begins by supposing a mind that imagines something increasing or aiding the body's power of acting, and proceeds to show that such a mind must, if it is in its power, persevere in doing so (E3p12d—G II, 150/12-17). There is no pretence of proving that a mind that finds itself ceasing to imagine things that increase the body's power must do things calculated to result in imagining them, unless that is the sort of mind it is, which it may not be. Neither in propositions 12 and 13, nor in those that follow from them, does Spinoza infer facts about conduct from facts about its results unless a mediating condition is satisfied.

At this point, it may be complained that what seemed to be non-trivial falsehoods have been reduced to trivial truths. Spinoza's reply is: wait and see what use I make of them!

8.3. Derivation of Affects That are Passions

In any human individual, the form taken by the *conatus* or appetite that is the proximate cause of an individual bit of behaviour is largely determined by modes of the specific sort Spinoza calls 'affects' ('*affectus*'). They are not to be confounded with affections (*affectiones*) or modes in general.[20]

> By affect [he writes] I understand affections [i.e. modes] of the Body by which the Body's power of acting is increased or diminished, aided or restrained, and at the same time, the ideas of these affections. (E3d3)

He adds a note: 'if we can be the adequate cause of any of these affections, I understand by the Affect an action; otherwise, a passion' (E3d3—G II, 139/17-19).

A human being's passive affects give form to his *conatus* according as they are increases or decreases in his power of acting. Those that are decreases will be resisted, because his *conatus* is directed to continuing to exercise the power he is losing; those that are increases will be accepted, because his *conatus* is directed to continuing to exercise whatever power he has gained. Spinoza's name for an increase in the power of acting of part of the body or mind is 'pleasure' (*'titillatio'*), and for one in that of the body or mind as a whole is 'cheerfulness' (*'hilaritas'*). His name for a localized decrease in power of acting is 'pain' (*'dolor'*), and for one that is not localized, 'melancholy' (*'melancholia'*) (G II, 149/6-9). He calls pleasure, considered simply with reference to the mind, 'joy' (*'laetitia'*), and pain so considered 'sadness' (*'tristitia'*). (G II, 149/1-4; cf. AD2,3).

In presenting Spinoza's theory of affects, it is convenient to confine oneself, as he did, largely to the attribute of thought. With respect to it, joy and sadness are the fundamental generic affects. They are objectless: you rejoice and are saddened *by* things which cause your joy and sadness, but you do not rejoice, and are not saddened, *at* those things. Joy and sadness thus resemble moods. And they involve change, for the better or the worse. However, Spinoza carefully explains that it does not follow that they involve ideas of change. No more is implied than that 'the idea which constitutes the form of the affect affirms of the body something which in fact involves more or less of reality than before' (E3AD—G II, 204/13-17). When you pass from a lesser to a greater power of thinking the passing is joy, whether or not you compare your later state with what preceded it and notice the difference; and likewise with sadness.

All other affects are derived genetically from joy and sadness, by way of being directed to objects through conceiving them as caused. The objects to which they are directed, as Matheron has shown, are of two sorts, dividing the affects into two classes.[21] The former are things so far as they act upon ourselves, and affects directed to them are self-regarding or personal. The latter are things so far as they affect other people, and affects directed to them are other-regarding or inter-personal. Other-regarding affects are derived from self-regarding ones by sympathy, according to the principle that 'if we imagine a thing like us, towards which we have had no affect, to be affected with some affect, we are thereby affected with a like affect' (E3p27). The self-regarding affects are therefore fundamental.

To the extent that human beings are capable of forming ideas of external bodies as causes of joy and sadness, those external bodies will become objects of two derivative affects, love (*amor*), or 'Joy, with the accompanying idea of an external cause', and hate (*odium*), or 'Sadness, with the accompanying idea of an external cause' (E3p13s; AD6,7). Whether the accompanying idea is true or false, the object it represents will be the object of that love or hate. Other self-regarding affects are generated from love and hate according to the law of association proved in *Ethics* II, that if a human individual's body has been acted on by two bodies at once, then when he imagines one of them afterwards, he will also imagine the other (E2p18).[22] It oftens happens that, when you imagine two bodies that once acted on you together, imagining one of them increases or diminishes your power of acting, that is, causes you joy or sadness, while imagining the other is affectively neutral, and does neither. Yet the neutral imagining, because it always carries the affectively potent one with it, also causes you joy or sadness, not *per se*, but *per accidens*. Consequently, if you form an idea of the cause *per accidens* of that joy or sadness, your mind will be affected with love or hate of that cause (E3p14,15,c). Love and hate can spread in this way from anything conceived as a cause *per se* of joy or hate to anything conceived as its cause *per accidens*. And since ideas of things that resemble one another are also apt to be associated, that two external objects resemble one another is often enough for one to be conceived as causing *per accidens* what the other causes *per se*, and hence for whatever love or hate is directed upon the latter to spread to the former (E3p16).

A different phenomenon occurs when you think of two similar external objects as producing opposite effects on your body, one increasing its power of acting, and the other decreasing it. Although thinking of the former *per se* increases your mind's power of acting and thinking of the latter *per se* decreases it, so that the one *per se* causes joy, and the other sadness, yet each, by virtue of its association with the other, *per accidens* has an affect opposite to that which it has *per se*. The result is that you both love and hate what you think to be the cause of each. And, since an individual affect of love cannot also be one of hate, the 'constitution' of mind that arises from loving and hating the same thing is a *'fluctuatio'* or vacillation. It is related to affective capacities as doubt is to imaginative ones (E3p17d,s).

A variety of other affects spring from love and hate because, as has been shown in *Ethics* II, human beings are affected both in body and in mind by things that are not present to them (E2p17). Defining a 'past thing' as a thing in so far as you have been affected by it, and a 'future thing' as a thing in so far as you will be affected by it, Spinoza points out that it follows from his earlier theorem that, even though by conjoining the image of a future thing with that of future time, or of a past one with that of past time, you imagine them as future or as past, since the bodily image of which that imagining is the idea is the same as if it were present, 'the affect of Joy or Sadness is the same, whether the image is of a thing past or future, or of a present thing' (E3p18d— G II, 154/19–23). However, since affects of which the objects are future or past things are apt, like imaginative ideas of those same things, to 'fluctuate' or vacillate, the love or hate that spreads from present objects to future or past ones is often inconstant. Hope (*spes*), for example, derives from love of a future thing, or an effect of a past thing, which you doubt will come about; and fear (*metus*) derives from hate of such a future thing. By removing doubt that what is loved or hated will come about, hope and fear are converted into confidence (*securitas*) and despair (*desperatio*). Considered without reference to their objects, confidence is a species of joy that may be called 'gladness' ('*gaudium*'), and despair a species of sadness that may be called 'remorse' ('*conscientiae morsus*') (E3p18s2, AD12–17).

Spinoza himself prefers to analyse hope and fear in terms of the fundamental affects of joy and sadness. Unfortunately, his subtly accurate definition obscures how love and hate mediate between them. He defines hope as 'an inconstant Joy which has arisen from the image of a future or past thing whose outcome we doubt', and fear as the inconstant sadness that is its opposite (E3p18s2—G II, 155/9–11). Although this is accurate, because joy or sadness 'arises from' an image of a thing only when we have an idea of that image as cause of our joy or sadness, and so love or hate the thing imaged, these definitions distract attention from what it ought to be drawn to: the fact that hope and fear can be derived from joy and sadness only through mediating affects in which they are accompanied by ideas of their causes, that is, through love and hate.

Love and hate can spread not only from the present things to future and past ones, but from things to their causes. It almost goes without saying that imagining the preservation of what you love and the destruction of what you hate helps you to imagine what you love and to cease to imagine what you hate, both of which have been shown to be joys (E3p19,20). It is a little less obvious why, on Spinoza's principles, imagining somebody you love to be affected with joy or sadness should give you joy or sadness; but since you conceive things you love as causing your power of acting to be increased, and since imagining them as joyful or sad is imagining their power of acting to be increased or decreased, the power of your mind to think joyful thoughts must both be increased by imagining that the power of what increases your power of acting has increased, and saddened by imagining that its power has decreased (E3p21). The opposite holds for imagining joy and sadness in those you hate: you rejoice in the former, and are saddened by the latter (E3p23). These affects spread to their causes. According as we imagine somebody causing joy or sadness in one we love, we love or hate him (E3p22); and according as we imagine somebody causing joy or sadness in one we hate, we hate or love him (E3p24).

These self-regarding affects, as modes of our bodies as well as of our minds, generate appetites and desires, that is, affects that tend to cause modifications of our behaviour and thinking. Generally, 'we strive (*conamur*) to promote the occurrence of whatever we imagine will lead to joy, and to avert or destroy what is contrary to it, or will lead to sadness' (E3p28). In both cases,

> the Mind's *conatus*, or power of thinking, is equal to and at one in nature with the Body's *conatus*, or power of acting (as clearly follows from E2p7c, 11c). Therefore, we strive absolutely, or (what, by E3p9s, is the same) we seek (*appetimur*) and intend that [whatever we imagine will lead to joy] should exist. (E3p28d—G II, 162/5-9)

In the same way, this double *conatus* is directed to promoting the joy and preventing the sadness of those we love and to promoting the sadness and preventing the joy of those we hate (E3p25,26). Once more, we must remind ourselves that the behaviour to which striving to promote something gives rise depends wholly on the power of thinking and acting of whoever thus strives. If he cannot think of anything that will promote what he desires to promote, his striving will be nothing but a readiness to act; if he can think of something, but thinks foolishly, his striving will be futile, intended to promote what it does not promote. Accidents apart, only if he thinks truly will his striving promote what he imagines will lead to joy.

Other-regarding affects are derived from love and hate by sympathy—the tendency of human beings to associate modes of their own bodies and minds with others like them, that is, with like modifications of like bodies and minds (E3p27d—G II, 160/13–20). Since affects are modes, 'if we imagine a thing like ourselves, towards which we have had no affect, to be affected with some affect, we are thereby affected with a like affect' (E3p27). Bennett correctly objects that Spinoza invalidly infers this from the proposition that nobody can have an idea of an external body without having an idea of his own (E2p16); for that proposition does not imply that he thinks of his own body as having the same modes as the external one.[23] However, the phenomenon asserted is well attested; and Spinoza's theory could be repaired by proving subsidiary theorems about association. There should be no difficulty in proving, for example, that if you remember your body having been affected with a certain affect, and if the idea of an external body affected with that same affect is always associated with an idea of your own body, it will also be associated with the memory of your own body's having that affect.

This sympathetic association of one's own affects with those of others gives rise both to sympathetic joy and to sympathetic sadness (E3p27). Spinoza names the latter 'pity' ('*commiseratio*'), defining it as 'Sadness that has arisen from injury to another' (E3p22s, AD18). These affects are directed not only to those we love, but also to those towards whom we are neutral, that is, neither to love nor hate. That is why the joy we gain from the sadness of those we hate 'can hardly be enduring and without conflict of mind' (E3p23s). And pity is a sadness the perceived cause of which we cannot hate; for we associate that cause with ourselves (E3p27c2). The desire that arises from pity is therefore not to destroy the pitied object, but to free it from its suffering (E3p27c3).

Other-regarding affects of a different sort, Spinoza observes, are generated by love of possession. For example, 'if we imagine that somebody enjoys [possessing] something that only one can possess, we shall strive to bring it about that he does not possess it' (E3p32). For, while we tend to love what others love (by E3p27), in such a case *ex hypothesi* we imagine his enjoyment to be an obstacle to ours, and so a cause of our sadness, which we strive to remove (E3p32d). That is why 'for the most part human nature is so constituted that men pity the unfortunate and envy the fortunate, and ... [envy them] with greater hate the more they love the thing they imagine the other to possess' (E3p32s—G II, 165/11–17). Paradoxically, envy as well as pity originates in sympathy.

8.4. Servitus Humana

Affects have power over human beings in so far as they are passions and not actions: and to the extent that they do, Spinoza describes the human condition as one of *servitus*—servitude or slavery, usually translated as 'bondage'. How far it is, and why, are explored in the first eighteen propositions of *Ethics* IV, the remaining fifty-five being devoted to 'what reason prescribes to us, which affects agree with the rules of human reason, and which, on the other hand, are contrary to those rules' (E4p18s—G II, 222/12–14). What human beings can do about those prescriptions is reserved for the first half of *Ethics* V.

Dismissing the scholastic doctrine that things are good or evil in themselves, Spinoza asserts in the Preface to *Ethics* IV that, since human beings both 'desire to form an idea of man, as a model of human nature we may look to' (G II, 208/15–17), and judge one another more or less perfect according as they approach or fall short of the model of human nature they set before themselves, the word 'good' ('*bonum*') may legitimately be used for 'what we certainly know to be a means whereby we may approach nearer and nearer to [that] model', and the word 'evil' ('*malum*') for 'what we certainly know hinders us from becoming like that model' (G II, 208/18–22). He therefore defines 'good' as 'what we certainly know (*scimus*) to be useful to us' (E4d1), and 'evil' as 'what we certainly know to hinder (*impedire*) us from being masters of some good' (E4d2). In so far as it is possible to derive from reason a model of what human nature can be, good and evil are real properties of things, although relational ones.

The theory of human servitude needs only one axiom: that 'there is no singular thing in nature than which there is not another more powerful and stronger. Whatever one is given, there is another by which the first can be destroyed' (E4a1). Within nature, human beings are relatively weak. Not only is each of us a part of nature, not the whole, and hence something to which things happen that can only be understood by referring to other parts of nature (E4p2), but the force by which we act is 'infinitely surpassed by the power of external causes' (E4p3). It is therefore impossible that human beings be wholly active (E4p4): they are 'necessarily always subject to passions, follow the common order of Nature and obey it, and accommodate [themselves] to it as much as the nature of things requires' (E4p4c).

In addition, a human being's power of acting can always be surpassed by the power of his externally caused passions. This follows from the fact that all inadequate ideas contain something positive (what they present) as well as something negative (what they exclude); and that to the extent that they contain something positive, they are true (cf. 7.5). For, since a true idea cannot be contrary to what is true in another idea, it cannot, in so far as it is true, remove what is positive in a false idea (E4p1). Just as an affect in a human individual's body, since it is caused externally, can be taken away only by some stronger external cause, so the idea of it in that individual's mind will be inadequate, and caused by ideas external to that mind. Hence that inadequate idea cannot be removed except by an idea of a contrary modification of the body produced by some other external cause (E4p5). That idea will therefore 'adhere tenaciously' to that individual (E4p6); and can be constrained or taken away only by a stronger opposite affect (Ep7).

Depressing conclusions about time and modality follow. The stronger affects tend to be unenterprising. Ideas of images imagined to be caused by present things are more intense than those that are not (E4p9d); and ideas of those imagined to be caused by things in the near future or past are more intense than those imagined to be caused by things in the distant future or past (E4p10d). Similar conclusions follow for modality: ideas of things imagined as necessary are more intense than ideas of those imagined not to be (E4p11d); and ideas of things imagined to be possible (that is, things of which we can imagine causes, without knowing whether those causes exist—cf. E4d4) are more intense than those of things imagined to be contingent (that is, things whose existence is perceived as neither necessarily posited nor excluded) (E4p12d). Hence affects whose causes are perceived to be actual or probable are apt to be stronger than those whose causes are perceived to depend on results of possible actions, even if there are past models for them.

Cognition of good and evil—that is, cognition of what is for (*prodest*) or opposed to (*obest*) the conservation[24] of one's power of acting—is in the same position as any other cognition (E4p8d). It can restrain only as an affect, not as a truth (E4p14). Hence a desire (that is, appetite or *conatus* together with consciousness of it) arising from true cognition of the good can be extinguished or restrained by desires that do not so arise (E4p15), the more so as the former arises from cognition of things that are future or contingent, and the latter of things that are enjoyed now (E4p16,17). Human beings are therefore fortunate in that, from one to another, the strength of their various appetites depends largely on their external circumstances, and not on conditions that are the same for all.

8.5. Ductus Rationis

Despite their inescapable servitude to their affects, human

beings have enough true ideas to be able to set before themselves a rational model of human nature, and to deduce a way of life that would enable them to approach nearer and nearer to it. Although widely denounced as 'the foundation, not of virtue and morality, but of immorality' (E4p18s—G II, 223/23-4), the fundamental principle of that way of life, as Spinoza formulates it, is

> that everyone love himself, seek his own advantage (*suum utile*), what is really useful (*utile*) to him, want (*appetat*) all that will really lead man to greater perfection, and absolutely, that everyone should strive as far as he can to conserve his own being. (E4p18s—G II, 222/18-21)

This is commonly considered egoist; and many continue to believe that Spinoza advanced it on psychological grounds which C. D. Broad has summed up as follows:

> Every emotion, volition, and action of a man is an expression of the Vital Impulse, which is his essence. And this Vital Impulse, like very other *conatus*, is a striving for *self*-maintenance and *self*-preservation and for nothing else.[25]

Yet Spinoza's principle, if it is egoist at all, cannot be egoist in the usual sense; for it asserts that you cannot will your own advantage without willing what will lead man (not just yourself) to greater perfection.

Moreover, as has been shown in 8.2, self-conservation as Spinoza conceives it is not unconditional self-preservation. True, Spinoza identifies 'acting absolutely from virtue' with 'acting, living, and conserving our being (these three signify the same thing) by the guidance of reason (*ex ductu ratonis*) from the foundation of seeking one's own advantage' (E4p24). But whether that identification is egoist or not depends on what reason guides us to do from that foundation. Obviously, it guides us to seek our advantage according to adequate ideas of what our advantage is (cf. E4p23d). Elementary reasoning shows, as Matheron points out, that it is not to our advantage to act, like brute animals, on a biological instinct of self-preservation, but as *homines oeconomici*, on rational calculations of what will maximize our benefits and minimize our costs.[26] Even at a primitive stage of development, reason is instrumental: its end is given to it by something outside itself, the affects of joy and sadness. But Spinoza proceeds to argue that reason demands more: 'What we strive for from reason is nothing but understanding (*intelligere*); nor does the Mind, insofar as it uses reason, judge anything useful to itself except what leads to understanding' (E4p26). In other words, the *conatus* of rational beings to persevere in their being, or to conserve themselves as rational, ultimately requires that their ends as well as their means shall be determined by adequate ideas. No limit is set to the rationality they strive to attain. Rational individuals go beyond economic rationality not only in their chief ends in life, but also in the principles on which they resolve conflicts between their lesser ends.[27]

Even with regard to external finite things, Spinoza argues, nothing is more advantageous to us than acting in association with one another. For of the external things whose natures, not being contrary to ours, are potentially useful to us,

> we can think of none more excellent than those that agree entirely with our nature. For if, for example, two individuals of entirely the same nature are joined to one another, they compose an individual twice as powerful as each one. To man, then, there is nothing more useful than man. Man, I say, can wish for nothing more helpful to the conservation of his being than that all should so agree in all things that the Minds and Bodies of all would compose, as it were, one Mind and one Body; that all should strive together, as far as they can, to conserve their being; and that all together should seek for themselves the common advantage of all. (E4p18s—G II, 223/5-14)

Bennett's regretful verdict is that this argument for collaborative morality is too good to be true: it 'fails at every step', because its conclusion depends on 'contingent facts about human nature and perhaps about human societies,' and so cannot be proved 'in a few short steps from basic, abstract metaphysics'.[28]

My own verdict is more favourable. Spinoza claims to prove that human beings, to the extent to which they are rational, will collaborate, not that some nostrum for promoting their collaboration would be efficacious. His proofs employ premises about practical rationality and the genetic structure of human affects, derived, not from 'basic, abstract metaphysics', but from systematic reflection on human life analogous to the systematic reflection on physical phenomena that produced the mechanical conception of nature. I do not see why, by their very nature, his conclusions cannot be true; and I think that, in large measure, they are true. Matheron, however, has justly remarked that, in expounding them, '*la concision nuit à la précision.*'[29]

Human beings who live by reason, Spinoza concludes, perceive that they and their fellows are contrary to one another, not *per se*, in having the passions they do, for in that they agree, but *per accidens*, in the objects to which some of their actual passions are directed: for example, in each loving the possession of the same individual thing. However, they perceive this accident, not as a case in which the limit of reason has been reached, but as a problem calling for a solution rationally acceptable to all parties. There can be such a solution if a set of rules governing the acquisition and transfer of possessions can be found that no human being can reject as unreasonable; for such a set can be rationally accepted as 'common to all', and '[can] be enjoyed by all equally' (E4p36). And that there is such a set of rules, Spinoza declares, 'arises from the very nature of reason, because it is deduced from the very essence of man, so far as it is defined by reason' (E4p36s—G II, 235/4–7).[30]

Can such a set of rules be found? It is not hard to see why Spinoza was confident that it can. Anarchy, a state of war of all against all, is not good even for those who are victors in that war. Nobody can rationally prefer anarchy to a lawful society unless a law-abiding member of that society can find himself consigned to a worse position than he would have if the society itself were destroyed. Spinoza took it to be evident that the prosperity of the republic of the Netherlands, despite the envious hostility of its neighbours, derived from rules of commerce that could be accepted, even by those worst off under them, as approximating to reasonableness, that is, as approximating to rules such that even the worst off could not rationally expect to be better off by replacing them with others.[31] He did not need to show that the laws of the Netherlands, or of any other society, satisfy all the demands of reason, but only that they attest that laws satisfying those demands can be found.

Spinoza's use of words like '*ductus*', '*dictamen*', and '*praeceptum*' in connection with reason is metaphorical, and Wernham has correctly described it as misleadingly so.[32] His 'dictates of reason' are not precepts, demonstrable by practical reason, which human beings are free to observe or not, and such that human beings flout their own nature as rational if, understanding them, they do not observe them. Since he held it to be rationally demonstrable that human beings are part of the common order of nature, and always act as they must, Spinoza would have contradicted himself if he had also held it to be rationally demonstrable that reason ever dictates that they should do otherwise. What he calls 'dictates of reason' are descriptions, in conditional form, of how a model human being who is the adequate cause of his own conduct, and whose ideas of his own conduct are adequate, conducts himself. Although metaphorically the model may be said to 'guide' or 'dictate' his conduct, those metaphors must not be taken literally.

Notes

[1] Voss (1981), pp. 168–70, 175.
[2] *Les Passions de l'âme* I, 17–27 (AT XI, 342–9).
[3] The following, among the many excellent recent studies of Hobbes' thought, will convey what the issues are: Howard Warrender, *The Political Philosophy of Hobbes* (Oxford: Clarendon Press, 1957); J. W. N. Watkins, *Hobbes's System of Ideas* (London: Hutchinson, 1965); F. S. McNeilly, *The Anatomy of Leviathan* (New York: St Martin's Press, 1969); Gauthier (1969); and Hampton (1987). *Studia Spinozana* 3 (1987) has 'Spinoza and Hobbes' as its central theme.
[4] Hobbes (1981) I, 6, 118/23.
[5] Hobbes (1981), I, 6, 120/24. My treatment of Hobbes has been influenced by Hampton (1987), ch. 2; and, in relation to Spinoza, my Matheron (1969), pp. 86–9.
[6] Voss (1981), pp. 171–4.
[7] See Curley's admirable note on E3AD20exp (C, 535 n.49).
[8] Descartes, *Princ. Phil* II, 31 (AT VIII-1, 57/9–25).
[9] Bennett (1984), p. 234.
[10] Bennett (1984), pp. 234–5.
[11] Bennett (1984, p. 235.
[12] Bennett views the essence of an individual non-Spinozistically, as the totality of its essential properties, exclusive of accidental ones (Bennett (1984), p. 236). For criticism see Mason (1986), pp. 332–9.

13 In interpreting *Ethics* III functionally, and with it E3p4, my largest debt is to Matheron (1969). Cf. also Allison (1987), p. 132.
14 Bennett (1984), pp. 240–6.
15 Bennett (1984), p. 242.
16 Bidney (1940), p. 96.
17 Matheron (1969), pp. 88–9.
18 Bennett (1984), p. 238.
19 Bennett (1984), p. 245. Bennett does not list the propositions he has in mind, but the following 11 fit his description: 12, 13, 25, 26, 27c3, 28, 29, 31c, 33, 39, 40c2. Perhaps 32 should be added, although it does not directly cite 12 or 13 (it does cite 28).
20 This is the rule; but, as Wolfson notes, Spinoza does not always observe it (Wolfson (1934) II, p. 194).
21 Matheron (1969), pp. 82–3, 616–7. Part II of this book is the best and most thorough examination of Spinoza's theory of affects that I have encountered.
22 Matheron distinguishes six derivative laws of association, both of ideas and of affects, that follow from Spinoza's fundamental law (E2p18)— Matheron (1969), pp. 114–6.
23 Bennett (1984), pp. 279–82; cf. 156–7.
24 Most anglophone commentators, including Curley, translate Spinoza's '*conservare*' as 'preserve'. 'Conserve' is preferable both etymologically (Spinoza does not use the non-classical '*praeservare*') and for its associations.
25 Broad (1930), p. 35. The best recent treatment of Spinoza as a rational egoist is Curley (1975). In rejecting egoist interpretations, I have been influenced by Diane Steinberg's deep analyses of E4p29-31, 35, and her bold interpretation of Spinoza's conception of the unity of human nature (Steinberg (1984), pp. 307–21).
26 Matheron (1969), pp. 247–50.
27 Cf. Matheron (1969), pp. 250–54.
28 Bennett (1984), p. 306.
29 Matheron (1969) p. 262, n.50. What follows simplifies themes in the same work, pp. 258–77.
30 Matheron (1969), pp. 272–7.
31 Spinoza's doctrine that 'the greatest good of those who seek virtue ... can be enjoyed by all equally' (E4p36) implies a Rawlsian concern for the worst off.
32 Wernham's treatment of Spinoza's transformation of the language of morals is masterly (Wr, 16–20, esp. 19–20.

9 Human Freedom

9.1. Living by the Dictates of Reason

To the extent that human beings are guided by reason, Spinoza has argued, there must be a 'convergence of their *conatus*'.[1] It 'follows from the necessity of [their] own nature' that, outside civil society, human beings not only judge by their own wits (*ex suo ingenio*) what is good and evil, that is, what is advantageous to them and what is not, but also strive to return evil for what they imagine to be evil done to them from hatred (by E3p40c2), to conserve what they love, and to destroy what they hate (by E3p28). It is therefore by 'the highest right of nature' ('*summum jus naturae*') that they do so (E4p37s2—G II, 237/20-2). Yet the more adequately they think, the more clearly they perceive that what is generally useful for others of their kind is also generally useful to themselves. That others should love what they love is hateful to them only when what they love is not a good common to all; but love for a good not common to all always springs from some affect, and not from reason (E4p37s1—G II, 236/8-15).

If all human beings lived according to the guidance of reason, nobody would harm anybody else; for nobody would either cause sadness to anybody else, of imagine anybody else to cause sadness to him. Unfortunately, it is beyond most human beings to live so: they are 'contrary to one another, even while they need one another's aid' (E4p37s2—G II, 237/29-32), because they are subject to affects whose power far surpasses theirs. Yet the conceivable human being who of himself would always follow the guidance of reason is the model of rational conduct for all of them. Spinoza therefore proceeds to delineate that model; for anybody who of himself follows the guidance of reason must be free from servitude to affects (E4p70,72).

The affect of joy, although directly good, can be indirectly evil when it is pleasure, that is, when it is the idea of an increase in power of acting localized in some parts of the body; for it can be excessive, that is, it can be the idea of an increase that in fact prevents the power of acting of other parts of the body from being increased. By the same reasoning, sadness, although directly evil, can be indirectly good; for it can restrain excessive pleasure (E4p41–3). Cheerfulness (*hilaritas*), an idea of an increase in which all parts of the body share, is the only variety of joy that cannot be excessive; but cheerfulness 'is more easily conceived than observed" (E4p44,s). Like joy, love and the desire it generates can also be excessive and so evil (E4p44); and if hate towards non-human things restrains such love and desire it is good. Hate directed towards human beings, however, cannot be good; for it is directed to the destruction of what is good for us, another human being. Nor can affects that are varieties of hate of other human beings— 'Envy, Mockery, Disdain, Anger, Vengeance, and the rest'—be good either (E4p45,c1).

Affects involving intellectual error, such as overestimation (*existimatio*), or 'thinking more highly of someone than is just, out of love' (E4AD21), and scorn (*despectus*), or 'thinking less highly of someone than is just, out of hate' (E4AD22), are obviously evil. Even worse are very great pride, that is, 'thinking more highly of oneself than is just, out of love of oneself' (E3AD28), and very great despondency, that is, 'thinking less highly of oneself that is just, out of Sadness' (E3AD29). For since the foundation of virtue is conserving one's being by the guidance of reason, you cannot be ignorant of yourself without being 'extremely weak-minded', and 'highly liable to affects' (E4p56d,c). Those who live according to reason will also strive to be independent of affects that arise from defects of cognition and lack of power in the mind, even when they involve no specific errors. Hope and fear are such affects. Others are confidence and despair, gladness and remorse (see 8.3), which arise in part from hope or fear (E4p47,s).

Another kind of affect from which the wise strive to free

themselves is sadness about what cannot be helped. It too takes many forms. For example, pity, or 'Sadness, accompanied by the idea of an evil that has happened to another whom we imagine to be like us' (E3AD18), is both 'evil of itself', as involving sadness, and 'in a man who lives according to the dictate of reason, useless', because he will be moved to give what aid he can without it (E4p50d). Anticipating misunderstanding, Spinoza warns readers that he is speaking only of those who live according to reason: those who do not would 'rightly be called inhuman' if they were not affected by pity (E4p50s). Other forms of sadness about what cannot be helped (E4p53,54) are humility (E3AD26), and repentance (E3AD27); and these too are affects to which it is well that those not guided by reason are subject. Civil peace demands that most people be humble and repentant; for 'the mob is terrifying, if unafraid' (E4p54s—G II, 250/16).

Love is not evil as such, as hate is. Spinoza recognizes three forms of it as never contrary to reason except when they arise from error (E4p51,52,58): favour (*favor*), or 'Love towards someone who has benefited another' (E3AD19); self-esteem (*acquiescentia in se ipso*), or 'Joy born from the fact that a man considers himself and his own power of acting' (3AD25); and love of esteem (*gloria*), or 'Joy accompanied by the idea of some action of ours which we imagine that others praise' (E3AD30). Unfortunately, all three can arise from error; and when they do, they are evil. Thus it is evil to favour an actor because you falsely believe that he has done heroic deeds of the sort his films depict him as having done; and radically evil to love the esteem of those whose praise you falsely believe is worth having. Since the esteem of the multitude is fickle, and usually gained by undermining the good name of rivals, love of it readily becomes a 'monstrous lust' (*'ingens libido'*) (E4p58s).

It is a fundamental principle of Spinoza that those who live according to reason will 'follow the greater of two goods, and the lesser of two evils' (E4p65). Indeed, since 'good and evil ... are said of things insofar as we compare them to one another' (E4pref), a lesser good by which a greater is prevented is evil, and a lesser evil by which a greater is avoided is good (E4p65c). So far as human beings think rationally, the idea of a thing will affect their minds equally, whether they conceive it as existing in the past, in the present or in the future (E4p62). Therefore it follows, according to the principle of the greater good, that 'from the guidance of reason we want a greater future good in preference to a lesser present one, and a lesser present evil in preference to a greater future one' (E4p66); and hence that 'we shall want a lesser present evil which is the cause of a greater future good, and pass over a lesser present good that is the cause of a greater future evil' (E4p66c). It also follows that, when the best that can be done is to avoid an evil rather than to overcome it by destroying its cause, we shall avoid it rather than attempt to overcome it (E4p69c).

Of course we often do not conduct ourselves rationally. True cognition of good and evil, which derives from common notions, is 'only abstract and universal', whereas our conclusions about what is good or evil derive from our imaginative judgements of 'the order of things and the connection of causes', and hence are often erroneous. For example, we cognize the duration of things imaginatively and inadequately, and images of present things often leave no room for images of future ones. When an idea of a present good excludes the idea of the greater evil that good will cause, desire for that present good will restrain desire to avoid that future evil (E4p62s).

Spinoza's portrait of a free human being, that is, of one 'who lives according to the dictate of reason alone' (E4p67d), consists of seven propositions. In the first, that 'A free man thinks of nothing less than death, and his wisdom is a meditation on life, not on death' (E4p67), he rejects the doctrine attributed in Plato's *Phaedo* to Socrates, that the life of a philosopher is a preparation for death. Whatever may remain of a human mind after death, and Spinoza believes that something of it does remain, as we shall see, a free man thinks of nothing less than it. He 'desires the good directly', that is, he 'acts, lives, and conserves his being from the foundation of seeking his own advantange' (E4p67d)—his advantage as rational of course, not his advantage as a mere animal.

That implies a proposition almost universally considered to be paradoxical from Spinoza's own point of view: that 'A free man never acts with bad faith (*dolo malo*), but always with good faith (*cum fide*)' (E4p72).[2] At first sight, it appears both to be defectively argued for, and to contradict the eighth 'head' in the Appendix to *Ethics* IV, that it 'is permissible for us to avert, in the way that seems safest, whatever there is in nature that we judge to be evil, or able to prevent us from being able to exist and enjoy a rational life' (G II, 268/10–13).[3] Since a free man always acts according to the dictates of reason, Spinoza argues, if he ever acts *dolo malo* it must be virtuous to do so, and everyone would be well advised to act as he does.

> That is [he continues] , men would be better advised to agree only in words, and be contrary to one another in fact. But this is absurd (by p31c). Therefore &c. (E4p72d)

To this, both Bennett and Allison object that even though 'reason is supposed to dictate in the same way to everyone, and to speak only in general terms with no reference to *particulars*', it may 'address itself to *special kinds* of case'.[4]

Their objection would be well taken if Spinoza were upholding the eccentric position into which Kant sometimes fell, that good faith makes no provision for special kinds of emergency which are not explicitly provided for when a person gives his word. But why suppose that? It is more reasonable to interpret Spinoza as asserting that free men are such that their word can be relied on, in matters of great importance, even when they undertake to do something which may cost their lives; and that to deny this is absurd. It is advantageous to be trusted when you undertake to do something that may lead to your death, even though your good faith may result in your freely dying. This doctrine is not rigorist about promises generally: it is not rigorist, for example, about petty ones in which unexpected emergencies are not provided for, or forced ones, or ones foolishly or wrongly given.

9.2. Why Free Human Beings Need to Live *in Statu Civili*

Human beings can live outside society (*societas*) with common laws—that is, they can live otherwise than in a state (*status*) they and their fellows have artificially brought into existence. Although they would 'live harmoniously and be of assistance to one another' in that non-artificial or natural (*naturalis*) state if they were free and guided by reason, they cannot, owing to their servitude to their passions. Hence they form political societies that, through a variety of arrangements, decide on, promulgate and enforce laws, and provide for the common defence against foreign attack. Spinoza described such societies as *'civitates'* or 'States', and membership of them as the 'civil state' (*'status civilis'*).[5] Like most people, he believed that only in the civil state, that is, only as members of States, or citizens (*cives*), can human beings live prosperously and in harmony with their fellows (E4p37s2—G II, 237/26-238/17).

In the *Tractatus Theologico-Politicus* he set out the rudiments of a theory of what a State is, how it can contribute to human blessedness, and what can hinder it from doing so; and drew out its implications for the place of religion in the State, especially with regard to what its citizens are free to inquire into, and to publish. In *Ethics* IV, 37 schol. 2, he sketched the same ideas, but more abstractly and compactly. And finally, in the *Tractatus Politicus*, which was incomplete when he died, he set out to lay down the principles of politics, and by reference to them to show how the three possible forms of State, monarchy, aristocracy and democracy, must be organized if they are to endure and serve the ends for which they were instituted.

Except with respect to its principles, Spinoza's political theory cannot be appraised simply as philosophy; for, as he acknowledged, all political theory must be tested by what he calls 'experience'—that is, by history, recent or remote. That is why *politici*, those who have been engaged in public business, like Machiavelli, have written much better about politics than philosophers (TP, 1, 2—G III, 274/6-7). It is generally agreed that he intended what he wrote about the forms of State to bear upon the politics of his own time, especially in the Netherlands. I do not know how informed he was about the political situations to which he intended his theory to apply: about production and trade, internal and external; about colonization and struggles to control overseas markets; about how war was conducted, and how armies were recruited, trained and supplied; and about cultural and religious differences between and within States. Whatever he knew appears directly in his writings only in details: like Machiavelli, he preferred to take his illustrations from ancient literature, either the Jewish Bible or the writings of the Roman historians.[6]

While Spinoza's debt to the work of Hobbes is evident, and implicitly acknowledged in a letter to his friend Jarig Jelles (Ep50—G IV, 238/25-293/4),[7] he radically criticizes Hobbes's theory of the nature of the contract by which States are instituted, and consequently takes a different view of what they both consider the fundamental political problem: the instability of free States.

Hobbes saw human politics as a predicament. On the one hand, we should all be better off if we acted according to what he called 'the Lawes of Nature' and Spinoza 'the guidance of reason', namely, *'Justice, Equity, Modesty, Mercy*, and (in Summe), *doing to others as we would be done to'*; but on the other, so acting is 'contrary to [the] naturall Passions' that determine what most of us do.[8] In our natural state, we cannot effectively agree or 'covenant' to observe the laws of nature; for 'Covenants, without the Sword, are but words, and of no strength to secure a man at all.'[9] Hence, unless a power can be established that can and will enforce agreements to observe the laws of nature, 'every man will and may lawfully rely on his own strength and art, for caution against all other men'.[10] That power must be strong enough both to keep those subject to it permanently 'in awe', and to repel any interference from outside.[11] And it can be brought into existence only on the condition that virtually everybody subject to it in effect says to every other,

I authorise and give up my Right of Governing my selfe, to this Man, or to this Assembly of men, on this condition, that thou give up thy Right to him, and Authorise all his Actions in like manner.

'This done', Hobbes continues, 'the Multitude so united in one Person, is called a COMMON-WEALTH, in latine CIVITAS'.[12] Commonwealths or States are either 'instituted' by common consent, or 'acquired' by natural force or war; but 'the Rights, and Consequences of Sovereignty are the same in both': namely, that sovereignty can neither be forfeited nor divided. No citizen or group of citizens has the right to judge the sovereign's discharge of his (or its) office. And that office itself, which is legislative, judicial and executive, is indivisible.[13]

Although Hobbes writes of this transfer of right to the sovereign as alienating it irrevocably, he restricts its scope. There are 'some Rights which no man can be understood by any words or other signes, to have abandoned or transferred', such as the right forcibly to resist those who assault him in order to kill or wound him, or to fetter or imprison him.[14] However, as Spinoza understood him, Hobbes maintains that, even *in statu naturali*, contracts can bind you to do what you judge to be to your disadvantage. What he says about how contracts are voided and invalidated explains why. The right of nature possessed by all human beings, as Hobbes defines it, is their liberty to use their own power, as they themselves will, for the preservation of their own natures.[15] Part of that liberty, as we have seen, cannot be alienated, namely, their liberty to defend themselves against death, wounds or imprisonment; but part of it can, namely, their liberty to use things or services in their power, providing that alienating it does not threaten death, wounds or imprisonment. Anybody may 'covenant' with others to alienate part of that liberty if those others convenant to do something from which he hopes to gain more than he loses. Such covenants are voided only by performance or forgiveness.[16]

Although Hobbes maintains that if you contract to perform your part first, you always have cause to fear that, having gained what he hoped for, the other will not perform his part, he also maintains that the other is obliged to, for he can no longer fear your non-performance.[17] The most striking cases of this are contracts to do something in return for being liberated from duress: 'if I be forced to redeem myselfe from a Theefe by promising him mony,' Hobbes declares, 'I am bound to pay it.' True, he adds that 'the Civill Law [may] discharge me' from this obligation; but *in statu naturali* there is no civil law.[18] Spinoza presumably accepted this as a well-considered part of Hobbes's theory, and not as a slip to be disregarded, because the liberty to make non-void contracts at will is treated by Hobbes as a fundamental part of everybody's right of nature.

There is a political application. Since you and your fellows, in binding one another to obey a sovereign who can and will enforce performance, do not bind yourselves to alienate your right to resist death, wounds or imprisonment, your contract is not void. Nor is it as a rule invalid; for you normally believe that the sovereign will enforce performance. Hobbes adds a further consideration. With respect to that part of their liberty social contractors can alienate, the contract that institutes a sovereign makes that sovereign their agent. '[E]very Subject is by this Institution [i.e. that of the State] Author of all the Actions, and Judgments of the Soveraigne instituted'; and therfore 'he that complaineth of injury from his Soveraigne, complaineth of that whereof he himself is Author.'[19]

In *Ethics* IV Spinoza adopts two of Hobbes's doctrines: that it is a dictate of reason that human beings strive to be *in statu civili*, and not *in statu naturali*; and that they cannot put themselves *in statu civili*, as opposed to being coerced, unless they 'give up their natural right', that is, their right of nature as it is exercised *in statu naturali*, by agreeing to be members of a society that arrogates to itself the sole right to decide what rules of conduct may be upheld by force, and to employ that force (E4p37s2—G II, 237/35-238/1, 9-16). States are instituted if and only if their citizens agree (*conveniunt*) among themselves that each of them is to exercise his right of nature (*jus naturae*) to seek his own advantage only in such a way that all his fellow-citizens can exercise their, that is, according to common laws (*communia jura*),[20] those who thus agree having together the common right (*jus commune*) to determine those laws (TP, 15-16, G III, 281/21-282/3).

Having recognized the common right of each to decide how to exercise his right of nature, those instituting a State may agree to vest that common right either in one person or in 'a council (*concilium*)', the council being composed either of 'certain selected [persons] only', or of 'the common multitude'. So vested, this common right is customarily called 'government' ('*imperium*').[21] In the first case the government is a monarchy, in the second an aristocracy, and in the third a democracy (TP, 2, 17). In any case, the government is empowered to regulate exercises of the individual right of nature that may prejudice peace or security: it must pass and enforce laws about property and personal security, and provide for the common defence against attack from outside.

At this point, Spinoza took Hobbes to have wrongly inferred that, in so empowering government, citizens surrender their right to 'do those things that follow from the necessity of their own nature' if doing them is legally forbidden, saving only their inalienable right to resist death, wounds or imprisonment (E4p37s3—G II, 237/21–1): an inference he utterly rejected. As he wrote to Jelles,

> the difference between Hobbes and me, about which you inquire, consists in this, that I always conserve natural Right intact (*sartum tectum*), and that I lay it down that the Supreme Magistrate in any City possesses no more right over subjects than is proportionate to the power by which he holds them in subjection, which is always the case in the Natural state. (Ep50—G IV, 238/25–239/4)

Natural right must always be conserved intact. It is a law 'so *firmly* written in human nature that it should be numbered among the eternal truths of which nobody can be ignorant' that

> no one forgoes anything he judges to be good, except from hope of a greater good, or fear of a greater loss: that is, everyone will choose what he judges to be the greater of two goods, or the lesser of two evils. (TT P, 16—G III, 191/34–192/4, 6–7)

From this it follows at once that

> no one will promise without deceit that he will yield his right to do everything, and absolutely no one will keep promises except from fear of a greater evil or hope of a greater good. (G III, 192/8–10)

To Spinoza, as Wernham has observed, Hobbes's doctrine that contracts are invalidated only by fear of non-performance is 'a flirtation with respectability': something 'more disreputable' is called for (Wr, 29).

Given the right of nature, 'an agreement can have no force except that of utility' (G III, 192/25–6). '[I]n instituting a State', therefore, the most important thing to remember is that 'it is foolish for anyone to demand that another keep faith with him forever if he does not at the same time strive to bring it about that from breaking the contract it will follow that the breaker incurs more loss than gain' (G III, 192/27–30; cf. TP, 2,3–12—G III, 276–80). Does it not also follow that those who institute a State covenant to alienate the inalienable? No, Spinoza replies, because, in contracting with others to give up the right to do part of what you do by the inalienable right of nature, in return for others' doing the same, both you and they expect that, as a result of contracting, it will not be advantageous to any of you to exercise that right as you did before. You believe that, by contracting, you will so change your condition that observing the contract and acting according to the right of nature will be the same: that the condition the contract brings about, your membership of a trustworthy group of free human beings, will be advantageous, even if situations may occur in which it requires you freely to give up your life. Yet, in contracting, you do not surrender the right of non-performance if you come to conclude that you have been deceived, and that the other members of your group are not free and so not trustworthy.

What then is the point of the contract? That all parties can co-ordinate what they do. Knowing that all agree to institute a State in itself gives each reason to predict that all or most will obey the State once instituted; and knowing that the State once instituted will have some power to coerce those who do not obey it gives them further reason. In other words: by contracting to institute a State, the parties change their situation from one in which they are in their natural state to one in which they are in a civil state, and they do so because they believe it will be to their advantage; but they surrender no part of their right to act, in either state, as they judge may be to their advantage.

The agreement by which a State is instituted binds those who make it, as all contracts do, solely because it is to their advantage to keep it. When citizens perceive that the State is weak, they withdraw their agreement to obey it; and they begin to suspect that it is weak when they find reason to think that their fellow citizens are withdrawing their agreement to obey it. Yet Spinoza derides Hobbes's attempt to break the circle by persuading the citizens of a weak State to support it; for it is contrary to their nature to do anything they judge to be disadvantageous, and it is disadvantageous for them to support a State that is perceived by their fellows to be weak. The circle can be broken only if those who govern a weak State can be persuaded to change their ways: to win the citizens' support by governing in a way that is advantageous to them. It is a principle of Spinoza's politics that

> sedition, wars, and contempt or violation of laws are to be imputed, not to the wickedness of subjects, but to the depraved condition of government (*imperii*). For citizens are not born, but made. (TP 5, 2—G III, 295/19–22)

States are instituted because human beings cannot live in peace and security in their natural state; but no agreement to institute a State becomes firm and habitual until life in that State has given its citizens confidence in its power to provide the peace and security they desire. Human beings become good citizens only because in good States they find that good citizenship is advantageous.

9.3. Liberty and Political Stability

In political societies, or States, the power or right to govern is either freely instituted or acquired by right of war. Hobbes professed to have demonstrated that, whether instituted or acquired, the power to govern cannot be divided without destroying itself, and that the person or body exercising the power cannot retain it if subjects are permitted to judge for themselves either what its laws or decrees mean, or which are to be obeyed and which not. Spinoza accepted both demonstrations (TT-P, 16—G III, 193/30-4; TP, 3, 3-4). For him, as for Hobbes, it is a political truism that a subject is bound, as a subject, to carry out lawful commands, even though he thinks them unjust (TP, 3, 5—G III, 286/10–11).

Spinoza largely confines himself to the only politics of practical interest to free human beings: that of States instituted by the common consent of their peoples, like those of western Europe in the seventeenth century (TP, 5, 6). Even in States so instituted, government can be so badly organized or exercised that its subjects must seriously consider withdrawing their consent to obey it. If it would dissolve the State, it would never be rational for them to do so; for reason itself teaches that peace is advantageous, that it can be attained only in States whose laws are kept, and that the peace of even a bad State is more advantageous for its citizens that the natural pre-political state. Hobbes, writing as an Englishman during the English Civil War, assumed that any serious civil disobedience would ultimately dissolve the State. Writing over twenty-five years later as a citizen of the Netherlands, Spinoza did not. Selective disobedience, he observed, has relieved hostility to bad governments. And States (e.g. the English kingdom) have remained intact while not only governments (e.g. that of King James II, after Spinoza died), but even forms of goverment (e.g. the pre-1688 Stuart monarchy) have been overthrown. 'From the discords and seditions that often arise in a State it never comes about that citizens dissolve the State (as often happens in non-political societies), but that they change its form to another' (TP, 6, 2—G III, 297/23-5).

There is a theoretical distinction between an agreement to institute a State, and a subsidiary agreement to institute a particular form of government; and because both citizens and those engaged in the business of governing sometimes draw that distinction, they can recognize that the subsidiary agreement has lapsed even though the former has not, and so can change a form of government without reverting to the natural state. Although his expressed attitudes to bad government are largely conservative,[22] Spinoza recognized that governments are likely to conduct themselves well in proportion as they have reason to fear the disaffection of their subjects. His rational citizen, although no rebel, remembers Seneca's lines,

violenta nemo imperia continuit diu,
moderata durant;[23]

and takes comfort that the passions of his fellows ensure that no individual or group can last as a government if it is perceived to govern contrary to the common good, whether from folly or from wickedness (TT-P, 16—G III, 194/5-16).

The fundamental principle of Spinoza's practical politics is that no form of government is stable unless it is so organized that the bulk of citizens, doing as always 'what they personally think to be in their best interests',[24] will continue to accept it. A State's authority is jeopardized if it commands its citizens to do what no one can be coerced into doing either by rewards or threats: whether it is something impossible by its very nature, for example giving up one's power of thinking for oneself, believing contrary to what one perceives or concludes by reasoning, or loving what one hates; or something 'human nature so abhors it that it considers it worse than any evil [that can be inflicted]', for example 'bearing witness against oneself, torturing oneself, killing one's own parents, making no attempt to avoid death, and things of that sort' (TP, 3, 8). Even when coercion is possible, Spinoza adds, commands that make numerous citizens indignant 'hardly fall within the right of the State' (TP, 3, 9—G III, 288/7-8); for 'the power and right of the State are diminished in proportion as it gives cause to many to conspire together' (G III, 288/12-13). Conversely, the power and right of the State are increased in proportion as it gives cause to many to consent to what it does.

Spinoza's defence of free speech in the *Tractatus Theologico-Politicus* is his most celebrated application of his fundamental principle. 'In a free State (*libera respublica*),' the title of its concluding chapter gives notice, 'everyone is allowed to be of what opinion (*sentire*) he chooses, and to say what it is' (TT-P, 20—G III, 239/2-3). Since governments, whether monarchical, aristocratic or democratic, are instituted 'to enable human beings to exercise their mental and physical powers in safety, to use their reason freely, and to prevent them from fighting through hatred, anger or bad faith, and from maliciously quarrelling with one another' (G III, 241/4-8), a government of any form that denies its citizens the right freely to form and express opinions thwarts one of the purposes for which it was instituted, and so undermines the agreement that was made to institute it. Yet liberty to express opinions, as Spinoza conceived it, confers no right to denounce the institution of the State, or to incite civil disobedience. Citizens may be prosecuted for accusing the magistrates of injustice in carrying out their duties, for making them hateful to the people, or for unlawfully trying to abrogate a law. Spinoza nevertheless firmly believed that, as long as it is done honestly and without malice or law-breaking, forming and expressing opinions about defects in the law or in the conduct of magistrates, far from harming the State, benefits it. Human nature being what it is, 'laws which proscribe opinions do not affect the wicked but the straightforward; they are passed not to coerce the crooked but to harass the honourable, and they cannot be upheld without great peril to government' (G III, 244/9-13).

Hubbeling draws attention to three principal devices Spinoza employs, for the most part more ingeniously than persuasively, in his political proposals.[25] Two are obvious and familiar. First, wherever possible, he advises that important and controversial tasks be done by large numbers of citizens. Secondly, he recommends that offices in goverment be held only for restricted periods. Although he never renounces Hobbes's doctrine that the powers of government cannot be divided without danger to the State, he finds it beneficial that they cannot in practice be exercised only by one person (monarchies, he remarks, are in fact aristocracies, but of the worst kind—covert ones). Thirdly, he advises that common interests be created among different interest-groups, and that divisive interests be removed. Here his specific proposals are least persuasive. For example, assuming that in aristocracies the ruling aristocrats profit from holding commands in war while the populace suffers, he suggests, on the one hand, that the ruling senators be assigned the proceeds of a duty on exports and imports, and, on the other, that both senators and ex-senators be prohibited from performing military duty. By these two measures, he explains, 'the senators will always have more to gain from peace than from war, and so will never advise war unless the highest necessity of goverment compels it' (TP, 8, 31—G III, 336/31-337/15).

9.4. The Mind's Power Over the Affects

Spinoza wrote the earliest of his surviving writings in a Platonic mood: weary of the world and persuaded that 'all the things that regularly occur in ordinary life are empty and futile'; and yet aspiring to find out 'whether there [is] something which, once found and acquired, would continuously give [him] the greatest joy, to eternity' (TdIE, 1—G II, 5/8-9, 14-16). He was then not more than thirty. What he finally offers in the *Ethics* is subtly different: the unfolding (*explicanda*) of 'those things that follow from the essence of

God, or the infinite and eternal Being', which 'can lead us, by the hand, as it were, to cognition of the human mind and the highest blessedness' (E2pref—G II, 84/8-9, 11-12). Although eternal, the highest blessedness the human mind can attain is not, as he unfolds it, a continuous state of the greatest joy. 'It is impossible', Spinoza argued, 'that a human being should not be part of Nature, or that he should undergo no changes except those than can be understood through his own nature alone' (E4p4); for 'the force by which he perseveres in being is limited, and infinitely surpassed by the power of external causes' (E4p3). The best endowed human beings, even if whatever he does is done well, may die before he does much. Even so, it is an error, and a grave one, 'to believe that Nature itself has failed or sinned, and left [that human being] imperfect' when you 'see something happen in nature which does not agree with the model [you] have conceived' of a human being living according to the guidance of reason (E4pref—G II, 206/17-19). There is nothing imperfect in nature; for what is perfect is whatever is necessary in nature, and everything that happens in nature is necessary. The very concept of sin is social: in the state of nature it cannot be conceived (E4p37s2—G II, 238/23).

In setting out to describe 'the means, or way, leading to Freedom', by demonstrating 'how great and of what kind' is the 'governing power (*imperium*)' of reason over the affects, 'for restraining and moderating them' (E5pref—G II, 277/8-9, 17-18), Spinoza takes pains both to remind his readers that he has proved that reason does not have an absolute governing power over the affects (G II, 277/19-20) and to scoff at Descartes's doctrine that 'there is no Soul so weak that is cannot—when it is well directed—acquire an absolute power of governing its Passions' (G II, 279/4-5, 17-19). Since mind and body cannot interact, so far as affects are physical, the mind has no power over them whatever. Yet the body, like the mind, is active as well as passive (cf. 8.1). To the extent that the mind has power over affects as mental, the body has power over them as physical (E5p1d).

The body's remedy for disadvantageous affects is to seek situations in which its power of action will be increased and avoid those in which it will be decreased; and its power to do so is proportionate to its capacity to form physical images of itself and its environment. The ideas of those images will be the mental counterpart of the body's power: the power over affects as mental possessed by the mind, 'considered only in itself' (E5p20s—G II, 293/4–17). In *Ethics* V, 2–9, this power as familiarly exercised is shown to depend on three facts. In the scholium to *Ethics* V, 20, the three reappear, differently ordered, as the first four of five constituents of the mind's power over the affects, the third fact appearing twice, in relation to affects of two different kinds.

The first fact (it reappears as the second constituent) is that since most affects—all those directed to objects—are states of love and hate, and most states of love and hate involve the idea of an external cause conceived confusedly, they can be destroyed to the extent that they can be separated from the thought of an external cause (E5p2d,p20s—G II, 282/2–4, 293/8–9). The joy and sadness they involve remain; but joy and sadness, not being as such directed to objects, do not have the effects on conduct of love and hate. Suppose that you are consumed with hate for the toothache you have as you are driving to the dentist. With the help of *Ethics* III, you can form a clear and distinct idea of its kind, hatred of bodily pain. That enables you to proceed to other true thoughts, such as that, given the human condition, bodily pain is inevitable through life, that treatment is available and that you will receive it, and that there are other things about which you can more advantageously think; and that will detach your sadness from the idea of your decayed tooth as cause, and so reduce or even remove your hate. Most people learn to remedy their hate of moderate pain in this way.

Spinoza's claims for this power are modest. He pretends neither that by it you can remove (say) your hate of having a tooth drilled here and now without an anaesthetic, nor that reducing your hate of what you believe to be the cause of a pain will relieve your pain. Yet it is a real power. By it, you can often reduce, and sometimes remove, hate of the cause of a pain.

The second and third of the facts on which the mind's power over its affects depends form a pair, and at first sight an incompatible pair. The second is that 'the more an affect is known (*notior*) to us, the more it is in our power, and the less the Mind is acted on by it' (E5p3c), which is a corollary of the theorem that 'an affect which is a passion ceases to be one as soon as we form a clear and distinct idea of it' (E5p3). Since it has been proved in *Ethics* IV that 'man is necessarily always subject to passions' (E4p4c), we can also infer from this theorem that there are affects of which we cannot form a clear and distinct idea. At first sight that contradicts the third of Spinoza's facts, that 'there is no affection of the Body of which we cannot form some (*aliquem*) clear and distinct concept' (E5p4); but only at first sight. The proof of the third fact, which depends on the premise that things common to all can only be conceived adequately (G II, 282/23–4), shows that it is about what is common to all, that is, about affects as kinds, not as actually existing individuals. Hence the two facts, as a pair, come to this: while the mind has little or no power to form an adequate idea of an individual affect that is a passion, it has unlimited power to form adequate ideas of the various kinds of affect, and that gives it limited power over individual affects.

Of the constituents of the mind's power over the affects on Spinoza's final list, the first, third and fourth depend on this pair of facts. About the first, 'cognition of the affects' (E5p20s—G II, 293/7), little need be said. Simply being aware of what kind of affect is rejoicing or saddening you reduces its power to harm you by inducing a false idea of itself.

The third constituent, 'the time by which the affections related to things we understand surpass those related to things we conceive confusedly' (G II, 293/10–12), applies only to affects arising from things regarded as absent: for example, hate of those who have done you harm, or whom you fear may do you harm. Many affects that poison life are of this sort. To the extent that you are able to form adequate ideas of permanent conditions of life that enable you to escape the harms you fear, those ideas can be kept longer before your kind than the ideas of absent hateful things that will arise in it unless excluded. Keeping those ideas before your mind will affects you with a confidence (cf. E3AD14) which will exclude the existence of the hateful objects, and to which your hate 'will have to accommodate [itself] ... more and more, until [it] is no longer contrary to it' (E4p7d—G II, 285/31-286/1). Thus, if you are troubled by images of cruelties you have suffered in the past from tormentors who have lost the power to harm you, a remedy is to train yourself to keep that fact in mind.

Here Bennett misrepresents Spinoza as 'say[ing] in effect that in a conflict between a reasoned affect and an unreasoned one, the former is an immovable object, because it must 'always' be present—while the latter is a resistable force'.[26] No such thing. Spinoza does not imply that your unreasoned hate for the highway patrolman who is now presenting you with a summons for exceeding the speed limit can be overcome by reflecting on the rationality of the speed limit, and the justice of the patrolman's action. He has not forgotten his doctrine that

> the true cognition we have of good and evil is only abstract or universal, and the judgement which we make about the order of things and the connection of causes, in order that we may be able to determine what in the present is good and evil for us, is imaginary rather than real. (E4p62s—G II, 257/28-32)

In most human beings, imaginative ideas of real things present to them and causing sadness will exclude abstract reasoned ideas of the harmfulness of the excessive pleasure that sadness will restrict.

The fourth of Spinoza's constituents, 'the multiplicity of the causes which foster affections that are referred to common properties or to God (GII, 13-14)'[27] enables you not to control the affects, but to endure them. Adequate ideas of general conditions of human life that cause you sadness are not contrary to affects referred to objects of inadequate ideas, and so do not exclude them; yet they can inhibit futile rage. Going further, and referring all your sadness to the course of nature, that is, to God, opens a further possibility, beyond the 'remedies for the affects' of which 'everyone in fact has experience, though they neither observe them accurately nor see them distinctly' (E5pref—G II, 280/22-4). It depends on the mind's power to 'order its affects and connect them to one another' (G II, 293/15-7). '[I]llnesses of mind and misfortunes originate above all in too much Love towards a thing which is liable to many variations and which we can never fully possess' (G II, 293/35-294/3). Such excessive love changes like its object, and is not possessed but possesses. The mind, however, has the power to form an adequate idea of an object, God, that is immutable and can be fully possessed, and that elicits an intellectual love that is stronger than other loves. While not excluded by this intellectual love, other loves pale by comparison with it, and have less power.

Notes

[1] Both phrase and thought are Matheron's (Matheron (1969), p. 274).
[2] E4p72 is translated by Curley freely, as 'A free man always acts honestly, not deceptively' (C,586). What I have to say about it is influenced by Diane Steinberg's related but different interpretation (Steinberg (1984), pp. 321-4).
[3] As Curley points out (C, 587 n. 37).
[4] Cf. Bennett (1984), pp. 317-8; Allison (1987), pp. 158-9.
[5] Unfortunately, the English word 'state' must be used both (i) for the Latin '*status*' (Dutch '*stand*'), when it means something more specific than 'condition' but less specific than 'status'; and (ii) for '*Civitas*' (in Dutch usually '*staat*', rarely '*burgerschap*'), when it means a political society (cf. C, 657, 667, 698). To reduce confusion, I render '*status*' by 'state', and '*civitas*' by 'State'.
[6] Much has been published in the last twenty-five years on Spinoza's political philosophy. Étienne Balibar, *Spinoza et la Politique* (Paris: Presses Universitaires de France, 1985) is an up-to-date introduction, with a well-chosen briefly annotated bibliography. *Studia Spinozana* 1 (1985), co-edited by Emilia Giancotti, Alexandre Matheron and Manfred Walther, admirably presents the present state of research on its 'central theme', Spinoza's Philosophy of Society. Books in French of special importance are: Matheron (1969) and (1971); Sylvain Zac, *Philosophie, Theologie, Politique dans l'Oeuvre de Spinoza* (Paris: Vrin, 1979); and André Tosel, *Spinoza ou le Crepuscule de la Servitude* (Paris: Aubier-Montaigne, 1984). In English, there are McShea (1968) and D. J. den Uyl, *Power, State and Freedom: an Interpretation of Spinoza's Political Philosophy* (Assen: van Gorcum, 1983).
[7] The writings of Hobbes that presumably influenced Spinoza were *De Cive* (1642) and *Leviathan* (1651).
[8] Hobbes (1981), 17, 223/85.
[9] Hobbes (1981), 17, 223/85.
[10] Hobbes (1981), 17, 224/85.
[11] Hobbes (1981), 17, 224-5/85-6.

Human Freedom 189

12 Hobbes (1981), 17, 227/87.
13 Hobbes (1981), 17, 228/88; 20, 252-3/102.
14 Hobbes (1981), 14, 192/66.
15 Hobbes (1981), 14, 189/64.
16 Hobbes (1981), 14, 196/69.
17 Hobbes (1981), 14, 198/69.
18 Hobbes (1981), 14, 198/69.
19 Hobbes (1981), 18, 232/90.
20 Wernham translates '*jura habent communia*' here and in the next section (G III, 281/32) as 'hold rights as a body' (Wr, 277). The plural '*jura*', however, usually means 'laws': cf. Wernham's own translations of '*jura statuendi*' (G III, 282/6—Wr, 279), of '*decreta seu iura*' (GIII, 285/33—Wr, 287), and of '*communia Civitatis jura*' (G III, 286/21-2—Wr, 298); and it is by exercising their inalienable *jus naturae* according to common laws that citizens live in peace. An example in which '*jura*' means 'rights' rather than 'laws' is '*imperii jura*' (TP, 7, 2—GIII, 308/12), which I take to mean 'the rights of government', and not 'civil right' (Wernham) or 'the constitution' (Hampshire)—cf. McShea (1968), p. 110.
21 In its political sense, '*imperium*' stands, in classical Latin, for the power of a major magistrate; and, in Spinoza's writings, for the power of the magistracy. I translate it as 'government', because one sense of 'government' in English is 'power of governing'. Curley's 'Dominion' is more exotic than '*imperium*' (C, 681).
22 On Spinoza's political conservatism see Hubbeling (1964), pp. 120-1.
23 'No one long retains powers of governing violently used; those used moderately endure' (*Troades*, 258-9). I owe the reference to Wernham, who points out that Spinoza also quotes the passage at TT-P, 5—G III, 74/4-5 (Wr, 94-5, 134-5).
24 Wr, 39. My debt to Wernham's discussion of the principle of Spinoza's model constitutions (Wr, 38-40) should be evident.
25 Hubbeling (1964), pp. 113-6; cf. Wr, 41.
26 Bennett (1984), p. 333.
27 My translation deserts the Latin passive '*a quibus ... foventur*' for the English active 'that foster ... '. Curley's 'are encouraged' for '*foventur*' is unhappy.

10 Last Things

10.1. Problems in Interpreting *Ethics* V, 21-42

Spinoza brings the *Ethics* to a close by considering 'those things which pertain to the Mind's existence[1] without relation to the body' E5p20s—G II, 294/23-4). For at least a century, this has scandalized his admirers, whether idealist or naturalist, most of whom have dismissed belief in the human mind's survival of the body as a popular error unworthy of a scientifically-minded thinker. Many follow Pollock, and suppress the scandal by interpreting inoffensively the passages that occasion it.[2] Others despair. Supposing Spinoza, vacillating between science and mysticism, to have vainly tried to combine them,[3] they cannot deny Bennett's verdict that the latter half of *Ethics* V is 'an unmitigated and seemingly unmotivated disaster'.[4]

These reactions become suspect when Spinoza's proofs of the six propositions of *Ethics* V in which the existence of the mind without the body is affirmed (21-3. 29-31) are studied without prejudice.[5] For when Spinoza's theory of the identity of individual human minds is juxtaposed with his theory of God's cognition of non-existent individuals, implications about the existence of individual human minds without relation to bodies leap to the eye;[6] and those theories are the two pillars supporting his conclusion that, after the body ceases to exist, part of the human mind 'remains' (E5p23). According to the first of those theories, individual human minds are not finite substances, but modes of thinking in the divine intellect; each is God, so far as God constitutes the idea of an individual human body actually existing, and nothing else (E2p10,11). According to the second, 'ideas of non-existent singular things or modes must be comprehended in the infinite idea of God' (E2p8). Certainly, there will be differences between God's idea of an individual human body actually existing, and God's idea of it as an essence before and after its actual existence; but on the face of it the two will have something in common. God's idea of it as an essence will be 'something of' it that neither begins to exist nor ceases to exist when the body of which is it the idea does (cf. E5p23).

10.2. The Identity of Individual Human Minds

Every human being, according to Spinoza, is a finite mode of nature as constituted by extension and thought: a body as extended, a mind as thinking. A human mind is the counterpart in thought of the human body in extension. Just as each human body is a finite mode of God as extended, differing from all others because its relative motion and rest are different, so each human mind is a finite mode of God as thinking, differing from all others usually because some of the objects of its ideas are different, and always because the ideas it shares with them are differently related (7.1–2).

As subject, every human mind is God: not God so far as he conceives himself as he is, but God so far as he constitutes the essence of that individual human mind (cf. E2p11c—G II, 94/33–95/1). So far, all God's ideas are either contained in that mind's primary constituent, the idea of an existing individual human body, and nothing else (E2p13), or are derived from it. As explained in 7.3, some of those ideas are primary ideas of the affections of that body, images caused in it being among those affections, and others are ideas derived from those primary ideas—whether of things common to the ideata of all of them (E2p38), of properties common both to that body and to external causes of effects in it (E2p39), or of other objects. Although normally the set of objects of which an individual human mind, say Peter's, has ideas is not the same as the set of which, say Paul's, has ideas, that is not the fundamental reason why they are not identical. Even if the objects of the ideas which Peter had were the same as those of the ideas which Paul had, so that neither had an idea of anything which the other did not, their minds would differ, because no object of a primary idea of Peter's mind would be an object of a primary idea of Paul's. Ultimately, individual human minds differ from one another because the individual bodies whose affections are the objects of their primary constituents are different.

The ideas of their bodies by which human beings' minds are primarily constituted are far from wholly adequate, as has been shown in 7.2. The essence of an individual human body is the fixed manner in which, from conception to death, its parts communicate motions to one another; but since nobody adequately cognizes the parts of his body, nobody can adequately cognize either the motions they communicate to one another, or the fixed manner in which they communicate them. The only adequate ideas human beings have of their bodies are constructed out of common notions and ideas of properties shared by affections of their bodies and their external causes (see 7.4), and most of those adequate ideas are not physical but functional (see 8.1). The complex idea that primarily constitutes a particular human being's mind will therefore be partly inadequate, consisting of imaginative ideas of his body's affections, and partly adequate, consisting of rational ideas of those affections and their part in his body's functioning.[7]

In *Ethics* III Spinoza proceeds to generalize the functional concept of a body as something whose parts tend to continue to communicate motions to one another in a certain unique manner. It is the essence of any individual constituted by any attribute to tend to persevere in whatever mode of functioning its being consists in, and that tendency or exercised power can be described as a '*conatus*' or striving (E3p7d—G II, 146/26-9). The power or *conatus* by which a human individual perseveres in being is complex and ordered: a power to exercise powers. Not only is it a power to exercise or not to exercise powers to do different things, like sitting, walking or running; it is also a power to acquire new powers, both by biological growth and by learning. Furthermore, since human bodies have not only the power, in a suitable environment, to grow to maturity, but also the power to persist as, through decay, they lose some of the powers they have acquired, it is of the essence of a human individual, as a continuing higher-order power of powers, that in the course of its life it will both acquire and lose lower-order powers, that is, that its various lower-order powers will at different times increase and decrease.

That is why, in *Ethics* IV, Spinoza distinguishes the *conatus* or power of acting by which a human individual perseveres in being, and which constitutes its essence, from the power of acting that increases and decreases in the course of that individual's life.

> [W]hen I say that someone passes from a lesser to a greater perfection, or the opposite [he writes], I do not understand that he is changed from one essence or form to another .... Rather, we conceive that his power of acting, insofar as it is understood through his nature, is increased or diminished. (E4pref—G II, 208/24–209/1)

He does not contradict himself. In *Ethics* III he is speaking of the higher-order power of powers that constitutes an individual's *conatus* or the power of acting by which it perseveres in existence; but in *Ethics* IV he is speaking of the lower-order power to do this or that, which may increase or decrease while the higher-order power to persevere in existence remains unchanged.

Spinoza was resigned to the gross inadequacy of the ideas that many people have of what they are. God cognizes the essence of Peter's body adequately; but he does so through his ideas of the external causes that at Peter's conception established the fixed manner in which its parts communicate their motions to one another, and not through his idea of that fixed manner *and nothing else*: that is, not through the idea of Peter's body he has in so far as he constitutes Peter's mind. In so far as God constitutes Peter's mind as a child, his idea of Peter's body will consist largely of simple bodily perceptions and recollections, and of elementary affects such as pain when hungry, desire to do what it is imagined will relieve that pain, and pleasure at its relief. He will cognize it in the only way Locke believes any human being can cognize his body, through remembered continuities, and the pleasures, pains, and other affects that accompany them. Yet Spinoza believed that adults can do better than that, although many do not. They can think of themselves functionally, both as bodies and as minds, as he himself did in *Ethics* II, III and IV. The ideas by which they can do so are neither primary ideas of the affections of their bodies, nor ideas of those ideas: they are either common notions or ideas of properties shared by affections of their bodies and their external causes. So far as they cognize their essences through such ideas, they do so adequately. The more active and less childish a human individual is, the more he will think of himself in this way: functionally and adequately.

The idea an active human individual, say Peter, forms of his own essence, although largely adequate, is not complete. No human individual can cognize his essence as God cognizes it, through the external causes that bring him into existence and enable him to survive. Yet whatever adequate functional cognition of his essence Peter attains is part of God's cognition of it: the part that God cognizes in so far as he constitutes the essence of Peter' mind.

10.3. God's Cognition of Non-Existent Individuals

The first of the pillars supporting Spinoza's conclusions about the human mind's existence without relation to the body is now in place. What of the second: his theory of God's cognition of non-existent individuals or 'singulars'? Some critics, arguing that his principle of mode identity, that 'the order and connection of ideas is the same as the order and connection of things' (E2p7), implies that the expressions of a mode under each of the attributes, extension and thought, must be strictly symmetrical, contend that he has denied himself the right to have such a theory.[8] According to that principle, they maintain, there cannot be existent ideas without existent bodies as counterparts. Since the counterparts of non-existent possible bodies are non-existent possible ideas, there cannot be in God existent ideas corresponding to non-existent things. Hence God cannot cognize non-existent bodies.

Immediately after stating his principle of mode identity, however, Spinoza excluded this interpretation of it by asserting that 'The ideas of singular things, or of modes, that do not exist, must be comprehended *in God's infinite idea* in the same way as the formal essences of the singular things, or modes, are contained in God's attributes' (E2p8—my emphasis). To elucidate, I cannot do better than translate Matheron's comment:

> God, inasmuch as he conceives himself, necessarily conceives all the consequences of his nature (E2p3); he conceives, in other words, all the essences of all the finite modes, and, by virtue of that totalization, the order in which they pass one after another into existence: so many essences of singular things, so many ideas which express them objectively in the infinite Understanding. Now these ideas are eternal without qualification: their claim to exist encounters no obstacle; for nothing prevents the infinite Understanding from thinking simultaneously the successive modes of Extension; simply from the fact that they are deduced from the nature of God, they exist, independently of all temporal conditions. The ideas of non-existent bodies therefore have a slightly different status from that of their ideata; the former exist only so far as they are comprehended *in the attribute Extension* (E2p8c), as being logical possibilities, conceivable combinations of motion and rest; the latter exist in so far as they are comprehended, not only in the attribute Thought, but *in God's infinite idea* (E2p8c), as being actual parts of that immediate infinite mode. The equivalent, in Thought, of the eternal essence of a body is not only the eternal essence of the corresponding idea: it is the eternal idea of the essence of that same body.[9]

The difference between the status of ideas of non-existent bodies and that of their ideata, which Matheron ironically calls 'slight' ('*peu*'), is momentous: there is all the difference in the world between possible existence in an attribute and actual existence in an eternal mode.

Spinoza himself contributed to the prevalent incomprehension of *Ethics* II, 8, by explaining less than clearly his own illustration of what he meant. Euclid has shown that, if A, C, F, and G are points on the circumference of a circle such that the lines AC and FG intersect at a point B within it, then the rectangle with base AB and height BC is equal in area with that of base BG and height BF (*Elements* III, 35).[10] Spinoza comments:

> So in a circle there are contained infinitely many rectangles equal to one another. Nevertheless, none of them can be said to exist except insofar as the circle exists, nor also can the idea of any of these rectangles be said to exist except insofar as it is comprehended in the idea of the circle. Now of these infinitely many [rectangles] let two only [viz. those formed from the

segments of lines AC and FG][11] exist. Of course their ideas also exist now, not only insofar as they are comprehended in the idea of the circle, but also insofar as they involve the existence of those rectangles. By this they are distinguished from the other ideas of the other rectangles. (E2p8s—G II, 91/18--28)

The clue to understanding this passage is that, according to Spinoza's theory of ideas, you understand a sentence by actually having the ideas it expresses, not by possibly having them. Thus, you cannot understand its first sentence, 'In a circle there are contained infinitely many rectangles equal to one another', without having *actual* ideas of the *possible* rectangles formed by the segments of the lines cutting the circle and intersecting at a point within it.

If this clue is kept in mind, it can be seen that Spinoza is asserting: (i) that you cannot have an actual idea of the possible rectangles formed by possible lines cutting an actual circle unless that circle actually exists; for if it did not exist, your idea would be of rectangles formed by lines cutting a possible circle, not an actual one; (ii) that you can have an actual idea of the possible rectangles formed by possible segments of possible lines cutting an actual circle; for if you could not, theorems could not be proved about them; (iii) that for a reason parallel to that for (i), you cannot have an actual idea of an actual rectangle formed by segments of an actual line cutting an actual circle unless that line actually exists and is actually divided into two segments; and (iv) that when you have an actual idea of actual rectangles formed by actual segments of actual lines cutting an actual circle, your ideas of them exist both as ideas of essences (that is, of things 'comprehended in the idea of the circle'), and as ideas of actual existents (that is, as ideas 'involv[ing] the existence of those rectangles').

Although in *Ethics* II Spinoza does not apply to God's cognition of non-existent bodies what he has said about non-existent individuals generally,[12] the application is evident. God, so far as he constitutes the idea of an actually existing human body, will have an idea of it both as comprehended in his infinite idea of nature as extended, and as involving the actual existence of that body. And when that body does not exist, whether before its conception or after its death, God will still constitute the idea of it: not as involving actual existence, but as comprehended in his actual infinite idea of nature as extended. Since, according to Spinoza (10.2), the mind of a living human being is identical with God's, so far as God's mind constitutes the idea of that human being's body and nothing else, it remains for him to inquire whether God's mind, so far as it constitutes the idea of the body of a human being who is dead or not yet born, and nothing else, is identical with the whole of that human being's mind, or only with part of it.

10.4. The Human Mind Without Relation to the Human Body

Spinoza begins by showing that, except in relation to an actually existing body, no individual mind can imagine or recollect anything (E5p21). The proof recalls his definitions of imagination and recollection (see 7.3). Imagining is having either primary ideas of actual affections of our bodies, or ideas derived from them about either our bodies or external things (E2p17s—G II, 106/7-11); and recollecting is 'nothing other than a certain connection of ideas involving the nature of things which are outside the human Body ... according to the order and connection of the affections of the human Body' (E2p18s—G II, 106/35-107/4).

Although it is uncontroversial that God cannot have ideas of a human body as actually existing unless it does actually exist, Spinoza is clear that God must have ideas of every body that once existed but now does not, or that will exist but does not yet. 'In God,' he declares, 'there is necessarily an idea that expresses the essence of this or that human body *sub aeternitatis specie*'[13] (E5p22). The proof is brief:

> God is the cause, not only of the existence of this or that human Body, but also of its essence (by E1p25), which therefore must be conceived through the very essence of God (by E1a4), by a certain eternal necessity (by E1p16), and this concept must be in God (by E2p3). Q.E.D. (G II, 295/7-12)

God causes the essence as well as the existence of things, because his essence determines not only what shall come into being, and for how long, but also what beings are possible—what formal as opposed to merely objective essences there are (see 4.2). Thus, God caused not only the existence of the circulatory system of the tyrannosaurus of whose bones there is a photograph in my *Encyclopaedia Britannica*, but also its essence—that is, that system as a natural possibility. Its existence was confined to an interval in the Jurassic Age, but its essence, which follows from the laws of nature alone, is confined to no time. There is necessarily in God an idea of every essence of which he is the cause, because there is necessarily in him 'an idea ... of everything that follows from his essence' (E2p3). And since what exists necessarily exists eternally, there is eternally in God an idea of the essence of each human body, whether that body actually exists or not.

Given that in God there are ideas expressing the essences of all the individual human bodies there have been, are, or will be, it seems probable that 'the human Mind cannot be absolutely destroyed with the Body, but something of it remains which is eternal' (E5p23). Spinoza enunciates it as a theorem. However, since his demonstration is clarified when restated as applying to an arbitrary human being who no longer exists, I now restate it as applied to Hannibal, whom Spinoza admired:[14]

> In God there is necessarily an idea which expresses the essence of Hannibal's body (by E5p22), an idea, therefore, which is necessarily something that belongs[15] to the essence of Hannibal's mind (by E2p13). But we do not attribute to Hannibal's mind any duration that can be defined by time, except in so far as it expresses the actual existence of Hannibal's body, which is explicated through duration, and can be defined by time, i.e. (by E2p8c), we do not attribute duration to it except while Hannibal's body endures. However, since what is conceived, with a certain eternal necessity, through God's essence itself (by E5p22) is nevertheless something, this something that belongs to the essence of Hannibal's mind will necessarily be eternal (cf. E5p23d—G II, 295/17–27).

Provided that it is remembered that Hannibal's essence, whether as extended (as a body) or as thinking (as a mind), is individual, and that ideas of what is possible are actual,[16] this proof is valid, although, on Spinoza's principles, one of its steps is questionable. Its steps are: (i) there is necessarily in

God an idea of the essence of Hannibal's body; (ii) that idea belongs to the essence of Hannibal's mind; (iii) Hannibal's mind endures for a time only so far as it is the idea of his actually existing body; (iv) the idea of the essence of Hannibal's body that is necessarily in God is something, and it belongs to the essence of Hannibal's mind; (v) and, since it exists necessarily, unlike Hannibal's idea of his actually existing body, it is eternal; (vi) therefore, something belonging to the essence of Hannibal's mind is eternal.

The questionable step in this proof is (ii): that the idea in God which expresses the essence of Hannibal's body belongs to the essence of Hannibal's mind. According to Spinoza, what belongs to the essence of Hannibal's mind is whatever, being given, Hannibal's mind is necessarily posited, and whatever, being taken away, Hannibal's mind is necessarily taken away (by E2d2). Now, if an idea that is necessarily in God is taken away, then God and everything else is taken away, including Hannibal's mind. But it is by no means evident that if the idea in God that expresses the essence of Hannibal's body is given, the essence of Hannibal's mind is necessarily posited. The idea in God's mind is wholly adequate; but the essence of Hannibal's mind is a possible individual consisting largely of inadequate ideas (cf. E2p19,27). How can an adequate idea in God be such that, if it is given, an inadequate one in Hannibal's mind is necessarily posited?

This difficulty can be removed by a slight amendment of Spinoza's proof. So far as Hannibal's idea of the essence of his body is imaginative and therefore mutilated, it is in God's mind, not *sub specie aeternitatis*, but only in so far as it constitutes the idea of Hannibal's body as actually existing in the present, and nothing else. On the other hand, so far as Hannibal's idea of the essence of his body is itself made up of common notions and ideas of properties common to his body and the external things that affect it, it too is *sub specie aeternitatis*, and so part of God's own idea of it. 'Whatever the Mind understands *sub specie aeternitatis* it understands not from the fact that it conceives the Body's present actual existence, but from the fact that it conceives the Body's essence *sub specie aeternitatis*' (E5p29).

When Hannibal died, God's mind ceased to constitute the

idea of his body as actually existing, and nothing else. It therefore ceased to contain ideas either of Hannibal's body as existing, or of the images that existed in his body, whether of that body itself or of things external to it, present or past; and it ceased to contain ideas of those ideas. Most of what constituted Hannibal's self-cognition as a child, so far as he remembered it, therefore vanished too. With them vanished all his ideas representing the essence of his body as a complex of parts of certain shapes, sizes and other elementary physical properties, communicating motions of certain quantities to one another in definite ways, so far as those ideas depended upon ideas of sensory images. But so far as his idea of himself was a functional one, along the lines of *Ethics* III and IV, which, although derived from his imaginative ideas of himself during his life, made use of none but common notions and ideas of properties common to the human and external things affecting it, it would be a part of the adequate idea of his essence eternally in God's mind, and so would remain. Hence to the extent that it was an adequate complex idea of himself as a person possibly existing in nature, Hannibal's mind can only be eternal.

So far as they coincide, the part of Hannibal's thinking that pertains to the essence of his mind, and is eternal, is absolutely identical with God's idea of the essence of his body, and his idea of that idea, and not something different with the same content. What is eternal in the ideas constituting Hannibal's mind, or those constituting that of anybody else, is nothing but God, so far as he constitutes what is eternal in Hannibal's idea of his body and of nothing else, along with an idea of that idea, and so on. And as for the subject of those ideas—the 'I' that accompanies them all, as Kant would put it—it is the subject of the ideas of every other human being, namely, the subject of the eternal mode Spinoza refers to as 'God's infinite idea' (E2p8).

10.5. *Mentis Humanae Summa Beatitudo*

'We feel and experience (*sentimus experimurque*) that we are eternal' (E5p23s—G II, 296/4): this remark has prompted many readers whom Spinoza's reasoning repels to interpret the final propositions of *Ethics* V as a report of his experience as a mystic. He himself did what he could to prevent this, by immediately explaining what he meant by 'feel and experience':

> the Mind feels those things that it conceives in the understanding no less than those it has in the memory. For the eyes of the mind, by which it sees and observes things, are simply demonstrations. (G II, 296/4-7)

Most people find it almost impossible to think of a world utterly without themselves, even as observers. Spinoza explains this, not in the fashion of psychotherapy today, as a 'defence mechanism', but as an inference, sometimes explicit but more commonly inchoate, from common notions we all have: those of substance; of thought as an attribute expressing an infinite essence, and hence of a common eternal subject of all ideas; and finally, of ideas God has *sub specie aeternitatis*, in particular, of his ideas of the essences of individual human bodies, and of whether they form part of the minds of the living human beings whose bodies they are.

What Spinoza says about the mind's existence without relation to the body is a naturalization of the religious doctrine of the four last things: death, judgement, heaven and hell. How he conceived death we have already seen. A body dies, or ceases to exist, when its parts cease to transmit motions to one another in the fixed manner that constitutes its essence. When that happens, the mind, as a composite idea primarily constituted by the idea of it actually existing, and nothing else, also ceases to exist. According to the principle of mode identity, that each enduring human body is the same mode as some enduring human mind, the duration of a human being's mind is the same as that of his body. However, to the extent that a human being, during life, forms an adequate functional idea of the essence of his body, that idea, although a component of his mind as enduring, is also more than that: it is the idea constituting his cognition of his identity through time, so far as it is adequate. That component, therefore, is eternally in God as a component of his infinite idea: an infinite and eternal mode expressed by the attribute thought (E5p23d—G

II, 295/17-20,24-7). Hence it is not destroyed with the body, but remains after the body dies, as it existed before it lived (E5p23s—G II, 296/7-11).

Spinoza repudiated, as ethical irrationality compounded by superstition, the Christian concept of God as a judge who, according to the moral law revealed to Moses, pronounces judgement of salvation or damnation on whatever remains of each human individual after death. It is irrational to 'prefer to curse and laugh at the Affects and actions of human beings, rather than to understand them' (E3pref—G II, 138/6-7); for, however tempting it is to believe it, it is false that 'man disturbs, rather than follows the order of nature, that he has absolute power over his actions, and that he is determined only by himself' (G II, 137/12-15). Error becomes evil in those who

> attribute ... human impotence and inconstancy, not to the common power of nature, but to I know not what vice of human nature [presumably, the doctrine of original sin], which they therefore bewail, or laugh at, or condemn, or (as usually happens) curse. And he who knows how to censure more eloquently or cunningly the impotence of the human Mind is held to be inspired by God. (G II, 137/15-20)

Since human beings necessarily follow the order of nature, rage at what they do, as well as ridicule, contempt and reprobation, are all misplaced. Of course, nobody can escape judging what his fellows do as good or evil: each, *in statu naturali*, judges the conduct of others as beneficial or harmful, and takes measures accordingly; and each, *in statu civili*, expects the State to promulgate a legal code and to enforce it. Such modes of thinking, however, can only be justified practically, not as 'indicat[ing some]thing positive in things' (E4pref—G II, 208/8-9). They therefore have no place in God, or in human minds after death.

Writing to Willem van Blijenbergh, who had asked him 'whether in relation to God, stealing is as good as being righteous' (Ep22—G IV, 140/19), Spinoza was comprehensive:

> if *good in relation to God* implies that the just man does some good to God, and the thief some evil, I answer that neither the just man nor the thief can cause either delight (*delectatio*) or disgust (*taedium*) in God. But if it is asked whether each of those actions, so far as it is something real

and caused by God, is not equally perfect, I say that if we attend to the actions alone, and in the way proposed, then it can turn out that each is equally perfect. Should you now ask whether the thief and the just man are equally perfect and blessed, I answer No. For I understand him to be just who steadfastly desires that each one shall possess what is his; which Desire I show in my *Ethics* (not yet published) necessarily to originate in the pious from the clear cognition they have of themselves and of God. And since the thief does not have a desire of that kind, he is necessarily destitute of cognition of himself and of God, which is what primarily makes us human.[17] (Ep23—G IV, 150/8-16, 151/1-6)

It follows from this that, although there will be no judgement, the eternal lot of the thief and the just man will not be the same.

Yet the lot of the guilty is no more a punishment than is that of the innocent a reward. The eternal lot of many innocents is not happy: for example, that of children who die in infancy:

[H]e who has passed from being an infant or a child to being a corpse is called unhappy (*infelix*). On the other hand, if we pass the whole length of our life with a sound Mind in a sound Body, that is considered happiness. And really, he who, like an infant or child, has a Body capable of very few things, and very heavily dependent on external causes, has a Mind which considered solely in itself is conscious of almost nothing of itself, or of God, or of things.... In this life, then, we strive especially that the infant's Body may change (as much as its nature allows and assists) into another, capable of a great many things and related to a Mind very much conscious of itself, of God, and of things. (E5p39s—G II, 305/20-6, 28-31)

Of course, Christians agree that you do not lead a happy or fortunate natural life if you die in infancy: their difference with Spinoza is about an infant's eternal life; for Spinoza consistently maintains that nobody can cognize anything eternally that he does not cognize during his life.

Since there is no Last Judgement, there is neither heaven nor hell. Yet there is a '*summa beatitudo*' or 'highest blessedness', which some human beings will attain, and others not. It is eternal; and it will be purely mental, because what survives death is a human being's idea of his or her own essence, so far as it is adequate. The ideas active adults have of their own essences, as we have seen, are adequate to a considerable extent. However, no mind can have an adequate idea of its own essence without having the rudiments of the idea of God—of an essence such that it exists necessarily, in Spinoza's naturalist sense. The highest blessedness consists primarily in understanding oneself and other finite things *sub specie aeternitatis*, from the point of view of God, with an adequate idea both of God's nature, and of how by virtue of that nature God, as *Natura naturata*, is immanently caused. This is the form of cognition Spinoza calls '*scientia intuitiva*' and 'cognition of the third kind' (see 7.4).

Cognition of this third kind is the highest blessedness, Spinoza argues, because from it 'there arises the highest *acquiescentia* of Mind there can be' (E5p27). The root concept of *acquiescentia* is that of *quies*: rest or peace. It is accurately rendered neither by 'acquiescence' which suggests putting up with, nor by Curley's 'satisfaction' which suggests having enough (C,661). Given his doctrine that nothing can be understood except as God, or as a mode of God (5.5), together with his identifications of virtue with power (8.6), of mind with the power to think, and of understanding with the exercise of that power (7.4—cf.E3p1,3), Spinoza has no difficulty in proving, in *Ethics* IV, that 'Cognition of God is the Mind's highest good, and the highest virtue of the Mind is to cognize God' (E4p28). Having attained the highest good it can attain, there is no other state in which an individual mind's power of acting can be greater (8.3), or its joy fuller: 'Joy born of the fact that [it] considers itself and its power of acting' (E3AD25). It must therefore be affected with the highest *acquiescentia* in its own condition that is rationally conceivable (E527d—G II, 297/22–3).

So far as it goes, there is no flaw in Spinoza's reasoning, but it does not go far enough. He must also inquire whether suffering can overpower this *acquiescentia*. Can somebody who has cognition of the third kind of God, himself and other things come to suffer agony so great that the sadness of considering it as necessary in the order of nature, and hence accompanied by the idea of God as cause, will be greater than the joy of considering the nature of God? If he can, then he will rather the whole of nature be annihilated than that his suffering continue: that is, hate of God will overcome love of God. This is not possible after death; for suffering involves inadequate ideas, and nothing remains of any human being after death except his idea of his own essence, so far as it is adequate. But is it possible in this life? Spinoza professes to show that it is not (E5p18).

Citing the final theorem in *Ethics* III, that 'Among all the affects that are related to the Mind insofar as it acts, there are none that are related to Joy or Desire' (E3p59), he argues that

> *insofar as* we consider God, we act (by E3p3). Consequently (by E3p59), there can be no Sadness accompanied by the idea of God, i.e. (by E3AD7), no one can hold God in hate. (E518d, my emphasis)

Unfortunately, this will not do. Since consciousness of being burned alive or being gassed by Zyklon B can, and presumably did, accompany consideration of God in the minds of many whom the Inquisition burned or the Nazis gassed, those who were thus burned or gassed were, so far as they were considering God, acting and not sad. On the other hand, so far as they were conscious of being burned or gassed, they were suffering as well as acting, and therefore sad as well as joyful. And a theorem in *Ethics* III, that 'A Desire which arises from a true cognition of good and evil can be extinguished or restrained by many other Desires which arise from affects by which we are tormented' (E3p15), implies that it is possible that love of God arising from cognition of the third kind can be 'extinguished or restrained' by hate of God arising from extreme suffering.

Spinoza's supplementary argument in the scholium to *Ethics* V, 18 has the same defect:

> insofar as we understand the causes of Sadness, it ceases (by E5p3) to be a passion, i.e. (by E3p59), to that extent it ceases to be Sadness. And so, insofar as we understand God to be the cause of Sadness, we rejoice. (G II, 292/2–5)

Although sadness as cognized through ideas of its causes is not a passion, nobody who suffers extreme pain cognizes wholly through its causes the decrease in his power of acting it constitutes: he also cognizes it imaginatively, as a passive affect; and that passive affect may possibly overpower active cognition of it as necessary in the course of nature.

It is true, on Spinoza's principles, that the more active a human individual's mind is, the more cognition of the third kind, and so of God, will have the chief place in it; but it is also true that by nothing he can do can anybody ensure that his mind will be more active than passive. The theorem of *Ethics* IV stands: 'It cannot come about that a man... could suffer no changes except those which can be understood through his nature alone, of which he is the adequate cause' (E4p4). Your mind may be so constituted that your active cognition of God generates a love that overcomes any suffering you endure. Judah the Faithful so loved God (although not Spinoza's God) that he sang as he was burned to death (cf.1.3—Ep76—G IV, 321-2). Love of Spinoza's God springing from cognition of the third kind can have that result, but it does not necessarily have it. When accompanied by enough suffering, cognizing that suffering as immanently caused by God may generate a hate of him that will extinguish love.

This correction is not radical. It exposes the austerity of Spinoza's doctrine, while retaining its essence. To love God is to accept what nature is, because nature cannot be otherwise. God's or nature's love of itself is the fullness of that acceptance, and is without any passive affect whatever towards its modes. It cannot be said of Spinoza's God: 'herein is love, not that we loved God, but that he first loved us.'[18] Yet if God is what Spinoza believed he is, there is nothing greater to which human beings can aspire than to love him without desiring that he should love them in return (E5p19). For that is 'the very Love with which God loves himself, not insofar as he is infinite, but insofar as he can be explicated by the human Mind's essence, considered *sub specie aeternitatis*' (E5p36). '*Acquiescentia*' is a fitting name for it.

Notes

[1] '*Existentiam*' is Meijer's emendation, accepted by Appuhn. The *Opera Posthuma* reads '*durationem*', and the *Nagelate Schriften* supports this reading (cf. G IV, 390; C, 606 n.13). Spinoza will go on to demonstrate the eternity of what of the mind 'remains' when the body is destroyed (E5p23). Hence, if he wrote '*durationem*', he did not mean it in the strict sense in which he has defined it (E2d5); and the sense in which he meant it is well captured by 'existence'.

[2] For an interpretation inoffensive to naturalists, see Pollock (1880), pp.

292–9; for others inoffensive to idealists, see Joachim (1903), pp. 298–303, and Harris (1973), pp. 243–5; for one inoffensive to contemporary philosophers generally, see Allison (1987), pp. 165–70.
3   For a respectful despairing interpretation, see Feuer (1964), pp. 221–7, 247–8.
4   Bennett (1984), p. 357.
5   Apart from those expressly discussed, among the treatments of Spinoza's argument that have influenced me are: Kneale (1968), Harris (1971), Friedman (1978 and 1986), Steinberg (1981), and Delahunty (1985).
6   Matheron (1969), pp. 574–6.
7   What follows about how we all to a greater or lesser extent form adequate ideas of the essences of our bodies is derived from Matheron's brief but rich treatment (Matheron (1969), pp. 576–83). Matheron follows Brunschvicg in rendering '*sub specie aeternitatis*' as '*sous la categorie de l'éternité*' (p. 576 n.11): but see above, ch. 6 n.18.
8   Cf. Bennett, who implies that Spinoza's doctrine of parallelism would 'fail' if 'some possibilities under one attribute have no counterparts under the other' (Bennett (1984), p. 358).
9   Matheron (1969), pp. 575–6.
10 I have drawn upon Curley's note on Spinoza's over-abridged statement of Euclid's theorem (C, 452 n.15).
11 Replacing the single letters 'D' and 'E' by which Spinoza denotes the intersecting lines.
12 '... *que Spinoza, depuis lors, avait à dessein laissé dans l'ombre*' (Matheron (1969), p. 575).
13 See ch. 6, note 24.
14 '[I]t is justly thought a remarkable virtue in Hannibal that no mutiny ever occurred in his army' (TP, 5, 3).
15 Translating '*pertinet*' as 'belonging', as Curley does in rendering E2d2.
16 Since Bennett denies that Spinoza held either, it is not surprising that, on his interpretation of what Spinoza has to say about the mind's existence without relation to the body, it is 'certainly false' and his 'whole line of thought ... wrong' (Bennett (1984), pp. 359, 361).
17 I translate from the Latin version probably made by Spinoza, and printed in OP, and not, like Wolf and Curley, the original Dutch letter (see G IV, 400–1; W1, 411; C, 352).
18 I John, 4:10.

Bibliography of Works Cited by Short Titles

(1) Spinoza's Writings

Curley, Edwin (ed. and tr.) (1985), *The Collected Works of Spinoza* (Princeton: Princeton University Press), vol. 1.
[In quoting in English from writings translated in this magnificent edition, the second volume of which has not yet appeared, I largely adopt Curley's renderings. Departures from them (mostly for the sake of literalness) are indicated only if philosophically significant.]
Eisenberg, Paul (ed. and tr.) (1977), '*Treatise on the Improvement of the Understanding:* Baruch de Spinoza'. In *Philosophy Research Archives*, 5 July 1977.
Gebhardt, Carl (ed.) (N.D.), *Spinoza Opera* (Heidelberg: Carl Winter). 4 vols.
Mignini, Filippo (ed. and tr. [into Italian]) (1986), *Korte Verhandeling van God, de Mensch en deszelvs Welstand/Breve Trattato su Dio, l'Uomo e il suo Bene* (L'Aquila: L. U. Japadre Editore).
Wernham, A. G. (ed. and tr.) (1958), *Spinoza: The Political Works. The* Tractatus Theologico-Politicus *in Part and the* Tractatus Politicus *in Full* (Oxford: Clarendon Press).
Wolf, A[braham] (tr.) (1966), *The Correspondence of Spinoza* (London: Frank Cass). Originally published 1928.
Translations of TT-P and TP are based on Wr, when available (it omits the non-political parts of TT-P); and translations from letters not translated in C, on W1. However, I often depart from both. A full translation of TT-P, from Bruder's superseded edition, may be found in R. H. M. Elwes, *The Chief Works of Benedict de Spinoza* (London: George Bell and Sons, 1883), vol. 1 (reprinted by Dover Publications, New York).

(2) Works of Reference

Giancotti [Boscherini], Emilia (1970), *Lexicon Spinozanum* (La Haye: Martinus Nijhoff). 2 vols.

Gueret, Michel, Robinet, André and Tombeur, Paul (1977), *Spinoza: Ethica, Concordances, Index, Listes de Frequences, Tables Comparatives* (Louvain-la-Neuve: Publications du Centre de Traitement Electronique des Documents, Université Catholique de Louvain).

(3) Philosophical Writings before 1850

Arnauld, Antoine *and* Nicole, Pierre (1970), *La Logique, ou l'Art de Penser* (Paris: Flammarion). [Based on the 5th edn: Paris: Guillaume Desprez, 1683.]

Bayle, Pierre (1720), *Dictionnaire Historique et Critique*. 3rd edn (Rotterdam: Michel Bohm). [Translations are based on those of Richard H Popkin in Pierre Bayle, *Historical and Critical Dictionary: Selections* (Indianapolis, Ind.: Bobbs Merrill, 1965).]

Descartes, Rene (1964–75), *Oeuvres de Descartes*. Ed. Charles Adam and Paul Tannery. Nouvelle Presentation, en Co-Edition avec le Centre National de la Recherche Scientifique (Paris: J. Vrin). 11 vols.
[For the most part I follow the good translations from AT in: Cottingham, John, Stoothoff, Robert and Murdoch, Dugald (eds and trs) (1985), *The Philosophical Writings of Descartes* (Cambridge: Cambridge University Press). 2 vols.]

Hobbes, Thomas (1981), *Leviathan*. Ed. C. B. Macpherson (Harmondsworth: Penguin Books [Pelican English Library]). A critical edition based on the 'Head' edition (London: Andrew Crooke, 1651). Page references are both to the Penguin edition (left of the stroke) and to the original (right of it).

Leibniz, Gottfried Wilhelm (1890), *Die Philosophischen Schriften*. Ed. C. I. Gerhardt (Berlin: Weidmann). 7 vols.

Maimonides, Moses (1963), *The Guide of the Perplexed*. Ed. and tr. Shlomo Pines (Chicago: University of Chicago Press).

(4) Philosophical Writings After 1850

[References to articles recorded as reprinted in collections are to the pages of those collections.]

Allison, Henry (1987), *Benedict de Spinoza: an Introduction*, Rev. edn. (New Haven: Yale University Press).

Barker, H. (1938), 'Notes on the second part of Spinoza's *Ethics*'. *Mind* 47. Reprinted in Kashap (ed.) (1972).

Bar-On, A. Z. (1983), 'The ontological proof—Spinoza's version in comparison with those of Anselm and Descartes'. In Rotenstreich and Schneider (eds) (1983).

Bennett, Jonathan (1984), *A Study of Spinoza's* Ethics (Cambridge: Cambridge University Press).

——— (1986), 'Spinoza on error'. *Philosophical Papers* 15: 59–73. A French translation, 'Spinoza et l'erreur' has appeared in *Studia Spinozana* 2: 197–217.

Bidney, David (1940), *The Psychology and Ethics of Spinoza* (New Haven: Yale University Press).

Broad, C. D. (1930), *Five Types of Ethical Theory* (London: Kegan Paul, Trench, and Trubner).

Brown, Stuart (1984), *Leibniz* (Brighton: Harvester Press).

Curley, Edwin (1969), *Spinoza's Metaphysics: an Essay in Interpretation* (Cambridge, Mass.: Harvard University Press).

———(1975), 'Descartes, Spinoza, and the ethics of belief'. In Freeman and Mandelbaum (eds) (1975), pp. 159–89.

———(1986), 'Spinoza's geometric method'. *Studia Spinozana* 2: 151–69.

———(1988), *Behind the Geometrical Method: A Reading of Spinoza's* Ethics (Princeton: Princeton University Press).

de Dijn, Hermann (1986), 'Spinoza's logic or art of perfect thinking'. *Studia Spinozana* 2: 15–25.

Delahunty, R. J. (1985), *Spinoza* (London: Routledge and Kegan Paul).

Deleuze, Gilles (1968), *Spinoza et le Problème de l'Expression*. (Paris: Editions de Minuit).

Doney, Willis (ed.) (1967), *Descartes: a Collection of Critical Essays* (New York: Doubleday).

Feuer, Lewis Samuel (1964), *Spinoza and the Rise of Liberalism* (Boston: Beacon Press). [Originally published 1958.]

Floistad, Guttorm (1969), 'Spinoza's theory of knowledge in the *Ethics*'. *Inquiry* 12: 41–65. Reprinted in Grene (ed.) (1973).

Freeman, Eugene *and* Mandelbaum, Maurice (eds) (1975), *Spinoza: Essays in Interpretation* (La Salle: Open Court).

Friedman, Joel I. (1978), 'An overview of Spinoza's *Ethics*'. *Synthèse* 37: 67–106.

———(1983) 'Spinoza's problem of "other minds"'. *Synthèse* 57: 99–126.

―――(1986) 'How the finite follows from the infinite in Spinoza's metaphysical system'. *Synthèse* 69: 371-407.
Garrett, Don (1986), 'Truth and ideas of imagination in the *Tractatus de Intellectus Emendatione*'. *Studia Spinozana* 2: 61-92.
Gauthier, David P. (1969), *The Logic of Leviathan: the Moral and Political Theory of Thomas Hobbes* (Oxford: Clarendon Press).
Gewirth, Alan (1943), 'Clearness and distinctness in Descartes'. *Philosophy* 18. Reprinted in Doney (ed.) (1967).
Grene, Marjorie (1985), *Descartes* (Brighton: Harvester Press).
――― (ed.) (1973), *Spinoza: a Collection of Critical Essays* (New York: Doubleday).
Grene, Marjorie *and* Nails, Debra (eds) (1986), *Spinoza and the Sciences* [Boston Studies in the Philosophy of Science, vol. 90] (Dordrecht: Reidel).
Gueroult, Martial (1968), *Spinoza. Dieu: Ethique, 1* (Paris: Aubier-Montaigne).
―――(1974), *Spinoza. L'âme: Ethique, 2* (Paris: Aubier-Montaigne).
―――(1984) *The Soul and God*. Tr. Roger Ariew (Minneapolis: University of Minnesota Press). [This is a translation of *Descartes selon l'Ordre des Raisons*, 2nd edn (Paris: Aubier-Montaigne, 1968), vol. 1.
Hacking, Ian (1975), *Why does Language Matter to Philosophy?* (Cambridge: Cambridge University Press).
Hall, A. Rupert and Hall, Marie Boas (1964), 'Philosophy and natural philosophy: Boyle and Spinoza'. In *Mélanges Alexandre Koyré. II: L'aventure de l'esprit* (Paris: Hermann), pp. 241-56.
Hallett, H. F. (1949), 'On a reputed equivoque in the philosophy of Spinoza'. *Review of Metaphysics* 3. Reprinted in Kashap (ed.) (1972).
―――(1957), *Benedict de Spinoza: the Elements of his Philosophy* (London: Athlone Press, University of London).
Hampshire, Stuart (1956), *Spinoza* (London: Faber and Faber). [Original ed. Pelican Books, 1951.]
Hampton, Jean (1986), *Hobbes and the Social Contract Tradition* (Cambridge: Cambridge University Press).
Hardin, C. L. (1977), 'Spinoza on immortality and time'. *Southwestern Journal of Philosophy* 8. Reprinted in Shahan and Biro (eds) (1978).
Harris, Errol E. (1971), 'Spinoza's theory of human immortality'. *Monist* 55. Reprinted in Freeman and Mandelbaum (eds) (1975).
―――(1973), *Salvation from Despair: a Reappraisal of Spinoza's Philosophy* (The Hague: Martinus Nijhoff).

―――(1978), *Is There an Esoteric Doctrine in the Tractatus Theologico-Politicus?* (Vanwege het Spinozahuis: Medelingen 38. Leiden: E. J. Brill).

Haserot, Francis S. (1953), 'Spinoza's definition of attribute'. *Philosophical Review* 62. Reprinted in Kashap (ed.) (1972).

Hessing, Siegfried (ed.) (1977), *Speculum Spinozanum 1677-1977* (London: Routledge and Kegan Paul).

Hubbeling, H. G. (1964), *Spinoza's Methodology* (Assen: van Gorcum).

―――(1986), 'The third way of knowledge (intuition) in Spinoza' *Studia Spinozana* 2: 219-31.

Joachim, H. H. (1903), *A Study of Spinoza's* Ethics (Oxford: Oxford University Press).

―――(1940), *Spinoza's* Tractatus de Intellectus Emendatione (Oxford: Oxford University Press).

Kashap, S. Paul (ed.) (1972), *Studies in Spinoza: Critical and Interpretive Essays* (Berkeley: University of California Press).

Kennington, Richard (ed.) (1980), *The Philosophy of Baruch Spinoza.* Studies in Philosophy and the History of Philosophy, vol. 7. (Washington, D. C.: Catholic University of America Press.)

Kenny, Anthony (1967), 'Descartes on ideas'. In Doney (ed.) (1967). This paper subsequently appeared as a chapter in Kenny's *Descartes: a Study of his Philosophy* (New York: Random House, 1968).

Klever, Wim (1986), 'Axioms in Spinoza's science and philosophy of science'. *Studia Spinozana* 2: 171-95.

Kline, George L. (1977), 'On the infinity of Spinoza's attributes'. In Hessing (ed.) (1977).

―――(1982), 'Absolute and relative senses of *liberum* and *libertas* in Spinoza'. In *Spinoza nel 350° Anniversario nella Nascita* (Urbino: Bibliopolis, N.D.), pp. 259-280.

Kneale, Martha (1968), 'Eternity and sempiternity'. *Proceedings of the Aristotelian Society* 69. Reprinted in Grene (ed.) (1973).

Kneale, William *and* Kneale, Martha (1984), *The Development of Logic.* Corr. imp. (Oxford: Clarendon Press).

Lachterman, David R. (1978), 'The physics of Spinoza's *Ethics*'. In Shahan and Biro (eds) (1978).

Macherey, Pierre (1979), *Hegel ou Spinoza* (Paris: Francois Maspero).

Marcus, Ruth Barcan (1983), 'Bar-On on Spinoza's ontological proof'. In Rotenstreich and Schneider (eds) (1983).

Mason, Richard (1986), 'Spinoza on modality'. *Philosophical Quarterly* 36: 313-42.

Mates, Benson (1986), *The Philosophy of Leibniz: Metaphysics and Language* (New York: Oxford University Press).

Matheron, Alexandre (1969), *Individu et Communauté chez Spinoza* (Paris: Editions de Minuit).

——(1971), *Le Christ et le Salut des Ignorants chez Spinoza* (Paris: Aubier-Montaigne).

——(1986), 'Spinoza and Euclidean arithmetic: the example of the fourth proportional'. Tr. David Lachterman. In Grene and Nails (eds) (1986).

Matson, Wallace I. (1971), 'Spinoza's theory of mind'. *Monist* 55. Reprinted in Freeman and Mandelbaum (eds) (1975).

McShea, Robert J. (1968), *The Political Philosophy of Spinoza* (New York: Columbia University Press).

Meinsma, K. O. (1983), tr. S. Rosenboorg, with Latin and German Appendices tr. by J.-P. Osier. *Spinoza et son Cercle* (Paris: J. Vrin). [Although Meinsma's text, originally published in 1896, is unchanged, it is supplemented with much new material in a different type, edited by Henri Méchoulan and Pierre-François Moreau.]

Mignini, Filippo (1986), 'Spinoza's theory on the active and passive nature of knowledge'. *Studia Spinozana* 2: 27-58.

Parkinson, G. H. R. (1953), *Spinoza's Theory of Knowledge* (Oxford: Clarendon Press).

——(1969), 'Language and knowledge in Spinoza'. *Inquiry* 12: 15-40. Reprinted in Grene (ed.) (1973).

Pollock, Frederick (1880), *Spinoza: his Life and Philosophy* (London: C. Kegan Paul). [I have used the photographic reprint published in Dubuque, Iowa, by Wm. C. Brown's Reprint Library.]

Popkin, Richard H. (1979), *The History of Scepticism from Erasmus to Spinoza* (Berkeley: University of California Press.)

——(1987), 'The religious background of seventeenth-century philosophy'. *Journal of the History of Philosophy* 25: 35–50.

Rotenstreich, Nathan *and* Schneider, Norma (eds) (1983), *Spinoza: His Thought and Work* (Jerusalem: the Israel Academy of Arts and Sciences).

Savan, David (1958), 'Spinoza and language'. *Philosophical Review* 67: 212-25. Reprinted in Grene (ed.) (1973).

——(1986), 'Spinoza: scientist and theorist of scientific method'. In Grene and Nails (eds) (1986).

Shahan, Robert W. *and* Biro, J. I. (eds) (1978), *Spinoza: New Perspectives* (Norman: University of Oklahoma Press).

Steinberg, Diane (1981), 'Spinoza's theory of the eternity of the

mind'. *Canadian Journal of Philosophy* 11: 35–68.
———(1984), 'Spinoza's ethical doctrine and the unity of human nature'. *Journal of the History of Philosophy* 22: 303–24.
Strauss, Leo (1952), *Persecution and the Art of Writing* (Glencoe, Illinois: Free Press).
———(1965), tr. E. M. Sinclair. *Spinoza's Critique of Religion* (New York: Schocken Books).
Voss, Stephen H. (1981), 'How Spinoza enumerated the affects'. *Archiv für Geschichte der Philosophie* 63: 167–79.
van der Bend, J. G. (ed.) (1974), *Spinoza on Knowing, Being and Freedom* (Assen: van Gorcum).
Wernham, A. G. (1974), 'Spinoza's account of cognition in *Ethics* Part II, Prop. 9–13'. In van der Bend (ed.) (1974).
Wetlesen, Jon (ed.) (1978), *Spinoza's Philosophy of Man: the Scandinavian Spinoza Symposium 1977* (Oslo: Universitetsforlaget).
Wilson, Margaret D. (1980), 'Objects, ideas, and "minds": comments on Spinoza's theory of mind'. In Kennington (ed.) (1980).
Wolfson, Harry Austryn (1934), *The Philosophy of Spinoza* (Cambridge, Mass.: Harvard University Press). 2 vols.

Index

Abraham ibn Ezra ('Aben Ezra'), 17–18
action (*actio*), 148
affection (*affectio*) of a substance, *see* mode
affect (*affectus*), 155–63
Akkerman, F., 11
Allison, Henry, 168 173, 207
Aquinas, Thomas, 55
Aristotle, 55, 66–7
Arnauld, Antoine, *and* Nicole, Pierre, 12, 55
association, law of, 157, 168
atomism, 62, 123
attribute, 19, 69–72, 78, 102–6. *See* extension; plenitude, criteria of; relation, trans-attribute; *and* thought

Bacon, Francis, 6, 19–20
Balling, Pieter, 2, 16
Balibar, Etienne, 56, 188
Barker, H., 145
Bar-On, A. Z., 94
Bayle, Pierre, 20, 35
be in, to, 63–4, 68, 90–1, 105–6
being (*ens, esse*), formal, 37–9, 43–5, 60
objective, 37–9
Bennett, Jonathan, 52, 56, 59, 73–6, 94, 98, 109, 113–15, 140–1, 144–5, 148–52, 154–5, 160, 165, 167–8, 189, 191, 207
Bidney, David, 168
blessedness (*beatitudo*), the highest, 122, 183–4, 187–8, 200–6
body (*corpus*), 62, 148–50. *See* physics
human, 122–5, 129–33, 153–4, 192–3, 197–8
simplest (*simplicissimum*), 123
Boxel, Hugo, 3, 15
Broad, C. D., 164, 168
Brown, Stuart, 76, 93–4

cause, 61–2
adequate, 148
immanent, 62–4, 68, 87–8, 91–2, 106–7, 113–15
of itself (*causa sui*), 60, 62, 91–2
transient (*transiens*), 62–3, 87, 114–15
Christianity, 10, 24–9, 32, 33, 203
cognition (*cognitio*)/cognize (*cognoscere*), 7–8, 64–5
first kind of (=imagination), 94, 97, 128–34, 137, 144
fundamental axiom of, 68
second kind of, 97–9, 136–9, 143–4
third kind of (=*scientia intuitiva*), 137–40, 204

Cohen, Hermann, 26, 31, 35
common notion (*notio communis*), 51, 60, 136
conception (*conceptus*)/conceive (*concipere*), 64, 69
Curley, Edwin, 11, 16–17, 46, 55–6, 75–6, 93–4, 120–1, 144–5, 167–8, 188–9, 206–7

de Dijn, Hermann, 76
Delahunty, R. J., 93, 113, 121, 207
Deleuze, Gilles, 94
den Uyl, D. J., 188
Descartes, Rene, 3–4, 6–8, 9, 19–20, 34, 36–44, 46–9, 53–5, 58–60, 62, 66–7, 74–6, 97–101, 104–7, 109, 123–4, 141, 144, 146–8, 167, 184
Desmarets, Samuel, 146
de Vries, Simon, 2, 9, 84–6
Doney, Willis, 55, 76
Duhem, Pierre, 67, 76
duration (*duratio*), 93, 108–9, 206

Eisenberg, Paul, 56
Englard, Izhak, 35
error, 43–4, 47–9, 142–4
essence, 43, 51–2, 57–60, 81–2, 87–9
  to belong to an, 59–60
  to constitute an, 88–9
  to express an, 89
eternity (*aeternitas*)/eternal, 92–3, 107–9, 111–13. See *sub specie aeternitatis*
Euclid's *Elements*, 54
extension/extended, 19–20. See physics
  as attribute of substance, 90–1, 99–101, 106–7, 109–10, 117

Feuer, L. S., 207
Floistad, Guttorm, 145
freedom (*libertas*)/free, 92, 172–4
  of speech, 182–3
Frege, Gottlob, 54, 56
Friedman, Joel I., 94, 207

Garrett, Don, 115, 121
Gebhart, Carl, 1, 4, 11, 206–7
Gewirth, Alan, 55, 56
Giancotti, Emilia, 75, 188
God or nature (*Deus sive natura*), 19–20, 33–4, 80–4, 88–93
  correction of accepted theological views of, 91–3
  humanly cognizable attributes of, 90, 96–7, 100–1, 116–18
  infinite intellect of, 19–20, 118–19, 126–7, 194–9
  naturans and naturata, 93, ch. 6 *passim*
  perfection of, 96–102, 202–3
good and evil, 162–3, 170–3, 179–80, 202–6
government (*imperium*), 29–30, 177–83, 189
Grene, Marjorie, 55, 99
Gueret, Michel; Robinet, Andre; *and* Tombeur, Paul, 75, 121
Gueroult, Martial, 55, 59, 69–70, 75–6, 94–5

Hacking, Ian, 7, 12, 36–7, 45
Hall, A. Rupert, 120, 145
Hall, Marie B., 145
Hallett, H. F., 11, 94, 112–13, 120, 134, 145
Hampton, Jean, 167

Harris, Errol E., 35, 94, 207
Haserot, Francis S., 76
Hobbes, Thomas, 54, 56, 146–8, 167, 175–81, 188–9
Hubbeling, H. G., 11, 51, 56, 94, 145, 183, 189
Hudde, Johannes, 3, 82–3
Huygens, Christiaan, 99

idea(s), 7–8, 36, 38–47, 60. *See* linkage of ideas
  adequate/inadequate, 68, 128–9, 136–40
  propositional counterpart(s) of, 52–3
ideatum, 8, 44, 47–8, 56, 60
incarnation, divine, 10
infinite, 83
  absolutely, 72, ch. 5 *passim*
  in its kind, 72, 88–9
intentionality, *see* representation/representativeness
interpretation, scriptural, 16–21
  universal rule of, 18, 27–8
  negative rule of truth in, 21

Jelles, Jarig, 2, 175, 178
Joachim, H. H., 11, 94, 112–13, 121, 123, 144, 207
Judah the Faithful, 10, 206
Judaism, 9–11, ch. 2 *passim*

Kenny, Anthony, 55
Klever, Wim, 56, 76
Kline, George, 76, 83, 94, 108
Kneale, Martha, 56, 121, 207
Kneale, William, 56
knowledge (*scientia*), intuitive, *see* cognition, third kind

Lachterman, David, 120
Land, J. P. N., 4, 11

Leibniz, G. W., 24, 54, 70, 74, 76, 84–5, 93–4, 112
linkage of ideas, 46, 134–5, 143–4
  by conjunction (compresence), 46, 52
  by exclusion, 47–9, 52
Locke, John, 7, 193

Macherey, Pierre, 56, 94–5, 114, 121
Machiavelli, Niccolo, 174–5
Maimonides, Moses, 57, 75, 109
Marcus, Ruth Barcan, 94
Mason, Richard, 75–6, 167
Mates, Benson, 81–2, 94
Matheron, Alexandre, 32, 35, 75, 93, 128, 138–9, 145, 153, 156–7, 164–7, 168, 195, 207
Maull, Nancy, 99
matter/material, *see* extension/extended
McShea, Robert J., 188–9
Meinsma, K. O., 11, 12, 34
Meyer, Lodewijk, 2, 4
Mignini, Filippo, 4–5, 11, 56
mind (*mens*), 118–19, 129–30
  human, 122, 125–6, 128–9, 132–4, 156–61, 191–4, 197–200
miracles, 15–16
mode, 68, 72, 105
  infinite and eternal, 102–7
  finite, *see* body, mind
morality, moral law, 25–6, 29–30, 166–7, 169–73, 202–3
motion (*motus*) and rest (*quies*), 104–5, *see* physics

Nails, Debra, 99
nature (=absolutely infinite substance), *see* God or nature

mechanical conception of, 19–20, 33–4, 62–3, *see* physics
nature (=that by which something is of a kind), 58, 60, 69, *see* essence
necessitarianism, 91–2, 113–16
Newton, Isaac, 6, 33
nominalism, 51–2

Oldenburg, Henry, 10, 16–17, 32–3, 34

parallelism, 87–8, 118–19, 126–7, 155–6, 194–7
  extra-cogitative, 140, 143, 145, 194, 201
  intra-cogitative, 118–19, 140–2, 145
Parkinson, G. H. R., 51, 56, 129, 145
perception (*perceptio*)/perceive (*percipere*), 69
physics, 66–8, 74–5, 97–101, 104–7, *see* nature, mechanical conception of
plenitude, principle of, 77–80, *see* substance plenitude, principle of
  criteria of, 77–8, 84–5
Pollock, Frederick, 12, 34, 126–7, 145, 207
Popkin, Richard H., 32, 35
Port Royal Logic, the, 7, 11–12, 36, 55
Priestley, Joseph, 8
prophecy, *see* revelation, divine

Quine, W. V., 76

rationalism, 73–5, 114–15
relation, trans-attribute, 87, 125
religion, *see* Christianity, Judaism, universal revealed faith
representation/representativeness, 38–41, *see* ch. 7 *passim*
revelation, divine, 15–16, 21–6, 32–3
Rieuwertsz, Jan, 3–4

Savan, David, 49, 55, 98
Schuller, G. H., 3, 103
Seneca, L. Annaeus, 134, 181, 189
Skinner, B. F., 134
state (*status*), 66–7
  natural (*naturalis*), 173–4, 177
  civil (*civilis*), 174–80
State (*civitas*), 174–83, *see* government
Steinberg, Diane, 115, 121, 207
Strauss, Leo, 14–15, 25, 26–7, 31, 34, 35
Suarez, Francisco, 37
sub specie aeternitatis, 112, 121, 197, 199, 201, 204, 206
substance, 69–73
  absolutely infinite. *See* God or nature
  essence of, 87–9
substance plenitude, Spinoza's principle of, 82–6, 91
superstition, 32

teleology, 115–16
thought (*cogitatio*)/think (*cogitare*), ch. 4 *passim*
time (*tempus*), 93, 109–11
truth, of ideas (material), 42–4, 46
truth, propositional, 45–6

universal revealed faith, 30–1

van Blijenbergh, Willem, 3, 33, 202

van den Ende, Francis, 9
van Velthuysen, Lambertus, 3, 35
van Vloten, J. V., 11
von Tschirnhaus, E. W., 99–101, 103–4, 118
Voss, Stephen H., 167

Walther, Manfred, 188
Wernham, A. G., 11, 167–8, 178, 189
Westerbrink, A. G., 11
Wilson, Margaret, 125, 127, 130, 144–5
Wolf, Abraham, 100, 207
Wolfson, H. A., 54, 56, 61, 75, 94, 168

Zeno (of Elea), 110, 148

DATE DUE

MY 3			

B   57082
3998
.D66   Donagan, Alan.
1989   Spinoza.

HIEBERT LIBRARY
Fresno Pacific College - M. B. Seminary
Fresno, Calif. 93702